Kizil, Niya, and Dandanoilik

Commemorating World Heritage Designation of
Silk Roads: the Routes Network of Chang'an–Tianshan

Edited by Yasutaka Kojima

Toho Shuppan

Research members, myself included, peering into a royal mummy, a great discovery (See page 79)

Full view of the Kizil grottoes before restoration (1986): Conservation work was conducted in a small way, photo by Y. Kojima

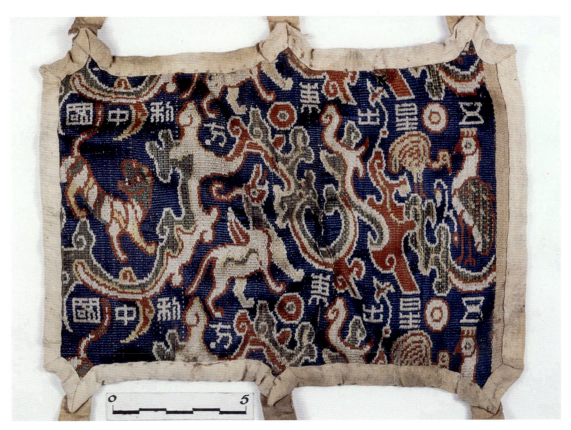

Silk brocade 五星出東方利中国 excavated by the Niya ruins research team which was designated as the national treasure of national treasures, photo by K. Sugimoto

Ruins having survived for a thousand and several hundred years in the desert, at the Dandanoilik ruins CD-1, photo by Y. Kojima

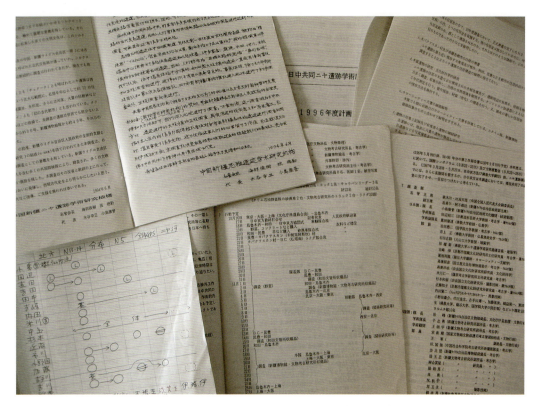

Research was conducted untiringly by various team members in accordance with detailed plans, the Niya research plans (a part), photo by Y. Kojima

Preparing supper before sunset in the desert, as it gets colder, "Oh, We can't wait!", photo by Y. Kojima

Even after supper whipping ourselves into measuring antiquities in a base camp, photo by Y. Kojima

Working in the desert is harsh, 15 degrees below zero in the morning and above 30 degrees in the afternoon, photo by H. Okuyama

Great challenge to find relics in the boundless desert, photo by Liu Guorui

A wide variety of related projects have been implemented, such as the outstanding awards for specialists, scholarship awards for university students, and educational support for grade-schoolers, photo by Y. Kojima

Many people working together
The Niya 1993 team entering into full-scale research with more members – front row right-to-left: Chinese leader Han Xiang (2nd), me (3rd), Japanese scholarly leader Taijun Inokuchi (4th), Chinese scholarly leader Wang Binghua (5th), and Japanese sub-leader Kodo Sanada (7th), photo by a Chinese member

The conservation and research projects of the ruins in Kizil, Niya, and Dandanoilik and their related activities would have never been implemented without supports and valuable efforts by a number of people. During the last three decades, some of them have regrettably passed away. I would like to dedicate this book to those mentors who have played irreplaceable roles.

DEDICATION in MEMORY

Wang Enmao 王恩茂 (1913 to 2001: the Secretary of the Xinjiang Uyghur Autonomous Regional CCP Committee and the Vice-Chairman of the National Committee of the Chinese People's Political Consultative Conference): In 1986 he gave me his seal of approval to offer funds to help restore and preserve the Kizil grottoes. This approval has led to launching the subsequent projects. He has also supported various activities of mine in every way.

Masajuro Shiokawa 塩川正十郎 (1921 to 2015: the Transportation Minister, the Education Minister, the Chief Cabinet Secretary, the Home Affairs Minister, the Chairman of the National Public Safety Commission, and the Finance Minister): I had received an exceptionally thoughtful mentorship since I established the Japan-China Friendship Association to Restore and Conserve the Kizil Grottoes in 1987, as well as in regard to the Japan-China joint scholarly research of the Niya ruins.

Koshi Uemura 上村晃史 (1924 to 1997: the President of C. Uyemura & Co., Ltd.): He exerted every effort for the fund-raising campaign as the Chairman of the Japan-China Friendship Association to Restore and Conserve the Kizil Grottoes which was established in 1987. This helped us clear the target amount of the donations.

Kosyo Mizutani 水谷幸正 (1928 to 2014: the President of Bukkyo University and the Chairman of Bukkyo Educational Institution): He supported the Japan-China joint scholarly research of the Niya and Dandanoilik ruins initiated in 1988 in various ways such as calling on Bukkyo University's Professors Kodo Sanada and Yoshika Ando and Ryukoku University's Emeritus Taijun Inokuchi for their involvements in this project.

Zhang Deqin 張徳勤 (1933 to 2015: the Director of the Chinese State Administration of Cultural Heritage): I had received his various considerations since I initiated the Japan-China joint scholarly research of the Niya ruins along with the Xinjiang party in 1988, especially when he directed to have the first-ever excavation certificate for a foreign explorer issued to me in 1994. I have been extremely obliged to it.

Yu Weichao 俞偉超 (1993 to 2003: the Director of the National Museum of Chinese History): He fully supported our Niya project as head of the Chinese archaeological world in various ways such as participating in the international symposium on the Japan-China joint scholarly research of the Niya ruins held in Urumqi in 2000.

Shouzo Tanabe 田辺昭三 (1933 to 2006: the Professor of Kyoto University of Art and Design): Starting in 1994, He was immeasurably supportive of our Niya projects in such manners as participating in the Japan-China joint research of the Niya ruins along with his many subordinates and played an active role as the second leader of the scholarly team from 1995. He made a huge contribution to desert archaeology.

Li Yuchun 李遇春 (1921 to 2003: the Vice-Director of the Museum of the Xinjiang Uyghur Autonomous Region): In 1959 he led the Autonomous Museum team and pressed ahead with the research of the Niya ruins in spite of poor conditions just after the establishment of the Autonomous Region. Our Japan-China joint team has learned a lot from his expedition.

ACKNOWLEDGEMENTS

Tiemuer Dawamaiti 鉄木尔・達瓦買提 (the Governor of the Xinjiang Uyghur Autonomous Region and the Vice-Chairman of the NPC): He kindly assumed the position of the Honorary Chairman for the Japan-China Joint scholarly research team of the Niya ruins and entirely supported us to conduct research at the Niya ruins. He is currently undergoing medical treatment due to the advanced age as 88. I sincerely pray for long life for this grand person.

Foreword

Sheng Chunshou 盛春寿
Director of the Cultural Heritage Administration Bureau of
the Xinjiang Uyghur Autonomous Region

I have been acquainted with Mr. Yasutaka Kojima 小島康誉 for almost 30 years. In 2013, he published a book about his 30-year long undertakings such as the conservation and research of those ruins in Kizil, Niya, and Dandanoilik, the presentation of the outstanding-performance awards for Xinjiang cultures and heritages, the grant of the scholarship for Xinjiang University, and others under the title of 新疆での世界的文化遺産保護研究事業と国際協力の意義 (The projects to conserve and research world-class cultural heritages in Xinjiang and the significance of international cooperation.) It is worthy of celebration, and when I read the book, bygone days came to mind. This book really doubled my pleasure and attachment to him.

Mr. Kojima told me that he was planning to publish a book in order to globally expand the awareness of significance to conserve and research cultural assets in Xinjiang trying to take the opportunity for the Kizil grottoes and others having been listed as one of the World Cultural Heritages. He said, "Since your names and photos appear here and there in this book, I would like to ask you to write a foreword." I was pleased to accept this offer without any hesitation.

Looking back over the time I encountered with Mr. Kojima in the summer of 1986, when he visited the Kizil grottoes for the first time and offered to contribute 100,000 CNY for the renovation of the grottoes. This was the first contribution ever offered by a foreigner in Xinjiang, China. And then he further proposed that he would launch a fund-raising campaign back in Japan for the restoration of the said grottoes. With his tremendous efforts, he established the Japan-China Friendship Association to Restore and Conserve the Kizil Grottoes with ex-Minister Taro Nakayama and Mr. Koshi Uemura as the Honorary Advisor and the Chairman respectively. Mr. Kojima devoted to this project as the managing director of the Association night and day to finally contribute funds amounting JPY 105.44 million, as well as research equipment to the Xinjiang Uyghur Autonomous Region, the People's Republic of China, for the renovation and conservation of the Kizil Thousand-Buddha grottoes.

In those days, I accompanied Mr. Kojima several times for his projects in Kizil as a staff member of the Assets Section of the Xinjiang Cultural Heritage Administration Bureau. Through these kinds of close and long-standing exchanges as mentioned above, I have been impressed with his passion and devotion for the conservation of cultural assets in Xinjiang. Thus, Mr. Kojima and I have been bound by deep friendship.

His personal contribution and fund-raising efforts for the Kizil grottoes turned out to be an opening stage for Mr. Kojima to be thoroughly involved in Xinjiang. Since that time, he has integrated himself into the vast Xinjiang land and infused his soul into the conservation activities of the ancient Chinese civilization, which has brought his life a great leap as we can see it now.

Mr. Yasutaka Kojima proposed a plan to organize a China-Japan joint research team in 1988 and put around JPY 200 million into large-scale scientific investigations of the Niya ruins extending over nine times for ten years. He spent almost all of his fortune. We encountered countless, painful hardships in the course of our investigations. On each occasion, he inspired our spirits as a monk as well as a mentor. Mr. Kojima turned in such outstanding performances not only as a leader of the Japanese team for archaeological research but as a role model for all the research team members through his discipline and perseverance to achieve his original goal. Through several researches, our projects have attained such a brilliant success as the Niya ruins site was designated as one of the Chinese Cultural Assets of Important Conservation, which means a very important cultural asset. It has also given an enormous international impact. The silk brocade Wu Xing Chu Dong Fang Li Zhong Guo 五星出東方利中国 (the five stars from the east beneficial to China) has been admired within and without China, and Niya studies have made a remarkable development.

In 1996, Dandanoilik was discovered again for the first time since its location had become unclear because of petroleum exploration activities. It was the valuable Buddhist ruins in the Tang dynasty period. In 2002, we organized a joint expedition team between China and Japan to research the Dandanoilik ruins. The Japanese group was represented by The Academic Research Organization for the Niya Ruins in Xinjiang, China, in Bukkyo University 佛教大学内ニヤ遺跡学術研究機構 (hereinafter called "the Academic Research Organization for the Niya ruins, Bukkyo University"). This was the first attempt for the Chinese Relics Archaeological Research Institution to research and excavate this ruins site. The team excavated beautiful murals such as so-called "Mona Lisa in the Western Regions" which has offered the latest material to research Buddhist arts in the Western Regions 西域 (currently the whole area of Xinjiang). After transferring murals detected in the ruins to the Xinjiang Archaeological Institute, Mr. Kojima organized a group of leading Japanese specialists and brought them to the Institute along with conserving and restoring staff for murals. They studied conserving methods of murals collaboratively with our staff here in Xinjiang. The level of our technology in the field of murals conservation has progressively matured.

Scholars from China and Japan held international scholarly symposiums in Peking University and Bukkyo University. The reports of research and studies on the Niya and the Dandanoilik ruins were published both in Chinese and Japanese. They have offered abundant materials for archaeological culture studies and given a great influence on them.

While Mr. Yasutaka Kojima has been engaged in conserving cultural assets in Xinjiang, he has realized the importance of developing human resources. Knowing of nurturing people as a crucial agenda for the long-term development of antiquities conservation and research in Xinjiang, he has enhanced the levels of Chinese researchers on antiquities conservation. In 1993, he established "The

Yasutaka Kojima Scholarship for the funds of Chinese antiquities conservation" through which he has contributed JPY 4.3 million every year to invite two relevant Xinjiang researchers to Japan to receive training programs. This has remarkably enhanced the standard and capabilities of those who research to conserve cultural assets in Xinjiang. Besides, Mr. Kojima and the Cultural Heritage Bureau of the Xinjiang Uyghur Autonomous Region signed to implement "the Kojima Yasutaka awards for outstanding performances for Xinjiang cultures and heritages" on July 3, 1999, for the purpose of constantly promoting activities for conservation and research of cultures in Xinjiang. For the decade from 1999 through 2008, CNY one million had been donated to annually offer 20 awards either for individuals or groups that made outstanding performances in the fields of conservation and research of cultural assets in Xinjiang. This worked out 200 awards for either individuals or groups in total for ten years. Award winners include: ordinary people working diligently for conservation, civil elderly artists trying to pass on each traditional culture, people working responsibly and earnestly at the forefront, high-level researchers on excavation and conservation of cultural assets, and front-line workers to protect cultural assets as a security guard to take a few examples.

In 2009, Mr. Yasutaka Kojima who aged 67 years signed the said agreement with the Cultural Heritage Administration Bureau of the Xinjiang Uyghur Autonomous Region to extend it for another five years. For five years from that year, he agreed to offer the awards as much as CNY one million. He said, "I'm already old. If I die, my wife will succeed this agreement. If she dies, this agreement will be terminated." That statement was referred to in this agreement. The establishment and donation of the awards have already achieved tremendously noteworthy results. They have encouraged people who have contributed to the conservation activities of cultural assets in Xinjiang and shed light on groups and people having made outstanding performances, and played a critical role for the development of activities for culture and art and antiquities conservation of each tribe in Xinjiang.

Mr. Kojima has been engaged in public relations to inform Xinjiang on an enormous scale as well as implemented various projects, including cultural enhancement, conservation of cultural heritages, and education and human resources development programs. He has made contact with various scholarly fields in Japan and frequently lectured in the media and at research institutions. His lectures always focus on Xinjiang, because Xinjiang is his second home.

He has written a number of books, most of which have touched on Xinjiang. His books have endorsed to Japanese people beautiful places in Xinjiang, drastic transformation since its market-opening reform and valuable sites on the Silk Road. These kinds of activities have given added impetus to our media as well. Mr. Kojima has been praised as Today's Abeno Nakamaro 現代の阿倍仲麻呂 by People's Daily 人民日報 for his bridging role of friendship between Chinese and Japanese.

Although Mr. Kojima has reached an advanced age, he's still been back and forth between Xinjiang and Japan numerous times every year. I said to him before,

"Please not try too hard." However, he still takes an active interest in the conservation activities of antiquities in Xinjiang and supports us. He places importance on scientific arrangement of data and has his heart in such activities as education of Xinjiang, publication of historical materials, and the relief of the poor. Furthermore, he is trying to raise international community's awareness for the conservation of important cultural assets on the Silk Road, as well as to encourage the sprit and scientific idea to conserve cultural heritages.

I have been invariably impressed with Mr. Kojima's dedication and accomplishments as mentioned above. His lofty virtue and cordial friendship for the people of each tribe in Xinjiang have been received with our deepest regards and solicitude. It's such a great honor for me to be blessed with this friendship.

Mr. Yasutaka Kojima has visited Xinjiang more than 140 times since 1982. He explains the reason why he has chosen this land is that passion and honesty of the people of each tribe and many world-class cultural assets in Xinjiang touched his heart enough to bestow his supreme devotion on Xinjiang. Therefore, he has outfaced the challenges to explore such ruins as Kizil, Niya, and Dandanoilik tirelessly without fearing a dusty wind.

This book refers to the outstanding accomplishments and contributions made by Mr. Yasutaka Kojima in the course of conserving and researching world-class cultural heritages in Xinjiang. In addition, a part of his life is condensed in these projects in Xinjiang. In the meantime, it is very significant in the way he offers a great deal of facts and rationale why we have to protect cultural assets collaboratively on the international scene. Though it may be in a random fashion, I'd like to put this as a foreword.

(He was transferred to the other organization in May 2015 after the submission of this paper.)

Preface

Yasukata Kojima 小島康誉

Representative of Academic Research Organization for Niya, Bukkyo University, Japan

Conservation and Research of World-class Cultural Heritages through
International Cooperation for 30 Years in the Silk Road far away from Japan
Expressing my hearty thanks for having the Kizil grottoes listed as the World Cultural
Heritage while having a high hope for an additional listing of the Niya ruins

To begin with, I am highly obliged to Director of the Cultural Heritage Administration of the Xinjiang Uyghur Autonomous Region Sheng Chunshou 盛春寿 for his passionate and generous congratulatory message. Amid copy-editing this thesis, Mr. Sheng Chunshou was transferred to the other organization as of May 2015. I wish him every success in his new job.

The 38th UNESCO World Heritage Committee officially decided in Doha, Qatar, on June 22, 2014, that Silk Roads: the Routes Network of Chang'an - Tianshan Corridor including the Kizil grottoes 克孜尔千仏洞 shall be declared a World Cultural Heritage Site. China, Kazakhstan and Kyrgyzstan have applied for this registration, which covers 33 ruins, including 22 in China, eight in Kazakhstan, and three in Kyrgyzstan. In the Xinjiang Uyghur Autonomous Region 新疆維吾尔自治区 of China, besides the Kizil grottoes 克孜尔千仏洞 in which I myself have been involved for restoration and conservation since 1986, the ancient cities of Gaochang 高昌故城, Jiao River 交河故城, Beiting 北庭故城, the Subashi Buddhist Temple Ruins 蘇巴什故城 and the Kizilgaha Beacon 克孜尓哈烽火台 were designated. This road network has long been regarded as a highway having contributed to transporting various civilizations and cultures, such as religions, as well as people and things. In addition, this omnibus registration extending across surrounding nations has implications for where the World Heritage Centre will head from now on.

As I wanted to know of this decision as soon as possible, I kept on watching the conference of the World Heritage Committee live on the Internet. Japan and several other nations expressed favorable opinions. When the Chairperson declared the decision at 4:50 pm (Japan Time), I cried, "Hurrah!" Mr. Tong Mingkan 童明康, the head of the Chinese delegation, expressed the gratitude in his speech in English. The representatives of Kazakhstan and Kyrgyzstan also made speeches. Bureau Director Sheng Chunshou 盛春寿 attended the conference as a member of the delegation as well. A number of participants rushed to the Chinese delegates' seats to shake hands. It was the moment I felt extremely happy. I immediately sent a congratulations fax to the Cultural Heritage Administration Bureau of the Xinjiang Uyghur Autonomous Region.

Kosaku Maeda, Professor Emeritus of Wako University specializing in Asian cultural history, commented in the Yomiuri newspaper's article reporting the registration recommendation by ICOMOS, or International Council on Monuments and Sites, that these efforts across borders for registration hold a great significance to promote peace in Asia and taking this opportunity, Japan should globally release the long-accumulated research work of the Silk Road Culture and strive to have Japanese cultural heritages extensionally designated as the terminal point of the Silk Road. Meanwhile, Tomioka Silk Mill and Related Sites that had been applied by Japan was also designated, following Fujisan, the sacred place and the source of artistic inspiration in 2013.

In August 2006, the preliminary conference was held to apply for the designation of the Silk Road as the World Heritage in Turpan, Xinjiang, with the participation of Tajikistan and Uzbekistan besides the said three countries. Cultural heritages which compose Xinjiang ruins' sites included Niya 尼雅, Loulan 楼蘭, Bezeklik 柏孜克里克, and others. Initially, the Chinese State Administration of Cultural Heritage and the Xinjiang Cultural Heritage Administration Bureau had tried to enhance conservation, improve environments and develop human resources in order to have them designated in 2012. When a party headed by Director of the Cultural Heritage Administration Bureau of the Xinjiang Uyghur Autonomous Region Sheng Chunshou came to Japan in March 2007, I accompanied them to visit Ikuo Hirayama 平山郁夫 who then assumed a role as the UNESCO Goodwill Ambassador in charge of conservation of cultural assets. And he gave us one valuable instruction, saying that the transboundary application of the Silk Road for the World Heritage site would entail a variety of troubles. Exactly as he told us, due to the delay in preparations in some countries, the application was postponed and scaled down like Loulan and Niya being procrastinated in the next phase. Finally, a formal application was made in January 2013. UNESCO dispatched specialists to conduct on-site examinations in October 2013 followed by ICOMOS issuing a registration recommendation in April 2014. As a result, the Silk Road was officially designated as a new World Heritage site in June, thanks to the enormous efforts by a whole variety of people.

On this special occasion, I have compiled this summary about Japan-China joint projects in research and conservation of world-class cultural heritages and their related activities. I have publicized some parts of my activity log in the Research Bulletin of Bukkyo University and later revised them partially, as well as added subsequent events, all of which were translated into English. On top of that, superb theses of several researchers, including Mr. Toshio Asaoka 浅岡俊夫, Ms. Yoshika Ando 安藤佳香, Mr. Shiro Ishida 石田志朗, Mr. Kiyomi Tanaka 田中清美, Mr. Shin Yoshizaki 吉崎伸, and I have also been contributed. The translation was made by Mr. & Mrs. Kazuyuki Takada and the designing was created by Mr. Toshihiko Saito and Mrs. Hideko Nakagawa. This book has been succcessfully published with the assistance of Toho Shuppan. I would like to express my appreciation to them all.

In the course of over 140 visits to Xinjiang since 1982, I have conducted research and conservation works in a Japan-China joint manner, having started with the Kizil grottoes for their restoration and conservation, followed by the ruins in Niya and Dandanoilik. I don't know what I could have done without guidance and cooperation afforded by people in China as well as in Japan. Thus, I'm extremely grateful to them all.

The achievements attained by the Japan-China joint team have already been made in public through reports and international symposiums. And thanks to ongoing developments in technology, cultural assets detected by the team will surely bring about lots of new insights from now on and will play an extraordinary role for Niya-Silkroad studies, covering Kizil, Niya, and Dandanoilik.

I can't lay too much emphasis on researching and conserving world-class cultural heritages and the significance of international cooperation, because, it definitely leads to the very existence of human beings. International cooperation maintains peace and deters war. Though many people understand it, it is no easy matter to realize it. Yet, we have put it into practice every chance we have got. In terms of Japan-China environments, a strained relationship has intermittently recurred. I have prided myself in making continued efforts for 30 years to solidly enhance mutual understanding considering that we should evolve from a ready-made catch-phrase Japan-China friendship 日中友好 to Japan-China understandings 日中理解 and further to Japan-China collaboration 日中共同.

Thinking back on my personal funds for the conservation of the Kizil grottoes followed by rushing around trying to establish an association, to raise contributions along with so many projects afterward, I am very pleased that the Kizil grottoes site has been designated as one of the World Heritage. The Niya ruins' registration as the World Heritage, which was postponed to the next phase due to scaling down the applied areas for this registration, is anticipated to realize soon.

Thanks a lot, everybody. Cheer!

Explanatory notes:
....

- The book is the English translation of *Shinkyou deno sekaiteki bunkaisan hogo kenkyu jigyou to kokusai kyouryoku no igi*『新疆での世界的文化遺産保護研究事業と国際協力の意義』(The projects to conserve and research world-class cultural heritages in Xinjiang, China, and the significance of international cooperation) written by Yasutaka Kojima and published by the Bukkyo University Museum of Religious Culture, 2013 with some minor revisions, as well as additions of subsequent events. And further, contributions were made in English from Toshio Asaoka, Yoshika Ando, Shirou Ishida, Kiyomi Tanaka, Shin Yoshizaki, and Yasutaka Kojima.
- An English translation of the book was made by Kazuyuki and Yoko Takada and its layout was created by Yoshika Ando, Toshihiko Saito, and Hideko Nakagawa.
- Commonly used names were employed for people and places because there are various indications.
- The number of the notes has been substantially reduced from 96 in the original to 25 in the English edition.
- Photographers were referred to in the captions. The photos shown are not necessarily those taken in the corresponding year.
- This thesis is the record as of December 2015. A part of it has been spared due to space limitations.
- Since I presume that there can be omissions of materials or my faulty memory, I would like to ask those Japanese and Chinese involved in the said projects to point them out to make a correction.

Contents

DEDICATION in MEMORY 9
ACKNOWLEDGEMENTS 10
Foreword Sheng Chunshou 11
Preface Yasutaka Kojima 15
Explanatory notes 18

The projects to conserve and research world-class cultural heritages in Xinjiang, China, and the significance of international cooperation Yasutaka Kojima

Introduction 21
I. The Xinjiang Uyghur Autonomous Region 25
II. The Japan-China Friendship Association to Restore and
   Conserve the Kizil Grottoes and the Outline 31
III. The Japan-China Joint Scholarly Research of the Niya Ruins and the Outline   57
IV. The Japan-China Joint Scholarly Research of the Dandanoilik Ruins
    and the Outline 105
V. Related Projects and the Outline 143
VI. The Significance of International Cooperation 151
Conclusion With My Life Mission in Mind 161
Summary of the Timeline 167
References 170

contribution 1 A Summarized Report on Dandan Oilik Ruins
   Toshio Asaoka 175

contribution 2 Changes in Buddhism and the Styles of Stupa along Xi-yu Nan-dao
   Toshio Asaoka 182

contribution 3 Lining in the painting of Xinjiang : from Silk Route down to Japan
   Yoshika Ando 188

contribution 4 Topography and Geology of the Niya Site
   Shiro Ishida 194

contribution 5 Remains related to Buddhism at the point 93A35 (N5), Niya, Xinjiang
   Kiyomi Tanaka 206

contribution 6 The remains of manufactories in the north of The Ruins of Niya
   Shin Yoshizaki 212

contribution 7 The Whole Story of Sir Marc Aurel Stein's 4th Expedition
   To Xinjiang in Central Asia
   Yasutaka Kojima 217

The Projects to Conserve and Research World-class Cultural Heritages in Xinjiang, China, And the Significance of International Cooperation

Yasukata Kojima 小島康誉

Representative of Academic Research Organization for Niya, Bukkyo University, Japan

Introduction

On June 22, 2014, the 38th UNESCO World Heritage Committee officially designated Silk Roads: the Routes Network of Chang'an-Tianshan Corridor including the Kizil grottoes in Xinjiang, China, as a World Cultural Heritage Site. The Site comprises 33 ruins, including 22 in China, eight in Kazakhstan, and three in Kyrgyzstan.

The Kizil grottoes are a commemorable site for me, because it gave me the first opportunity to involve in conservation and research work in Xinjiang, which began in 1986. This opportunity has led me to further cooperate in conserving and researching activities afterward.

Taking this occasion of having been listed as the World Cultural Heritage, I have made final adjustments to those Japanese papers that had been publicized in the Research Bulletin of Bukkyo University to summarize my conserving and researching undertakings of world-class cultural heritages and their related activities in order to have them be translated into English.[1]

I have visited the Xinjiang Uyghur Autonomous Region, China, more than 140 times since 1982, and there I have initiated research, conservation and studies of world-class cultural heritages having survived in Xinjiang in a Japan-China joint manner receiving the guidance and support of researchers and conservation specialists both in Japan and China as well as such organizations as the Japanese Ministry of Education, Culture, Sports, Science and Technology (MEXT), Bukkyo University, the Chinese State Administration of Cultural Heritage (hereinafter called SACH, China), the People's Government of the Xinjiang Uyghur Autonomous Region, the Cultural Agency of the Xinjiang Uyghur Autonomous Region, the Cultural Heritage Administration Bureau of the Xinjiang Uygur Autonomous Region, and the Xinjiang Archaeological Institute. I would like to express my cordial appreciation to them all.

Some of the examples of these activities are the restoration and conservation of the Kizil grottoes, the research of the Niya ruins, the research of the Dandanoilik ruins and the conservation of their mural paintings, the presentation of the awards for outstanding performances for Xinjiang cultures and relics, provision of educational support for grade-schoolers in the area along the Silk Road, operation of the website to conserve Chinese historical, cultural heritages, publishing archives, funding both the scholarship for Xinjiang University and the

Downtown Urumqi in 1985, provided by Yang Xincai

The same downtown in 2008, photo by Yang Xincai

Chinese Cultural Resources News reporting with the highest commendation, photo by Y. Kojima

Bill with the image of Chairman Chiang Kaishek 蔣介石 issued in 1949 by Bank of Xinjiang, photo by Y. Kojima

construction of Hope Elementary Schools, dispatching and inviting delegates of various groups, and acting as intermediary in Xinjiang for various people.[2]

In the past, the official paper of SACH, China, named Chinese Cultural Resources News, carried a full-page feature on March 19, 2010 to report the conservation and research of the ruins as well as scholarly exchanges in Niya and Dandanoilik with the highest level of evaluation as being referred to "a textbook example of the joint activity between China and a foreign country," "the collaborative work for research and conservation in the multiple scholarly spheres and archaeology in the Western Regions," and "the excellent joint efforts among Chinese and foreign scholars." I am overjoyed as one of those who have devoted their energy to Xinjinag. The same paper wrote up using almost a full page as a major article on June 16, 2010, "Yasutaka Kojima; A Japanese who is devoting his entire life to Xinjiang has really touched our heart."

Besides the Kizil grottoes listed as the World Heritage Site, the Niya ruins which had been included in the initial phase of the application for the World Heritage was postponed to the next phase because this application was scaled down due to a huge number of sites submitted by surrounding nations.[3] This underlines how valuable those Japan-China joint projects for conservation and research I have been involved in are.

Such admiring remarks would come from the fact that Japanese and Chinese specialists had made up their own teams to implement research, studies, and conservation and simultaneously published and released those results in the symposiums at venues, including Bukkyo University, World Plaza Urumqi Hotel and Peking University. And the antiquities excavated in the course of research were found as a level high enough to be exhibited not only in Tokyo, Kyoto, Osaka, Kobe, and Okayama but in Urumqi, Beijing, Shanghai, Hangzhou, Hong Kong,

Taipei, and even farther in London, Rome, New York, Huston, Soul, and other cities.

Notes:
....

(1) (2) My manuscripts include: *Chousa no keiki to keika*「調査の契機と経過」(The opportunity and the transition of research) in *Nicchu-Chunichi Niya iseki gakujutsuchousa houkokusho*『日中・中日共同ニヤ遺跡学術調査報告書』第一巻 (The report of the Japan-China joint scholarly research of the Niya ruins. Vol. 1). Kyoto: Hozokan法蔵館, 1996; *Chousa no keii*「調査の経緯」(The background of research) in *Nicchu-Chunichi Niya iseki gakujutsuchousa houkokusho*『日中・中日共同ニヤ遺跡学術調査報告書』第二巻 (The report of the Japan-China joint scholarly research of the Niya ruins. Vol. 2). Kyoto: Nakamura Printing 中村印刷, 1999; *Nicchu kyoudou Niya iseki gakujutsuchousa no gaiyou*「日中共同ニヤ遺跡学術調査の概要」(The outline of Japan-China joint scholarly research of the Niya ruins) in *Shirukurodo Niya iseki no nazo*『シルクロード・ニヤ遺跡の謎』(The mysteries of the Niya ruins on the Silk Road). Osaka: Toho Publishing Inc. 東方出版, 2002; *Kijiru Senbutsudou kara Niya, Dandanuiriku iseki he*「キジル千仏洞からニヤ・ダンダンウイリク遺跡へ」(From the Kizil grottoes through the Niya ruins to the Dandanoilik ruins) in *Shin Sirukuroudo*『新シルクロード』第三巻 (The New Silk Road. Vol. 3), Tokyo: NHK Publishing Co., Ltd. 日本放送出版協会, 2005; *Chousa no Keii*「調査の経緯」(The background of research) in *Nicchu-Chunichi Kyoudou Niya iseki gakujutsuchousa houkokusho*『日中・中日共同ニヤ遺跡学術調査報告書』第三巻 (The report of the Japan-China joint scholarly research of the Niya ruins. Vol. 3), Kyoto: Shinyosha 真陽社, 2007; *Nicchu kyoudou Dandanuiriku iseki gakujutsukenkyu purojekuto gaiyou*「日中共同ダンダンウイリク遺跡学術研究プロジェクト概要」(The outline of the Japan-China joint scholarly research project of the Dandanoilik ruins) in *Nicchu-Chunichi Dandanuiriku iseki gakujutsuchousa houkokusho*『日中・中日共同ダンダンウイリク遺跡学術調査報告書』(The report of the Japan-China joint scholarly research of the Dandanoilik ruins), Kyoto: Shinyosha 真陽社, 2007; *Shinkyou deno sekaiteki bunkaisan no hogo kenkyu to kokusaikyoryoku no igi*『新疆での世界的文化遺産の保護研究事業と国際協力の意義』(The projects to conserve and research world-class cultural heritages in Xinjiang, China, and the significance of international cooperation), Kyoto: the Bukkyo University Museum of Religious Culture 佛教大学宗教文化ミュージアム, 2013.

(3)「関于開展絲綢之路申遺準備工作的情況介紹」(The information on launching preparation work for the Silk Road exhibition) (Apr. 29, 2007) and「絲綢之路申報世界遺産国内遺産選点推荐名単及其評議意見」(The review on the recommendation for the Silk Road to be selected as the World Cultural Heritage) (Feb. 15, 2008): The electronic edition of the Cultural Heritage Administration Bureau of the Xinjiang Uyghur Autonomous Region.

I. The Xinjiang Uyghur Autonomous Region
―新疆維吾尔自治区―

I. The Xinjiang Uyghur Autonomous Region

Those of you who read the subtitle of this thesis and can create some image out of it should be the specialist of or well-versed in the Silk Road. They are the geographical names of the Xinjiang Uyghur Autonomous Region. This area is not familiar with outsiders. For example, we often misuse the Chinese character of 疆 (jiang) for a similar-shaped character, 彊 (jiang), with a different meaning, take the name of Uyghur for the similar country's name of Uruguay, call this region with the old name, The Xinjiang province 新疆省, or use it as an official name here, in Japan. Even in China, I have sometimes encountered these kinds of misunderstandings, for example, being often referred to as the Xinjinag Uyghur Tribe Autonomous Region. That's why I would like to introduce the Xinjiang Uyghur Autonomous Region first. This is nothing but my role as a cultural adviser to the Xinjiang Government.

The Xinjiang Uyghur Autonomous Region was established on October 1, 1955. It is located in the center of the Silk Road where cultures from the north, the south, the east and the west have interacted. It has borders with Mongol, Russia, Kazakhstan, Kyrgyzstan, Tajikistan, Afghanistan, Pakistan and India, extending around 5,600 km. This Region has been seen as a geopolitically important area and a strategic point between East and West. Thus, information warfare called "the Great Game" was developed among the Western nations aimed at territory grabbing for the period between the end of the 19th century and the beginning of the 20th century.⁽⁴⁾ Currently, it holds great political significance as one of contact points from the Chinese side in the light of "the Shanghai Cooperation Organization." ⁽⁵⁾

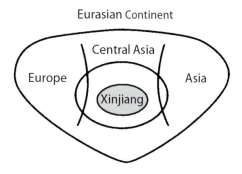

Geographical concept diagram of Xinjiang, China in Eurasia (The scope of Central Asia defined by UNESCO, drawn by the author)

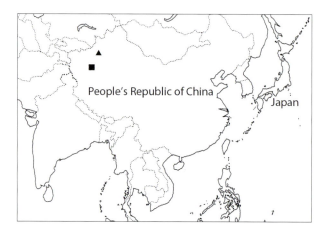

General locations of the Kizil grottoes, the Niya ruins, and the Dandanoilik ruins, reprinted from 日中共同ニヤ遺跡学術調査報告書 (The report of Japan-China scholarly research of the Niya ruins) (partially revised)   ▲ = The Kizil grottoes ■ = The Niya ruins and the Dandanoilik ruins

Simplified map of the Xinjiang Uyghur Autonomous Region and its surroundings

The Region has an area about 1.66 million square kilometers, occupies around one sixth of China and is approximately 4.4 times larger than Japan. It's also nearly 6.8 times of England, 2.6 times of France, 4.6 times of Germany and sixth part of the U. S. Such three great mountains as Altai, Tianshan, and Kunlun surround the Dzungaria Basin and the Taklamakan. The peaks of those mountains reaching as high as 5,000 to 7,000 meters are covered with eternal snows and the glaciers. The grassland like Bayinbuluke is filled with blooming alpine plants, where sheep, cattle, horses and goats are pastured.

The four key words to understand Xinjiang can be described as; the Silk Road, a multiethnic community, natural resources, and the center of the Central Asian Economic Sphere. This is where a whole variety of cultures have been interacting and world-class cultural heritages represented by Loulan, Kizil, and Niya are found all around. Those who have brought in civilizations and cultures are such people as Uyghur, Han, Kazakh, Hui, Mongol, Kirgiz, Xibe, Tajik, Manchu, Tartar, Uzbek, Daur, Russian, and others, in total 47 ethnics with the population of approximately 22 million as of end-October, 2010. They are working together for their daily lives. This variety reminds us of the bygone days' interactions. Vast natural resources like petroleum, natural gas, coal, rare metals, and water lie here and their development has just started. Whereas the Taklamakan Desert used to be called "the death sea," at present it has turned out to be "the hope sea." The central city of Urumqi is bristled with high-rise buildings and enjoys booming transactions with neighboring nations. Foreign firms' advancement is still going on now.

That Xinjiang became widely known in Japan was when lots of mysteries were unwrapped by the pool coverage program *Sirukuroudo* シルクロード (The Silk Road) released jointly by NHK (Japan Broadcasting Corporation) and the China Central Television, which had been broadcast from 1980 through 1981. It became a sort of social phenomenon along with a theme music composed by a distinguished composer, or Kitaro, and a narration made by a famous actor, or Koji Ishizaka. Since then, this phenomenon has garnered lots of enthusiastic fans even as being called the Silk Road syndrome. In 2005, *Shin Sirukuroudo* 新シルクロード (The New Silk Road) was televised and gathered as much attention as before. [6] The Chinese economic development has been so remarkably successful since the reform and door-opening policies 30 years ago that it has made even Xinjiang teem with business people and sightseers from a number of places around the world thanks to booms in investment and tourism. As many as approximately 50 thousand Japanese were also said to have visited there in the peak year.

As intensively reported in the media, the Uyghur insurrection in Urumqi in July 2009 followed by a large-scale demonstration by Han people in September attracted worldwide attention. [7] In place of Wang Lequan 王楽泉 who was then the Head of Xinjiang, or the Secretary of the Chinese Communist Party (hereinafter called CCP) in charge of the Xinjiang Uyghur Autonomous Region, Zhang Chunxian 張春賢 assumed this position in April 2010. In accordance with this transition, Chinese Government's massive and all-out support started and brought about historically drastic transformations in Xinjang. While investors and tourists once having extremely decreased due to the unrests there are beginning to return, there still have been various incidents arisen sporadically. For instance, explosions occurred in Urumqi and other places in April, May and September in 2014. In the meantime, China, including Xinjiang, has radically changed as a result of its reform and door-opening policies. [8] Moreover, Chinese President Xi Jinping recently advocated the Silk Road Economic Belt, the 21st Century Maritime Silk Road and Asian Infrastructure Investment Bank, and the significance of Xinjiang is growing day by day. But rapid growth has also caused a wide variety of distortions. I assume that it could go through further historical shifts.

Notes:

(4) The Xinjiang area was involved in a chaotic situation during the period from the end of Qing Dynasty through the foundation of the Republic of China. Old Russia took a strategy of southward expansion seeking for ice-free ports and England took a strategy of northward expansion as it had controlled India. Since the collision point between them was Xinjiang, both nations established their consulates in Kashgar to wage intelligence operations to grab a territory. It is recorded that a number of both British and Russian resided in Xinjiang. While England demanded to take over Kashgar, Russia stationed its soldiers there. It turned out to be nothing but a settlement. Military officers were dispatched from Japan as well. Thus it could be said that the exploration operation and the intelligence operations to grab a territory complicated relations among these nations.

(5) This was developed from the Shanghai Five initiated by five nations, such as China, Russia, Kazakhstan, Kyrgyzstan, and Tajikistan in 1996. Currently, Uzbekistan joined it along with Mongol, India, and Pakistan, and Iran being participating as observers, as well as several nations being on the list of partners. The joint military exercise was also carried out.

(6) I fully supported various negotiations with the Party, the Autonomous Region, the Cultural Heritage Administration Bureau, etc., in Xinjiang for *The New Silk Road* and its related programs, as well as the Exhibition of the New Silk Road by making the most use of my personal connections.

(7) Just after the Urumqi riots, the communication between Xinjiang and the outside was restricted in such ways as telephone, fax, and the Internet were cut off. Gradually, however, they were loosened and finally recovered entirely in the middle of May 2010.

(8) The visit to Japan in 1978 by Vice-Governor of the Central Committee of the Chinese Communist Party Deng Xiaoping 鄧小平 had turned out to be one of the most significant steps to launch market-opening reform policies which led to an enormous development of China after having been ravaged by the Cultural Revolution. For instance, China Youth Daily reported on Dec. 23, 2008 that the market-opening policies would have been totally different from what it is now without Japan.

II. The Japan-China Friendship Association To Restore and Conserve The Kizil Grottoes and the Outline

―日中友好キジル千仏洞修復保存協力会とその概要―

The western area of the Kizil grottoes before restoration (1986), photo by Y. Kojima

Implementation of full-scale restoration and conservation work (1989), photo by Y. Kojima

Shining brighter, the World Heritage Kizil grottoes (2014), photo by Yang Xincai

II. The Japan-China Friendship Association to Restore and Conserve the Kizil Grottoes and the Outline

1. Two moving stories and guide's joke

I had sourced jewelries at such places like the Canton Fair since Japan-China relations restored in 1972 to market them in Japan. On one occasion, as a trade house informed me of quality gems being available in Xinjiang, I visited Xinjiang for the first time in June 1982. Although my business was not successful, I was so attracted to people's humble, warm heart, as well as abundant cultural assets when I went on a sightseeing trip to Turpan.

Riding back on a freight due to traffic being closed, photo by Y. Terao

In May 1986, I can't forget how I was impressed when I first visited grottoes in Kizil 克孜尔 meaning red in Uyghur. They are one of the four great Chinese grottoes, including Dunhuang, Yungang, and Longmen, located about 70 km west of Kuqa 库车 at the south foot of Tianshan 天山 in the area of 41 degrees 47 minutes northern latitude and 82 degrees 31 minutes eastern longitude at a height of approximately 1,110 m above sea level. At that time, Kuqa was not open up to the world to the degree as I was made to receive the travel documents for foreigners to visit there.

I was extremely inspired by the story of Shakyamuni's previous life depicted in lapis lazuli's blue: firing his own hand for a traveler straying after dark; serving himself for starving lion's family; and others. There still has remained a cumulative total of 10 thousand square meters' murals depicted in most of 236 grottoes (having increased up to 300 or so by the subsequent restoration work). I have learned that the earliest ones had been constructed in the 3rd century with its heyday lasting from 6th through 7th century.

My instinct told me that this should be a world-class heritage site, imagining people who first wished to build grottoes, contributed huge funds, concentrated the wisdom to depict murals, preached Buddhism, disciplined themselves, and supported their lives there for over hundred, five hundred, and hundred of thousand years, during which sun rose and set going through natural hardships, other pagans, and lootings. The murals depicting people's wishes still remain vividly there.

In spite of households being so poor as not to be able to make a living, the people there worked until they were exhausted trying to conserve these national-treasure-class ruins (designated as the Major Historical and Cultural Site Protected at the National Level in 1961). In the innermost region of China some 30 years ago, where people lived in shanties, wore patched clothing, and had little to eat. I saw them slowly yet diligently engaged in conservation activities.

Ladder to caves: Risky conditions even to climb (appearance of the Kizil grottoes valley west ward in 1986), photo by Y. Kojima

Painfully stripped mural (the 38th cave of the Kizil grottoes), photo by Y. Kojima

On our way back, Wang Shitian, a staff member of Xinjiang Craftwork Bureau, said to me, "If Mr. Kojima kindly offers CNY 100,000, we will make a practice cave for Kojima's exclusive use," CNY 100, 000 was approximately equivalent to JPY 4.5 million or USD 27,000 at the time. Though he was not serious at all, I instantly responded, "All right, I will offer that amount" because of having seen a couple of moving scenes as mentioned above. He was astonished to hear this response of a foreigner with whom he met just a few times. With the same sense as calling a big money like "JPY 100 million or USD one million" he cited CNY100, 000. It sounded like that huge money in Xinjiang in those days.

I reiterated, "I don't want my own practice cave, so will you use it for restoration." He responded suspecting my real intention, "I was joking, so just forget it." He couldn't believe such an offer as to contribute unexpected huge amount of money without seeking any return. On our way back to Urumqi, our conversations of "I don't want my own practice cave, so will you use it for conservation." and "I was joking, so just forget it." went on and on for two days. After confirming again and again, he finally came to understand my true intention to conserve cultural heritages, saying "Now I have well understood your intention, yet I can't receive your money, instead I'll ask Mr. Sheng to introduce a relevant government institution."

At that time, Sheng Chunshou 盛春寿, fresh from Xinjiang University, began to work for the Assets Section of the Xinjiang Cultural Agency (who has been the Director of the Cultural Heritage Administration Bureau of the Xinjiang Uyghur Autonomous Region since 2001). He looked like more of a watcher for foreigners visiting Kizil, only listening to our conversation than just a guide. At the time, it was extremely rare for foreigners to visit Xinjiang, to say nothing of its ruins.

The person I was introduced was Han Xiang 韓翔, the Manager of the Assets Section at the Cultural Agency of the Xinjiang Uyghur Autonomous Region, who said to me again and again, "Why? Are you serious? What's your real intention?" I returned to Japan after having signed a simple note and then in the following month, Mr. Han Xiang, a person responsible for Xinjiang Art Crafts Company and I signed the memorandum of agreement. (The Memorandum Agreement between the Xinjiang Cultural Agency and Yasutaka Kojima on Jul. 16, 1986) However, the notice of a bank account took a long time to reach me. At last, I could remit the conserving contribution to the bank account on October 31, 1986 (the receipt of the Xinjiang Cultural Agency dated Oct. 31, 1986). Being the first foreigner to offer a contribution to Xinjiang in any form, including economics and culture, they only half-believed it and I had trouble receiving permission to make a donation due to their fear that I had another intention. I was told later that Wang Enmao 王恩茂, the Vice-Chairman of the National Committee of the Chinese People's Political Consultative Conference, or the Head of Xinjiang at that time (the Secretary of the Xinjiang Uyghur Autonomous Regional CCP Committee until 1985), had given a final approval.[9]

When I visited Xinjiang again after a brief interval, I heard that the Chinese Government had put up CNY 20 million to conduct a full-fledged restoration of the Kizil grottoes in considering they were highly valued by a foreigner. While activities for restoration and conservation had sparsely been continued over the years, their physical environment presented that even scholarly work could incur a sizable risk. And if we left it as it had been, destruction would have been aggravated and the valuable cultural heritages of humanity would have been buried into history. While construction for restoration and conservation was being considered in order to stop this situation and make it available for sightseeing, the contribution made by a foreigner might have triggered the said full-fledged restoration.

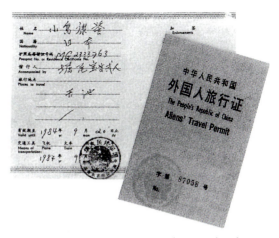

Foreigner's Travel Permit, 1984: The special authorization required even to visit Kizil and Tianch reprinted from my book シルクロードの点と線 (Points and lines on the Silk Road)

If that's the case, since CNY 100,000 was not enough, I offered to contribute another JPY 100 million by launching a fund-raising campaign across Japan. In terms of the local commodity prices those days, this amount is worth of such a great value as being equivalent to the current CNY 100 million (approximately JPY 2,000 million or USD 16 million as of July 2015). Everyone including the Director-General of the Xinjiang Cultural Agency was again so shockingly stunned and actually screamed, "What!?" In fact, I made this offer having reflected on how the Otani exploration team 大谷探検隊 from Japan had involved in devastation of this area's cultural heritages such as the Kizil grottoes. (10)

The memorandum agreement signed at the presence of Vice-Chairman Wang Enmao (rear row, 4th from left), photo by the Xinjiang Cultural Agency

The devastation of the ruins was mainly caused by: exporting mural paintings by exploration teams from Germany, Russia, and France other than Japan; peeling away of gilt by the local people of that time; destructions by infidels; age-long decay.

The Kizil grottoes can be likened to an exquisite flower bloomed in the desert of the Silk Road and is a precious cultural heritage expected to be thoroughly researched from a whole variety of fields, such as archaeology, ethnology, history of cultural exchange between East and West, art history, Buddhist studies, linguistics, and conservation science.

In those days, among these majestic grottoes, 236 were numbered for conservation, of which 104 were relatively well preserved, 74 had murals survived almost unhurt, 20 were open to scholars, and six were available for tourists. The opened grottoes were very few because it was next to impossible or too risky even to approach. Except for the Kizil grottoes, the other three Chinese Great Caves had already been basically restored. Thus, I made this offer with the view that the

Kizil grottoes were not just for the cultural heritage of China, but immeasurably valuable for mankind in terms of scale and quality.

But once again, it took a long time to obtain an endorsement. Finally, however, we could welcome Vice-Chairman Wang Enmao 王恩茂 at the signing ceremony at the Xinjiang Guest Palace on May 20, 1987. Vice-Chairman Wang read every word of the leaflet for the fund-raising campaign written in Chinese and added the word "Cultural" to that of Heritage. I was impressed with his scrupulous attitude. He has since been a sympathetic supporter of mine. Vice-Director-General of the Xinjiang Cultural Agency Wang Chengwen 王成文 and I signed the memorandum of agreement.

2. The characteristics of the murals

Located in the westernmost and established earliest among the Chinese Four Great Grottoes, the Kizil grottoes are rock-cut caves along the northern bank of the Muzat River extending 3 km, which originates in the Tian Shan Mountains and vanishes into the Taklamakan Desert 塔克拉玛干沙漠. For such a long period as from the 3rd through the 13th century (according to Manager Hang Xiang), the grottoes have been constructed by the ancient Kuqa and Uyghur. They cut into rather soft river bank to make a cave, inside of which was coated with stucco made of mixed mud. Buddhists and animals were depicted on the wall. It may have taken several years to complete a big cave.

The form of a grotto consists of separated caves for a mainstay, a Buddha statue, a square, and a monastery. Though the mainstay cave used to be constituted of three parts, namely a front chamber, a main chamber, and a rear chamber, the front chamber was demolished at most of grottoes.

The Kizil grottoes are characterized by voluminous depictions of the Jataka Tales, which were created to honor the achievements of Shakyamuni. They are described in diamond-shaped lattice patterns. The lapis lazuli's ultramarine color gives us a brilliant impression.

These murals surely must have nursed millions of people's souls for a long time.

3. The outline of the restoration and conservation project
(from the plan document of that time)

The construction supervisor: the Xinjiang Cultural Agency. The construction period: five years from 1986. The preparation process: to start streamlining an approach lane, as well as proceeding with the construction of electricity, water supply and lodgment in 1986 to complete them within 1987, meanwhile, making a survey, experiments of restoring and conserving methods, and strength tests in order to decide a construction method in the first half of 1987. We will invite relevant specialists from Beijing and Lanzhou for consultation of these tests in order to get the project under way.

The first process: The west cliff area is to be flattened by removing about 3 million cubic meters of landslides having accumulated over years. Grottoes buried in

Five-string Biwa depicted in the 8th cave, photo by Y. Kojima

Buddha's First Sermon depicted in the 224th cave, photo by Y. Kojima

Construction drawing (a part), photo by Y. Kojima

Leaflet for fund-raising to restore and preserve the Kizil grottoes (a part), photo by Y. Kojima

the sediment could be discovered in this process. As for grottoes possibly buried further down, we will discuss the matter later in the light of costs and construction methods as there is quite a high possibility that they would be discovered here. This process is to begin in April 1988. The east cliff area will follow suit, but inner cliff area's landslides will not be removed. The rear mountain area is seen as a difficult work to deal with because construction need to be focused on stairs and corridors due to its location as the top of a mountain.

The second process: This process is to encase cliff surface and the periphery of grottoes in concrete by covering them with reinforced nets and then spraying concrete all over them in order to solidify mountain surfaces which are seen as easy to crumble. The construction method to solidify the inside of grottoes and their periphery is to perfuse special chemical liquid. The insides of grottoes are to be straightened as well. This process is to complete by 1990.

The third process: This process is to restore murals within grottoes. Each of detached flakes will be put back in its original place one by one. Since it requires long-term construction, the restoration is to be partially completed in 1990 and the rest is to be continued. In the meantime, sightseeing is allowed even during construction and the grottoes free from construction are to be opened. After completing construction, grottoes should be opened as many as possible except for hazardous locations.

The budget: CNY 20 million (equivalent to JPY 800 million at the rate as of Oct. 1987).

4. The fund-raising campaign of the Association that got through every single challenge

Having been inspired by then Education Minister Masajuro Shiokawa 塩川正十郎, I established the Japan-China Friendship Association to Restore and Conserve the Kizil Grottoes in November 1987 and set up the secretariat at Tsurukame Corporation (currently called As-me Estelle) where I used to serve as the president. I then asked Taro Nakayama 中山太郎, a Lower House Member, the ex-Director of the Office of the Prime Minister's Office and the ex-Director General of Okinawa Development Agency; Koshi Uemura 上村晃史, the President of C. Uyemura & Co., Ltd.; and Kosyo Mizutani; 水谷幸正 the President of Bukkyo University (who later has become the chairman of the board of directors) to assume the positions of Honorary Adviser, Chairman and Vice-Chairman, respectively. Other important positions were filled by many other grand people from fields such as religion, business, and academia. I myself was in charge of the representative director. [11]

Fund-raising leaflet (a part), photo by Y. Kojima

We launched the fund-raising campaign in December and created leaflets, postcards, and calling cards with the slogan, "Let's hand down the Kizil grottoes to future generations." But most people were scarcely familiar with the Kizil grottoes, unlikely Dunhuang 敦煌. Then we asked the media, including newspapers, television, and radio, to cover this campaign. Being the president of the said company, I asked my business partners to make donations. (Chunichi Shimbun, Dec. 11, 1987; Nihon Keizai Shimbun, Dec. 14, 1987; Mainichi Shimbun Feb. 16, 1988; Chubu Yomiuri Shimbun, Feb. 28, 1988; Asahi Shimbun, Mar. 5, 1988; Yomiuri Shimbun, Apr. 30, 1988) Also, each member of directors made tremendous efforts. For example, Chairman Uemura kindly held a surface processing technology workshop and donated all of the proceeds. The secretariat staff members, such as Hayashi Maruyama, Yohei Ichikawa, Satoko Kojima, Toshikatsu Matsuo, Tatsumi Aoyama, Yasuo Sekiguchi, Kenji Katou, Chosaku Ueoka, and Hiroyuki Kitano, made immeasurable contributions.

Voluminous publicity activities (a part), photo by Y. Kojima

Ceremony to transfer the memorial due to its aging, photo by Yang Xincai

We donated JPY 62.01 million in total: JPY 35 million in cash and eight trucks valued at JPY 27.01 million at the first presentation ceremony held in Xinjiang People Hall in the presence of Vice-Governor of the Xinjiang Huang Baozhang 黄宝璋 on April 28, 1988. Vice-Governor Huang greeted saying that the donation to fund restoration of the Kizil grottoes with the history of 1,700 years expresses Japanese concern to the valuable historical, cultural heritage for all humankind as well as symbolizes the friendship between Chinese and Japanese. Each of our Xinjiang tribes' people places importance on this kind of friendship, in particular. [12] (Xinjiang Daily News and Urumqi Evening News, Apr. 30, 1988; Nihonkeizai Shimbun, May 15, 1988; Chugoku Shimbun and Nikkankogyou Shimbun, May 20, 1988; Chugainippou,

Jun. 21, Jul. 1, 1988, and Jun. 6, 1989; Chunichi Shimbun on Apr. 11, 1989) Vice-Chairman of the Association Tetsumyo Matsubara 松原哲明, the Chief Priest of Ryugenji Temple and I participated in this ceremony together with other 40 delegates. We, meanwhile, visited a number of ruins other than the Kizil grottoes. The Yomiuri Shimbun accompanied us to cover a story and reported it under the title of the Western Regions covering 2,000 km. (Yomiuri Shimbun, eight days during Jun. 6 through 17, 1988)

And the second ceremony was held in the presence of Vice-Chairman Wang Enmao on August 30, 1989 and we donated JPY 43.43 million despite our activities having been adversely affected by the Tiananmen Square Incident 天安門事件 in June 1989. [13] (Xinjiang Daily News, Aug. 31, 1989) Rev. Matsubara and I participated in the ceremony together with other 22 delegates and visited the Kizil grottoes and other ruins afterward. On these two occasions we contributed JPY 105.44 million to the Xinjiang Government. The funds were raised from voluntary contributions from both individuals and companies numbering more than 3,000. (Xinjiang Daily News on Oct. 23, 1990) Vice-Chairman Wang Enmao wrote to me, stating, "Each of our Xinjiang tribes' people can never forget that you have made an earnest endeavor without sparing toil to donate as much as JPY 100 million in a way having taken close to three years in order to restore the Kizil grottoes to conserve valuable historical, cultural heritages as an emissary of the friendship and the cultural exchange between Chinese and Japanese. I would like to passionately celebrate Honorary Adviser Taro Nakayama to have become the foreign minister and welcome him here in Xinjiang."

I would like to express my renewed, cordial appreciation to these individuals and companies having donated funds, as well as all of the directors of the

Donated very useful eight vehicles for construction work, photo by Y. Kojima

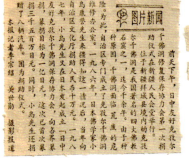

Urumqi Evening News reporting the first donation

Association and the secretariat staff members having made such great exertions,.

Thanks to these contributions as well as the untiring dedication of the Chinese Government and the people involved, the Kizil grottoes have recovered so admirably that a great number of people including Japanese and other foreign nationals are now visiting there. A monument was built at the site and Vice-Chairman Wang Enmao wrote an inscription on it explaining how the Japanese contributions had made this recovery possible. Contributors' names were also inscribed on the monument. Later the statue of Kumarajiva was built there in memory of his country, Kuqa.

Donation report (omitting donated individuals, companies, and amounts due to a paper being narrow in width), photo by Y. Kojima

Kizil grottoes restoration/preservation work [Picture left] Start with foundation work 1 (Standpipe construction), 1987 [Picture right] Start with foundation work 2 (sewer installation), 1988, photo by Y. Kojima

Testing materials to reinforce a cliff by specialists from Beijing and Lanzhou, photo by Y. Kojima

In September 1992, I reported to Governor of the Xinjiang Tiemuer Dawamaiti 鉄木尔·達瓦買提 (who later became the Vice-Chairman of the NPC) how the restoration work of the Kizil grottoes had developed. Governor Tiemuer kindly appointed me as a cultural adviser to the Xinjiang Autonomous Region. He told me that Secretary of the Xinjiang Committee of the Chinese Communist Party Song Hanliang 宋漢良 also agreed to it.

In June 1993, while I visited Vice-Chairman Wang Enmao and Governor Tiemuer to thank them for their supports in having completed the restoration of the Kizil grottoes, I introduced them Vice-Chairman of ITOUCHU Corporation Tadayoshi Nakazawa and other members in order to have both parties sign the Comprehensive Friendship Agreement. (Xinjiang Daily News Jun. 15–19, 1993; Monthly Metals Report of ITOUCHU, Jan. issue, 1994)

In September 1994, we, the Cultural Sightseeing Group, participated in the International symposium in commemoration of 1,650th anniversary of the birth of Kumarajiva 鳩摩羅什. Professor Emeritus of Tokyo University Shigeo Kamata and Secretary of the Xinjiang Cultural Agency (Vice-Director-General) Wang Zhongjun who separately visited there cut a ribbon and made speeches along with me. Including Professor of Kacho Junior College Toshinori Ochiai (currently professor of International College for Postgraduate Buddhist Studies) and Associate Professor of Nagoya University Ikuko Nakagawara, about 140 people from various places like China, Korea, France, and Germany as well as various parts of Japan gathered to celebrate. The ceremony ended in a great success. (Xinjiang Daily News, Sep. 19, 1994; Chugainippou, Sep. 27, 1994)

In December 1996, the publication ceremony of the Diary of Wang Enmao 王恩茂日記 (Japanese version: translated by Sun Zongming and Pi Xigeng, published by Shubunsha) which was released jointly with the Chinese side partly because of paying a tribute to the support given by him, was magnificently held with the participation of a number of high echelons, such as from the party, the military, and the government. Wang Enmao who had then been hospitalized expressed in writing his gratitude for this ceremony and Secretary of the Xinjiang Committee

Cliff reinforcement and corridor installation, 1989, photo by Y. Kojima

Construction to conserve the mural (the 8th cave), 1989, photo by Y. Kojima

of CCP Wang Lequan emphasized the significance of this book. I myself talked about my ties with Vice-Chairman Wang Enmao. (Xinjiang Daily News and Xinjiang Economics Report, Dec. 12, 1996)

In August 2006, the preliminary conference was held for the Silk Road application by SACH, China and the World Heritage Centre in Turpan. Besides China, Kazakhstan, Kyrgyzstan, Tadzhikistan, Uzbekistan, and other countries participated in this conference and decided an action plan. The joint application project extending across national boundaries was commenced.

In 2007, SACH, China, decided to file 48 sites in six provinces. In Xinjiang, 12 sites were included, such as the Lolan ruins 楼蘭, the ancient cities of Jiao River 交河故城 and Gaochang 高昌故城, the Astana tombs 阿斯塔那古墳, the Subashi Buddhist Temple Ruins 蘇巴什故城, and the Kumutula grottoes 庫木吐拉千仏洞 as well as the Kizil grottoes and the Niya ruins 尼雅遺址. While preparation activities were smoothly carried out in various places in China, such as conserving treatments, environmental improvements, and human resources development, some delay was found in some other countries. Though authorization was initially intended to garner from the World Heritage Committee in the summer of 2012, it was procrastinated.

In March 2007, when Director of the Xinjiang Cultural Assets Bureau Sheng Chunshou came to Japan, he and I paid a courtesy call on UNESCO Goodwill Ambassador Ikuo Hirayama 平山郁夫 (in charge of cultural assets' conservation) at home and received a valuable suggestion as to the application of the Silk Road for a World Heritage Site.

Receiving full support of the Xinjiang Cultural Heritage Administration Bureau along with me, Professor of Bukkyo University Yoshika Ando began a collaborating study in August 2007 and was scheduled to proceed with the second stage of research also in September 2008. Due to the incidents in Xinjiang and Beijing, however, the Japanese Foreign Ministry has upgraded so called "risk information" one step further, which suspended her study. This suspension still seems to continue for some time.

Observing Professor of Kyoto City University of Arts Michio Miyamoto's reproduction, photo by Yang Xincai

In 2010, on the occasion of the 25th anniversary of the Xinjiang Kuqa Research Academy, the memorial ceremony was held at the Kizil grottoes on August 15 while the symposium on Kuqa culture under the control of Han and Tang was also convened at Kuqa Hotel. The 25th anniversary convention of the Xinjiang Kuqa Research Academy was taken place with the master of ceremony Sheng Chunshou, the Director of the Xinjiang Cultural Heritage Administration Bureau. Followed by the speeches of Vice-Director of the Institute Zhan Guoling 張国領 (as the Director being absent) and Secretary of the Xinjiang Cultural Agency Han Ziyong 韓子勇, I was also privileged to deliver a commemorative lecture titled "Kizil in 1986 and My Starting Point—With a Lifelong Mission for Conservation and Research of Chinese Cultural Heritages." About 100 people, including professors from Peking University and Shanghai Normal University who saw the photographs of the cave before restoration, the restoration construction and the fund-raising campaign in Japan exhibited there for the first time, were thrilled with them a lot. Bureau Director Sheng said, "Mr. Kojima's funds had saved us enormously when Xinjiang was lacking financial resources. Now that we have become better off economically, we must learn from Mr. Kojima's spirit of dedication to people." When the announcement that I would donate a commuting bus for academy's staffers commemorating the 25th anniversary was made, the audiences exploded with applause. (Xinjiang Daily News, Aug.18 and Sep. 6, 2010; www.chinanews.com, www.fjnet.com, www.xinmin.cn, and www.sohu.com, Aug. 26, 2010) In return for this, I received a reproduction of a mural from Vice-Director Zhan. Some Japanese professors remarked, "We really admire such excellent foresight as to have recognized the importance of conservation of

Kizil grottoes valley westward appearance and the statue of Rev. Kumarajiva 鳩摩羅什 after restoration, 2003, photo by Y. Kojima

this site for two decades."

In September 2011, the Xinjiang Government sponsored the 30th anniversary of Mr. Yasutaka Kojima's visit to Xinjiang. As a part of its celebrations, the monument for contribution of the restoration fund which had been deteriorated with age was renovated. The ceremony was held before an audience of 30 people including me. The names of contributors and the executive members of the Association were inscribed on the monument as they had been. The German scholars who had happened to be there also participated in this ceremony. Incidentally, it was a big surprise to meet those same German again when I was invited by the British Library to make a speech at the International Conference on Archaeology of the Southern Taklamakan in November 2012, under the title "Niya and Dandanoilik Research–My Life-Long Mission for Conservation and Research of World-class Cultural Heritage Sites," touching upon the restoration and conservation projects of the ruins, those of Kizil included.

Besides Kizil, there still remain lots of cave temples, including Kumutula, Senmusaimu, Taitair, Kizilgaha, Mazhabohe, Subashi, Wenbashi, and Tuogilake. They are administered by the Xinjiang Kuqa Research Academy which is under the control of the Xinjiang Cultural Heritage Administration Bureau. (It had been originally established as the Xinjiang Kuqa Grottoes Research Center in 1985 and went through being renamed time and again until this particular name was decided in June 2009)

The scholarly research of murals in these grottoes is much to be awaited. The Chinese scholars such as Professors of Peking University Su Bai and Ma Shichang are now conducting a comprehensive research and the Japanese counterparts like

Venue of the 25th anniversary convention of the Xinjiang Kuqa Research Academy (the Kizil grottoes), photo by Yang Xincai

Donated a commuting bus for the institution's staffers, photo by Y. Kojima

Professor Emeritus of Nagoya University Akira Miyaji and Associate Professor Ikuko Nakagawara have long been engaged in researching the field of Buddhist art. Zhang Aihong, the painter at Xinjiang Art Academy, and Professor of Kyoto City University of Arts Michio Miyamoto are active in the field of reproductive art. In the field of painting materials and methodology, Professor of Tokyo National University of Fine Arts and Music Ichiro Sato and others are collaborating with their counterparts at the Xinjiang Art Academy.

In June 2014, the Kizil grottoes have become one of the World Heritage Site. Accordingly, Hiroshi Nagano and Kazuo Nakamura had launched a website, or culture.adc-g.co.jp, in which I posted "Kizil Grottoes registered as a World Heritage Site: A briefing on its restoration and preservation with thanks to many" and "My improvisation to thank for the decision." Mr. Masao Shiratori posted "The significance of the Silk Road as the World Cultural Heritage underlies that 'this Road leads to Peace and International Interaction.'" Professor Yoshika Ando and Mr. Duan Yuezhong offered "The attractiveness of the Kizil grottoes" and "The Silk Road is the road for mutual understanding," respectively. Also, the articles from "There is no boundary in eternal love," "The fate and friendship – Yasutaka Kojima on My Mind" by Bureau Director Sheng Chunshou and "The Buddha's providence bestowed in Kizil" by Vice-Director Zhang Guoling were reposted. Besides these works, the booklet has been printed in an emergency manner with a title "Commemoration of the Kizil grottoes designated as a World Cultural Heritage with congratulations as well as thanks" (ADC Cultural News Agency), including "The Japanese having cooperated for conserving the Kizil grottoes with smile, tears, and agony" written by Hiroshi Nagano.

In July the same year, the Xinjiang Uyghur Autonomous Government held a press conference for the designation of the World Cultural Heritage at the Xinjiang Museum. Bureau Director Sheng Chunshou addressed, "Success in registration marks a new beginning, unlikely a destination. We would boost efforts to enhance conservation and utilization living up to the World Heritage." In

October, *Sirukuroudo no Gendai Nihonjin Retsuden* シルクロードの現代日本人列伝 Biographies of the Present-Day Japanese dedicated to the Silk Road (printed by Sangokan) written by Masao Shiratori was published. It has taken up such people as Ikuo Hirayama, Kosaku Maeda, Kyuzou Kato along with me under the theme that "Why have these people tried so hard for conserving cultural assets?"

From October through November the same year, thanks to a heartfelt arrangement by Bureau Director Sheng, I visited six World Heritage Sites in Xinjiang, including the Kizil grottoes, the ancient cities of Gaochang, Jiao River, and Beiting, the Kizilgaha Beacon, and the Subash Buddhist Temple Ruins for celebration and encouragement for the staff there. We shared the joy of winning the designation of the World Heritage. I kept trying to emphasize the significance to conserve world-class cultural heritages, including the Kizil grottoes, through the lectures at the Beijing Forum in November and the International Symposium on Kharosthi at School of Foreign Languages, Peking University in December.

In August 2015, alongside the Asian Documentary Center I launched a shooting initiative in Kizil and other places for a TV program to appeal the importance of conserving world cultural heritages like the Kizil grottoes under the title of *Tenzan wo iku hyouga no megumi shirukuroudo monogatari* 『天山を往く 氷河の恵み シルクロード物語』 (Heading for Tianshan, blessings of the glacier and a Silk Road story) This is the collaboration with the Xinjiang Cultural Assets Bureau. (This program was broadcast enjoying a solid reputation at the BS station of Fuji Television Network in February 2016)

In September 2015, the Xinjiang Cultural Assets Bureau joining forces with me published both a large-sized photo collection called *Shinkyou sekai bunka isan zukan* 『新疆世界文化遺産図鑑』(A guide to World Cultural Heritage sites in Xinjiang) and a set of picture postcards focusing on the six World Cultural Heritage sites in Xinjiang, the Kizil grottoes included, which were presented to the Chinese part in order to raise funds to help conserve them. They have been well-received for their densely full-color photos. (The Japanese version of this collection was released in April 2016.)

The 38th UNESCO World Heritage Committee officially decided in Doha, Qatar, on June 22, 2014, that Silk Roads: the Routes Network of Chang'an-Tianshan Corridor, including the Kizil grottoes 克孜尔千仏洞 shall be declared a World Heritage Site. In the Xinjiang Uyghur Autonomous Region of China, besides the Kizil grottoes 克孜尔千仏洞, the ruins of Gaochang 高昌故城, Jiao River 交河故城, Beiting 北庭故城, the Subashi Buddhist Temple 蘇巴什故城 and the Kizilgaha Beacon Tower 克孜尔尕哈烽火台 were designated.

Photos of those five ruins are shown on the next page.

Ancient City of Gaochang 高昌故城, photo by Y. Kojima

Ancient City of Jiao River 交河故城, photo by Yang Xincai

Ancient City of Beiting 北庭故城, photo by Yang Xincai

Subashi Buddhist Temple Ruins 蘇巴什故城, photo by Y. Kojima

Kizilgaha Beacon Tower 克孜尔尕哈烽火台, photo by Yang Xincai

Notes:
....

(9) Wang Enmao (1913–2001): He was born in Jiangxi province, joined the Long Marches along with Wang Zhen 王震 (later to be the Vice-Premier and then the National Vice-Chairman), and became the Vice-Admiral of the People's Liberation Army to emancipate Xinjiang. He stayed in Xinjiang afterward to build up foundations for the development of Xinjiang. He held positions such as: the Commander of the Xinjiang military district; the Secretary of the Xinjiang Uyghur Autonomous Region (from 1952 through the Cultural Revolution and from 1981 through 1985); the First Secretary of

Jilin province; the Vice-Chairman of the National Committee of the Chinese People's Political Consultative Conference. His autobiography, 『王恩茂日記』 (The diary of Wang Enmao) (in five volumes), records the Long Marches in detail.

(10) The Otani exploration team operated in a wide area including Kizil for three times during the period from 1902 through 1914 and exported cultural assets. They are preserved at Ryukoku University, the Tokyo National Museum, the Hirayama Ikuo Silk Road Museum, the Beijing Library of China, the Lushun Museum, the National Museum of Korea, and private individuals. A part of them is said to have been auctioned and sold. For your information, the mural unearthed in the Dandanoilik ruins is preserved at the Hirayama Ikuo Silk Road Museum.

(11) The board members other than those mentioned in this paper include: as for the Vice-Chairpersons being assumed by Shigeru Ioki (the Vice-President of Mitsubishi Corporation); Noboru Ooka (the Vice-President of Obayashi Corporation); Masamichi Okuzumi (the Director of Okuzumi Management Institute Co., Ltd.); Motoo Kawasaki (the ex-President of Konan University); Eiichi Kimura (the former President of Osaka City University); Toru Kurihara (the Senior Executive of Nihonshinpan); Isamu Koyama (the Junior Executive of Chunichi Shimbun); Takeshi Suga (the Vice-President of Nomura Securities Co., Ltd.); Takashi Suzuki (the Chairman of Tokai Television Broadcasting Co., Ltd.); Shigekiyo Nakashima (the former Vice-Governor of the National Federation of Small Business Associations); Toshio Nishikawa (the President of UNY Co., Ltd.); Tatsuo Nozaki (the Vice-President of Yasuda Fire and Marine Insurance Co., Ltd.); Hiroko Hayashi (or Chikage Oogi, the Member of the House of Councilors); Tetsumyo Matsubara (the Monk of Ryugenji of the Myoshinnji Temple school of the Rinzai Sect); Eiin Yasuda (the Chief Steward of Yakushiji Temple); Masao Yokose (the Senior Executive of Sumitomo Metal Mining Co., Ltd.); Nobuatsu Watanabe (Professor Emeritus of Kyoto University); as for the Special Advisers being assumed by Nobusuke Kanda (the Vice-President of the Sanwa Bank, Ltd.); Hisaya Nara (the Vice-President of the Mitsubishi Bank, Ltd.); Takeshi Morita (the Vice-President of the Mitsui Bank, Ltd.); as for the directors being assumed by Sachiko Endo (in charge of auditing, a staff member at Japan Fire Insurance Co., Ltd.); Jitsurou Sugiura (in charge of general affairs, the President of PLAS); Yasunari Takaki (in charge of accounting, the Deputy Director of Shinnippon-hoki Publishing Co., Ltd.); Takara Horio (in charge of China affairs, the Director of Terao Shokai); Takeshi Murakami (the Director of Shinto Tsushin). (The names of companies and the positions are those used at that time.) Many of them have already passed away. I pray for their happiness in the next life.

(12) The interim report of the fund-raising campaign to restore and conserve the Kizil grottoes, the Japan-China Friendship Association to Restore and Conserve the Kizil Grottoes, May 31, 1988.

(13) The final report of the fund-raising campaign to restore and conserve the Kizil grottoes, the Japan-China Friendship Association to Restore and Conserve the Kizil Grottoes, May 26, 1989

III. The Japan-China Joint Scholarly Research of The Niya Ruins and the Outline

―日中共同ニヤ遺跡学術調査とその概要―

92A11 = Stein N8 of the Niya ruins having survived in the Taklamakan Desert (2015), photo by Y. Kojima

Emergency bivouacking, so exhausting (1988), photo by T. Horio

Proceeding with conservation of the stupa towards an additional registration to the World Heritage Silk Road (2015), photo by Y. Kojima

III. The Japan-China Joint Scholarly Research of The Niya Ruins and the Outline

1. The transition of research

The ruins of Niya 尼雅 (Though it is said to originally come from "niña" referred to in the literatures written in ancient Khotanese or to be named after the meaning of "a place far away" in ancient Uyghur, it is not clear.) are the remain of an ancient city, which was located approximately 100 km north of a small city called Minfeng 民豊 (renamed in 1947 from the old name of Niya) at the south edge of the Taklamakan Desert, having flourished during the age from the 1st century BC through the 5th century AD. They are identified as Jing Jue Guo 精絶国 according to Hanshu 漢書 (the Book of Han). [14]

The relics sprawl over such a wide area as extending roughly 7 km from east to west and 25 km from north to south (including the surrounding area). Centering on the Buddhist stupa situated at 37 degrees 58 minutes 34 seconds northern latitude and 82 degrees 43 minutes 15 seconds eastern longitude, there lie 220 or so relics, including temples, dwellings, production facilities, graveyards, orchards, reservoirs, barns, bridge-like relics, building-material yards, fences, a castle wall, and a line of trees, about 10 places with survived remains, and more such as riverbed and huge amounts of decayed woods. [15]

While Niya was a medium-sized city-state among so called 36 kingdoms in the Western Regions 西域36国, it is the remain of the largest state-city still surviving today because most of the other remains were buried to build another new city on them. Also, it holds a prominent position in the studies of the ancient Western Regions. Thus the Niya ruins are surely one of world-class cultural heritages in terms of its value as well as size and so it is called "Pompeii on the Silk Road" or "the lost ancient city." The sea level in the vicinity is more or less 1,200 m.

In the process to restore and preserve the Kizil grottoes, Manager Han said to me, "We have three historically significant ruins in Xinjiang, including Kizil, Loulan, and Niya. Though Loulan has completed basic research and Kizil is now being restored with Japanese financial assistance, a full investigation has yet to be made in Niya due to its size being too massive."

When I heard this, I instantaneously proposed a collaborative investigation. Whether it is the case of Kizil or this Niya, I think myself incurably goosy. Back in my junior high school days, I used to read biographies of Schliemann, Stein and others, so that the name of the Niya ruins has been engraved in my memory. He quickly agreed with me. But again, they would not easily accept my offer. That was not only because foreigners including Japanese exported cultural assets, but because ruins per se belonged to an unexploited area in the Western Regions. As it was the days when working toward constructing a new China and only 50 years or so had passed since Stein's fourth expedition, there was an overwhelmingly negative reaction to a joint investigation with foreigners. The Xinjiang Cultural Agency pulled up all the stops to persuade the Xinjiang Government and the

Liberation Army. In Japan, I proposed President of Bukkyo University Kosyo Mizutani to promote activities for research and conservation and garnered his basic acceptance.

I invited a group headed by Manager of the Xinjiang Cultural Agency Han Xiang in order to have them understand our nation's basic policy toward conservation of cultural heritages in July 1988. On 19th of the same month, Manager Han Xiang and I signed the memorandum regarding research of the ruins, including the Niya ruins, the Dandanoilik ruins, and the area around the Western Regions' Southern Route. The favorable recognition of our contribution to the restoration of the Kizil grottoes resulted in their approval of joint research in the name of "sightseeing."

The so-called Silk Road which connects Rome and Istanbul in the west and Chang'an 長安 (currently 西安 Xian) in the east holds extremely significant meaning since a variety of civilizations and cultures have been interacted here. The terminal point in the east can be Nara in Japan. Many of civilizations and cultures that had reached Japan have underlain a close tie with the Silk Road. In the Western Regions situated in the middle of the Silk Road, there ran three trade routes, named the Tianshan Northern Route 天山北路, the Western Regions' Northern Route 西域北道 and the Western Regions' Southern Route 西域南道, all of which had connected ancient cities. This research focused on the Niya ruins as its subject, which have been hypothesized to locate around the area on the Western Regions' Southern Route. [16]

The person who discovered this relic and named it as the Niya ruins 尼雅(ニヤ)遺跡 in January 1901 was Sir Mark Aurel Stein (1862–1943) born in Hungary and later naturalized in England who was explorer and archaeologist. He also researched the Niya ruins in 1906, 1913 and 1931 and exported huge amounts of antiquities like as many as 700 or more of Kharosthi documents as well as 50 or more of Chinese papers. His research was then-excellent and released in detailed reports. [17] Zuicho Tachibana 橘瑞超, a member of the second Otani exploration team of Japan, attempted to advance to the Niya ruins in 1909 and reached Imam Dadick Mazar which is the graveyard to worship the Islamic Saint Sadick. But he seems to have failed to reach the Niya ruins heatwise or itinerarywise. [18] The Vice-Director of the Xinjiang Museum Li Yuchun 李遇春 conducted research there and excavated the tomb of a couple-mummy burial in the north of the ruins.[19] Besides these, only an observation level of research and field works were conducted.

These researches and studies have resulted in clarifying that Niya as a west-edge oasis for the Kingdom of Loulan 楼蘭(鄯善) played the part of the centralized government maintaining the system of taxations, contracts, and postal service centered on Kroraina 扞泥城 in the period from the 3rd to the 4th century. After two thousand years, dwelling pillars and others still have survived there, which has made it

Aurel Stein who discovered the Niya ruins, reprinted from 近代外国探検家新疆考古档案史料 (The archaeological archives of Xinjiang by modern foreign explorers)

command considerable attention and well-known as the largest and most important ruins in the Taklamakan desert. Since it is situated far deep in the great desert, it has never been systematically investigated. Thus full-fledged research had been long-awaited.

2. The initiation of research

The Japan-China joint scholarly research of the Niya ruins (hosted by the Xinjiang Cultural Bureau <the Assets Section of the Xinjiang Cultural Agency until March 1997> the Academic Research Organization for the Niya ruins, Bukkyo University, and ratified by SACH, China, and subsidized by the Japanese Education and Science Ministry) was commenced by three Japanese members who left Japan on October 29, 1988. (Mainichi Shimbun, Jan. 20, 1996)

The first preliminary research was literally "exploration" without modern equipment such as a desert-specific vehicle and the GPS (global positioning system). It took 12 hours to reach a small oasis called Kapakeasican 卡巴克阿斯坎 from Minfeng. Because we had to drive on virtually trackless paths and vehicle's wheels were mired in the sand time and again. I happened to come across people putting water with cows' and sheep's dung floating on in a rusty tank. I asked if it was for camels. They answered it was for humans. I got nothing but stunned. Loading equipment on camels, we also rode on them to set out for the ruins.

What we relied on were only a simple chart depicted in the Stein's report and memories of a research staff member of the Xinjiang Relics Archaeological Institute Yidilisi Abuduresule 伊弟利斯·阿不都熱蘇勒 (Later having been the Director and currently being the Honorary Director). He guided the Japan-China joint news crews in 1980 along with a camel master, Kurubang. Although I brought up the idea of moving up the desert in accordance with the Stein's key map, it was decided that we would take the route along the bank of tamarix suggested by the Chinese side. The periodic message sent by a radio operator who had been dispatched for our safety by the Government: "Though we cannot orient ourselves geographically, we are all safe." It took almost an hour to set up the antenna for Morse each time. (Later, a satellite phone was introduced.) In the early morning on June 6, we

Cutting a path, 12 hours for 90 km: The way from Minfeng to Kapakeasican, photo by T. Horio

Proceeding from Kapakeasican into the Niya ruins by camels, photo by Y. Kojima

Using this polluted water for meal after boiling it. Humans survive, photo by Y. Kojima

"Though the present location is unidentified, we are all fine" sent in Morse, photo by Y. Kojima

finally found our way to stupa taking three days on camels over saying "right or left" along the bank of tamarix. Epoch-making research started right at this very moment. I still can't forget the sensation I felt then.

It was just a two-day stay, though, we walked around the center of the ruins for observation so as to come to grips with an outline and began collecting antiquities scattered around in pieces on the ground. We, Japanese and Chinese, found that it was imperative to research. Director-General of the Xinjiang Cultural Agency Maimaitizunong Maimaitiaili 買買提祖農·買買提艾力 and I signed the memorandum to continue to research further on 14th of the same month.

The itineraries of research on a yearly basis are as follows.

1988 research (the first research in a preliminary phase)
    Schedule: October 29 through November 16
    Participants (14 in total): (3 Japanese members) Yasutaka Kojima, Takara Horio, Hiroyuki Kitano
    (5 Chinese members) Han Xiang, Wang Jingkui, Yidilisi Abuduresule, Rejiebu Yusufu, Sheng Chunshou
    (6 assistants) camel masters, drivers, and a radio man
    Itinerary: Oct. 29–Nov. 2: Departure of the Japanese team, a welcome party hosted by the Xinjiang Government, Japan-China meetings and preparations in Urumqi and Hotan, arrival in Minfeng; Nov. 3: Taking 12 hours or so to reach Kapakeasican being about 90 km away by 3 vehicles including a truck and 2 four-wheel drives; Nov. 4: Advancing to the Taklamakan Desert to reach the Niya stupa about 30 km away by 20 camels, taking 3 days to finally reach the stupa; Nov. 6–7: Making a survey on the stupa and the Stein's relics numbers, including N1, N2, N3, N4, and N9 and collecting antiquities scattered in pieces on the ground; Nov. 7: Leaving Niya; Nov. 9: Arrival in Hotan; Nov. 14: Signing the memorandum for upcoming research and holding a return party hosted by the Japanese team; Nov. 16: Return to Japan.
    Investigation: Road mapping; grasping of the ruins' outline; and collecting antiquities scattered in pieces on the ground.

The first team that made a step toward an epoch-making research. The downward arrow (↓) far left showing the stupa, photo by H. Kitano

It is also to be noted that two researchers of the Tokyo National Museum had been initially scheduled to participate in this preliminary research. Regrettably, however, it was cancelled just before departure. After having completed research, once we showed Kosyo Mizutani 水谷幸正 and Secretary General of Bukkyo University Koji Takahashi 高橋弘次 (later to be the president) several antiquities borrowed with permission from the Chinese side, they immediately set a policy of conducting research, saying, "These are Buddhist antiquities. We should collaborate to research with Chinese by all means," This interested Professor of Bukkyo University Kodo Sanada 真田康道 as well. There also were Kharosthi documents among these antiquities, so that we urged Professor Emeritus of Ryukoku University Taijun Inokuchi 井ノ口泰淳 to involve in this project, since he was a recognized authority on this field.

We continued our preliminary researches in 1990 and 1991 and examined on how we could conduct research on a vast desert, which would be unparalleled by other. From the research in 1990, we started creating pattern diagrams of dwelling sites, along with opening a road for truck transportation. Maimaitizunong Maimaitiaili and I signed a memorandum to subsequently proceed with research on November 11, 1991. From the research in 1991, we began a distributional survey based on registration of ruins' location via GPS, introduced a desert vehicle on a trial basis, and started to build up conserving capabilities, such as increasing the number of personnel for administering ruins.

1990 research (the second research in a preliminary phase)
Schedule: October 27 through November 17
Participants (16 in total)**:** (5 Japanese members) Yasutaka Kojima,
　　　Taijun Inokuchi, Kodo Sanada, Takara Horio, Kenryu Kubota

Stupa located in the center of the ruins. Kowtow by the author, photo by T. Horio

Scattered relics (92B9 = Stein's serial number N3), photo by Y. Kojima

(5 Chinese members) Han Xiang, Wang Jingkui, Yidilisi Abuduresule, Li Xiao, Liu Wenzhen

(6 Assistants) camel masters and drivers

Itinerary: Oct. 27: Departure of the Chinese advance team; Oct. 29–Nov. 2: Departure of the Japanese team, a welcome party hosted by the Xinjiang Autonomous Region, Japan-China meetings and preparations in Urumqi and Hotan, arrival in Kapakeasican via Minfeng; Nov. 3: Setting off by 22 camels; Nov. 5: Arrival at the stupa taking two days and a half, the set-up of a base camp (hereinafter called as BC), encountering sand storm, truck drivers who had been left

The 1990 team with Professors Taijun Inokuchi and Kodo Sanada, photo by T. Horio

Exposed skull – *Namu Ami Dabutsu* (May his or her soul rest in peace), photo by Y. Kojima

behind at Kapakeasican opened a 10-kilometer road; Nov. 6: Making a survey of the stupa, N1, N2, N3, N4, N9, N11, and N12; Nov. 7: Leaving Niya to reach Kapakeasican; Nov. 8–10: Arrival in Hotan, observing neighboring ruins, leaving for Urumqi; Nov. 11: Signing a memorandum for the upcoming research and a return party hosted by the Japanese team; Nov. 12–13: Leaving China to fly back to Japan via Shanghai; Nov. 17: the Chinese vehicles team back to Urumqi.

Investigation: Creating pattern diagrams of dwelling sites; starting distributional research; and collecting antiquities scattered in pieces on the ground, such as Kharosthi wood slips.

1991 research (the third research in a preliminary phase)

Schedule: October 12 through November 6

Participants (21 in total): (7 Japanese members) Taijun Inokuchi, Kazutoshi Nagasawa, Kodo Sanada, Teruhiko Takahashi, Jun Aoki, Masachika Ogata, Yoshihide Izawa

(6 Chinese members) Wang Binghua, Yu Zhiyong, Ahemaiti Rexiti, Zhang Tienan, Shen Chunshou, Lie Wenshen

(8 assistants/other members) camel masters, drivers, and reporters

Itinerary: Oct. 12: Departure of the Chinese advance team; Oct. 14–19: Departure of the Japanese team, a welcome party hosted by the Xinjiang Autonomous Region, Japan-China meetings and preparations in Urumqi and Hotan, arrival in Minfeng; Oct. 20: Advancing by two desert vehicles even without accompanying a camel team, the vehicles being so big like 15 tons that we all were really exhausted to open a road; Oct. 23: Setting up a BC far south away from the stupa; Oct. 24–27: Making a survey on foot centering on the stupa and the southern part of the ruins; Oct. 28–30: Leaving Niya and arrival in Hotan via Minfeng; Oct. 31–Nov. 2: Staying at Hotan, observing neighboring ruins, leaving for Urumqi; Nov. 3: Japan-China meetings and a return party hosted by the Japanese team; Nov. 4–5:

Flying back to Japan via Beijing; Nov. 6: The Chinese vehicles team back to Urumqi.

Investigation: Distributional research via GPS; measuring a location of the stupa situated in the center of the ruins which has played a significant role to expedite advance into this area as well as to secure safety afterward; creating pattern diagrams of dwelling sites; collecting antiquities scattered in pieces on the ground, such as Kharosthi wood slips; besides the investigation, the China Petroleum Periodical and Tokai Television accompanied us to report.

3. Full-fledged Research

As the performances of these three preliminary researches were highly valued, we could receive the official certificate of approval from the SACH, China on April 14, 1992. Maimaitizunong Maimaitiaili 買買提祖農·買買提艾力 and I, on behalf of China and Japan, respectively, signed the memorandum of agreement in order to conduct comprehensive research of the Niya ruins (for 1992 and 1993) in the presence of Vice-Governor of the Xinjiang Autonomous Region Keyoumu Bawudong 克尤木·巴吾東 on April 28. (Urumqi Evening News, May 2, 1992; Xinjiang Daily News, May 3, 1992) The official name was decided as "The Japan-China (or China-Japan) joint scholarly research of the Niya ruins." In the 1992 research, we continued to conduct distributional research and create pattern diagrams of dwelling sites. Architectural research was also launched. (Asahi Shimbun, Sankei Shimbun, and Kyoto Shimbun, Jun. 4, 1992; Mainichi Shimbun, Jul. 20, 1992; Chunichi Shimbun, Oct. 4, Nov. 21, Dec. 18, 1992; Nihonkeizai Shimbun, May 4, 1993)

Besides the field work, we also implemented research of unearthed antiquities of the Niya ruins at the Xinjiang Museum and others. Thanks to tremendous efforts made by the people concerned, the subsidy of the Education Ministry (the present Ministry of Education, Culture, Sports, Science and Technology) for scientific research was commenced. (Head of research: Kodo Sanada).

1992 research (the fourth research)

Schedule: October 13 through November 11

Participants (27 in total): (8 Japanese members) Yasutaka Kojima, Kodo Sanada, Teruhiko Takahashi, Kenryu Kubota, Sun Yuexin, Masachika Ogata, Toshitaka Hasuike, Yoshihide Izawa

(8 Chinese members) Wang Binghua, Shabiti Ahemaiti, Wang Jingkui, Yu Zhiyong, Ahemaiti Rexiti, Zhang Tienan, Liu Yusheng, Shen Chunshou

(11 assistants/other members) camel masters, drivers, and reporters

Itinerary: Oct. 13: Departure of the Chinese advance team; Oct. 15–19: Departure of the Japanese team, a welcome party hosted by the Xinjiang Autonomous Region, Japan-China meetings and preparations in Urumqi, due to the closing of the Hotan airport arriving in

Desert vehicle often stuck in the powder sand of the Taklamakan Desert, photo by Y. Kojima

Hard and demanding research in the vast desert, the BC of the 1994 team, photo by Y. Kojima

Minfeng via Kashi instead; Oct. 20: Advancing by two desert vehicles and two trucks; Oct. 21: Reaching the stupa and setting up a BC, but moving it down south due to a sick person; Oct. 22–26: Mainly conducting distributional research along with making a survey on water system further west of the ruins; Oct. 27–28: Leaving Niya and arrival in Hotan via Minfeng; Oct. 29–30: Observing the Rawaq ruins; Oct. 31: Shooting pictures of antiquities and creating maps, a part of the Japanese team heading for Kashi; Nov. 2: The main unit arriving in Urumqi via Aksu, a part of the Japanese team visiting the Xinjiang Autonomous Region and SACH, China to make a report, holding a return party and then returning home; Nov. 3–5: A return party hosted by the Japanese team and so on; Nov. 6–7: The Japanese team leaving China for Japan via Beijing while the antiquities research group remaining there to shoot pictures of antiquities; Nov. 11: The Japanese antiquities research group arriving in Japan.

Investigation: Creating pattern diagrams of dwelling sites; distributional research; water system research on the western part of the Niya ruins; launching architectural research; collecting antiquities scattered in pieces on the ground, such as Kharosthi wood slips; besides the investigation, the China Petroleum Periodical and Tokai Television accompanied us to report.

As research being made fully fledged from the 1993 research on, the scale of the joint expedition expanded to as many as 60 or so members including a supporting team and the period of research work was also prolonged for as long as three weeks or so. We continued to conduct distributional research, create pattern diagrams of dwelling sites, launched measuring large-scale dwelling sites, 92B4 (N2) and geometrical research, and made a survey on the northern part of the ruins. With the permission of the Chinese side, we brought back analysis samples to study in Japan. From this year on, we fully adopted a Mercedes Benz desert truck called Unimog, which enabled us to relatively easily reach the ruins than before. After arrival, however, we used camels on site in order to conserve the ruins.

While fully supported by the Xinjiang Autonomous Region from the initial stage, we were fortunate enough to have Governor of the Xinjiang Tiemuer Dawamaiti 鉄木尔·達瓦買提 assume the position of the Honorary Chairman (Honorary Vice-Governor: Vice-Governor of the Xinjiang Wufuer Abudula 吾甫尔·阿不都拉; Special Adviser: Professor of Peking University Li Xianliu 季羡林; and others) from this year on. The Environmental Resources Conservation Committee of the National People's Congress (hereinafter called NPC), dispatched a reporting team comprising Xinhuashe 新華社, Central Television 中央電視台 and China Petroleum Daily. From then on, the Niya ruins research was widely reported within and outside China. (Bun Wai Hou, Oct. 19, 1993 and Nov. 18, 1993; Xinjiang Daily News, Oct. 20, 1993; People's Daily for overseas, Xinhua Daily Telegram and Ta Kung Pao, Nov. 18, 1993; Yomiuri Shimbun, Nihon Keizaishimbun, Nov. 19, 1993; Mainichi Shimbun, Nov. 20, 1993; China Daily, Nov. 23, 1993 and May 18, 1994; China's Social News, Nov. 30, 1993; People's China, Feb. 1994 issue; Asahi Shimbun, May 23, 1994; Sankei Shimbun, Oct. 1, 1995; The Washington Post's two-page coverage, Oct. 11, 1995; The Japan Times, Jan. 7, 1996) Tokai Television also reported in 1991 and 1992 in a row.

1993 research (the fifth research)
Schedule: October 8 through November 27
Participants (56 in total): (15 Japanese members) Yasutaka Kojima, Taijun Inokuchi, Kodo Sanada, Teruhiko Takahashi, Sun Yuexin, Fumitaka Yoneda, Masahide Furukawa, Toru Kaigara, Toshitaka Hasuike, Yoshihide Izawa, Tsuguo Arima, Mariko Hayashi, Akinori Uesugi, Kanae Kamemoto, Kouji Otani

(15 Chinese members) Han Xiang, Wang Binhua, Liu Yusheng, Shabiti·Ahemaiti, Wang Jingkui, Yu Zhiyong, Ahemati Rexiti, Zhang Tienan, Jing Ai, Liu Shuren, Chen Yun, Wang Bo, Xiao Xiaoyong, Yi Li, Tong Wenkang

(26 assistants/other members) camel masters, drivers, and reporters

Itinerary: Oct. 8: Departure of the Chinese advance team; Oct. 16–21: Departure of the Japanese team, announcing the Governor of the Xinjiang Autonomous Region Tiemuer Dawamaiti to assume the position of the Honorary Chairman for the Japan-China joint scholarly research team of the Niya ruins at the press conference, a welcome party hosted by the Xinjiang Autonomous Region, Japan-China meetings and preparations in Urumqi and Hotan, arrival in Minfeng; Oct. 22: Advancing by four desert vehicles to reach the stupa on the same day and on our way presenting clothes and school supplies at Kapakeasican (These activities have continued from the next year on); Oct. 23–Nov. 11: Dividing into a surveying group, a distributional group, a geographical and geometrical group, and a excavating preparation group to conduct research, from this year we adopted a diesel generator to improve daily life as well as to be

Bitter to conduct a large-scale research in the inhabited desert. Under a limited researching period due to the weather, we must carry in a huge amount of things, organize each participating party, put in a large capital, etc. You cannot survive without a tenacious spirit, tremendous stamina, and a cooperative attitude. The 1993 team, photo by a Chinese member

able to organize study-related materials at night, adopting to use charcoal and propane gas for cooking instead of using deadwood as part of ruins' conservation and environmental protection, setting up a toilet (Oct. 25: Arrival of the Chinese second party; Oct. 30: A part of the Japanese team leaving for Japan; Nov. 3: Report to the Xinjiang Autonomous Region, hosting a return party; Nov. 4: Reporting to SACH, China, hosting a return party; Nov. 5: Arriving in Japan); Nov. 12–17: The main unit leaving Niya to reach Urumqi via Minfeng and Hotan, researching at the Xinjiang Archaeological Institute and the Xinjiang Museum, and sponsoring a return party; Nov. 18–20: The Japanese team leaving China for Japan via Shanghai while the antiquities research group still remaining there; Nov. 27: The antiquities research group of the Japanese team arriving in Japan.

Investigation: Creating pattern diagrams of dwelling sites; distributional research; measuring 92B4 (N2); setting a basic point; surveying sedimented rock strata; confirming Buddhist temple relics; making a survey on the northern ruins; tidying up an exposed graveyard for conservation; architectural research; collecting antiquities scattered in pieces on the ground, such as Kharosthi wood slips; besides the investigation, Xinhuashe, Central Television, the China Petroleum Periodical, and Tokai Television accompanied us to report.

In recognition of the performances as mentioned above, SACH, China which had fully endorsed the Niya ruins' research, or the largest ever joint research operation between China and a foreign country, issued the excavation certificate under the name of Director Zhang Deqin 張德勤 on January 29, 1994 after having been ratified by the relevant authority.[20] (Asahi Shimbun, May 23, 1994; Kyoto Shimbun, Sep. 27, 1994; Xinjiang Daily News, Oct. 7, 1994) I was told that this was the first excavation certificate ever issued for a foreign explorer by SACH, China.

This was the certificate both Japanese and Chinese teams were long waiting for. Secretary of the Xinjiang Cultural Agency Xie Yaohua 解耀華 (Han Xiang for the Japanese version) and I signed the three-year memorandum of agreement (1994-1996), in the presence of Vice-Governor of the Xinjiang Autonomous Region Li Donghui 李東輝 on the same day. In order to implement full-fledged and long-term research, we have established the Academic Research Organization for the Niya ruins, Bukkyo University 佛教大学内ニヤ遺跡学術研究機構 with ex-Prime Minister Toshiki Kaifu 海部俊樹 and Director of SACH, China Zhang Deqin as Honorary Chairmen, then-Lower House member Masajuro Shiokawa 塩川正十郎 as a Special Adviser, and Bukkyo University President Kosyo Mizutani 水谷幸正 (to be followed by Shinkou Nakai 中井真孝, Ryuzen Fukuhara 福原隆善, and then Yoshika Ando 安藤佳香) and I as a representative in April 1994. (Chugai Nippou, Aug. 30, 1994) In May the same year, the environmental resources conservation committee of the NPC held a photo exhibition titled "Niya; an ancient kingdom disappeared in a desert" where Bukkyo University part-time lecturer Sun Yuexin (later collaborative research member at Kyoto University) and Xinhua reporter Li Xiguang 李希光 (later to be a group leader of the international communication at Tsinghua University) made their presentations on the Niya ruins' research for Chief of the Committee of the NPC and Nobel Laureate Li Zhengdao 李政道. (People's Daily, May 23 and Aug. 3, 1994; Xinjiang Daily News, Jun. 9, 1994) The Central Television broadcast nationwide on the research of the Niya ruins for half an hour in June.

Excavation certificate by SACH, China, photo by Y. Kojima

In the midst of such an increased interest, a party headed by Director Zhang Deqin and Su Bai was invited to Japan in July by the Japan Foundation. They had talks with Honorary Chairman Toshiki Kaifu and then-Chairperson of House of Representatives Takako Doi and visited Bukkyo University to exchange views on how to enhance the Niya ruins' research. On September 1, Director of the Xinjiang Archaeological Institute Wang Binghua 王炳華 and I signed a detailed memorandum of agreement on excavation for 1994. From the 1994 research on, excavations, the researches of wood and relevant urban dwellings started with the participation of Professor of Kyoto University of Art and Design Shouzou Tanabe 田辺昭三 who had received the Japan Academy award in order to boost the archaeological area of studies.

Unearthed antiquities from each ruin Mural, photo by Y. Kojima

Pottery, photo by Y. Kojima

Wood strips, photo by Y. Kojima

Corals, photo by K. Sugimoto

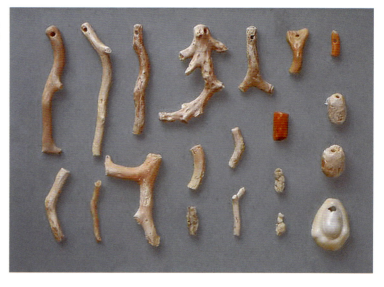

Widely covered in Japan and overseas, photo by Y. Kojima

Surveying dwelling sites (92B4 = N2), photo by Y. Kojima

[Picture left] Shooting from a scaffold (92B4=N2)
[Picture right] Positioning via big GPS (East of the stupa), photo by Y. Kojima

1994 research (the sixth research)

Schedule: September 25 through November 5

Participants (56 in total): (15 Japanese members) Yasutaka Kojima, Taijun Inokuchi, Shouzou Tanabe, Kodo Sanada, Takao Itoh, Teruhiko Takahashi, Sun Yuexin, Toshio Asaoka, Shin Yoshizaki, Yousei Kouzuma, Toshitaka Hasuike, Gosuke Onoda, Yoshifumi Ichikawa, Jinichi Yonekawa, Masahiko Gotou

(16 Chinese members) Han Xiang, Wang Binghua, Li Ji, Yang Lin, Shabiti・Ahemaiti, Wang Jingkui, Yu Zhiyong, Ahemaiti Rexiti, Zhang Tienan, Yang Yichou, Wang Shouchun, Wang Bangwei, Liu Yusheng, Tong Wenkang, Li Wenying, Wang Zonglei

(25 assistants) camel masters and drivers

Itinerary: Sep. 25–30: Departure of the Japanese advance team, research of relevant urban dwellings in Kashi and others; Sep. 27–Oct. 1: Departure of the Japanese team, Japan-China meetings and preparations in Urumqi, a welcome party hosted by the Xinjiang Autonomous Region, and arrival in Minfeng via Hotan; Oct. 2: Leaving by four desert vehicles, a vehicle fire breakout troubling our advancement, arrival at the stupa, setting up a BC, a plenary meeting, joining a camel team; Oct. 5–20: Dividing into an archaeological group, a distributional group, a wood group, and a geological group to conduct research, explaining the outline of the ruins and collaborating framework of the joint research to Li Ji and Yang Lin of SACH, China (Oct. 8: A part of both Japanese and Chinese teams leaving for home); Oct. 9: Information-sharing with the French team investigating the Kara-dong ruins; Oct. 11: Reporting to Governor of the Xinjiang Autonomous Region Tiemuer Dawamaiti (Xinjiang Daily News, Oct. 12, 1994), a return party; Oct. 13: Reporting to SACH, China, a return party; Oct. 14: Leaving for home, a part of the Chinese team leaving for home); Oct. 21: The main unit leaving for home, arrival in Hotan via Minfeng, observing the neighboring ruins; Oct. 24: Arrival in Urumqi, reporting to the Xinjiang Cultural Agency, a return party; Oct. 26–27: The Japanese team going home via Shanghai, the antiquities research group remaining after the main unit's return home; Nov. 4–5: The Japanese antiquities research group going home via Shanghai.

Investigation: Continuation of distributional research as well as geometrical and geological research; complementary measurement, detailed examination, and excavation of 92B4 (N2); excavation of 93A27 (N37); making a survey on vineyards; launching wood science research, initiating the research of relevant urban dwellings; confirming Buddhist temple relics 93A35 (N5); besides investigations, we donated clothes for welfare facilities in Urumqi, Hotan and Minfeng.

4. Excavation of the tomb of a king

In April 1995, a party headed by Governor of the Xinjiang Autonomous Region Tiemuer Dawamaiti and Commander of the Xinjiang Production and Construction Corps Jin Yunhui 金雲輝 visited Japan at the invitation of ITOCHU Corporation and me to sign the comprehensive agreement between ITOCHU and the Xinjiang Corps. They had talks with Chairman of the Japan-China Friendship Association Ikuo Hirayama and deepened the understanding of Japanese culture in Nara and other places. (Nihonkeizai Shimbun, Apr. 24, 1995; Nara Shimbun, Apr. 26, 1995; Reports of Benevolent Sinophilia of 2001) In May, The Mirage on Wind-Blown Sand – the Japan-China Joint Research of the Niya Ruins that had been locally covered by Tokai Television during the period of 1991 through 1993 was televised nationwide by the Fuji Television network. (Chunichi Shimbun, May 5, 1995) At the same time, the Chinese Ethnic Publishing House released the photograph collection of the Niya ruins titled "Dreamy Niya 夢幻尼雅." I met with Vice-Chairman of the NPC Wang Bingqian 王丙乾 at the NPC Hall to report the research of the Niya ruins; meanwhile, I was presented the Honor Award of the Environmental Resources' Committee of the NPC in the presence of the Japanese Minister and Director Zhang Deqin. (Yomiuri Shimbun, Mainichi Shimbun, People's Daily, China Daily, and Guang Ming Daily, May 23, 1995; Beijing Evening News, May 30, 1995; Chunichi Shimbun, Jun. 11, 1995; Xinjiang Daily News, Dec. 22, 1995) From this year onward, the Japanese team has started to research collected antiquities at the Xinjiang Archaeological Institute besides researches on site. In 1995, the study and the photo shootings of Kharosthi wood slips and others were conducted.

Schedule: July 17 through July 22
Participants: Taijun Inokuchi, Teruhiko Takahashi, Toshitaka Hasuike, Migifumi Sato

Research members, the author included, peering into a royal mummy, a great discovery, photo by a Japanese member

The detailed memorandum of agreement for the excavation and research for 1995 was signed between Maimaitizunong Maimaitiaili and me on August 18. In September, I met with Vice-Chairman of the NPC Tian Jinyun 田紀雲 to report the research at the NPC Hall.

Having been concerned that low-key research without a significant achievement makes continuation hard, we started the 7th research with high hopes and expectations. (Sankei Shimbun, Oct. 1, 1995) And at long last, a very great discovery was made during the research in 1995. A member of the Chinese team heading northwestern part of the ruins found a part of an exposed wooden coffin. Although we registered a number of tombs before, this coffin was totally different from those. Under the instruction of Director of the Xinjiang Archaeological Institute

Toward a research site together with Shouzo Tanabe, the second Japanese scholarly leader (far right) and others, photo by a Japanese member

Wang Binghua, the Chinese team mainly made a survey and an excavation. And then finally, the time came to open up the coffin. A research member of the Xinjiang Archaeological Institute Yu Zhiyong 于志勇 (currently the Chief) peered through the barely opened coffin and cried out, "Wow, it's wonderful" and read aloud, "Wang Hou He Hum Qian Qiu Wang Sui 王侯合昏千秋萬歲 (Best wishes for the King's marriage) and there's something more." All members both of the Japanese and Chinese teams present there raised their fists yelling, "Hurrah!"

The base camp on that night was filled with awesome excitement. Following Manager of the Assets Section of the Xinjiang Cultural Agency Yue Feng 岳峰, I was urged to make a toasting speech and said, "Today is the best day for us since we launched the Japan-China joint research of the Niya ruins in 1988. All of the members of both the Japanese and Chinese teams have endeavored to make this dream come true. Cheers!" I drank down baijiu which I rarely drink, again and again. During the period of this research, I attended the 40th anniversary of the Xinjiang Uyghur Autonomous Government and donated funds for the escape-from-poverty scheme of Hotan district and for the construction of the Hotan Museum as well. (The Donation Memorandum of Agreement between the Xinjiang Autonomous Region and Yasutaka Kojima on Oct. 2, 1995; Xinjiang Daily News and Xinjiang Urban Report, Oct. 3, 1995; Hotan News, Oct. 12, 1995)

1995 research (the seventh research)

Schedule: September 28 through November 5

Participants (56 in total): (16 Japanese members) Yasutaka Kojima, Shouzou Tanabe, Kodo Sanada, Teruhiko Takahashi, Sun Yuexin, Toshio Asaoka, Shin Yoshizaki, Yousei Kouzuma, Toshitaka Hasuike, Minao Nakajima, Gosuke Onoda, Yoshifumi Ichikawa, Jinichi Yonekawa,

Mikinari Ooyama, Toshiharu Kobayashi, Kazuki Sugimoto

(18 Chinese members) Yue Feng, Wang Binghua, Ren Shinan, Meng Fanren, Qi Dongfang, Yang Jing, Shabiti Ahemaiti, Wang Jinkui, Yu Zhiyong, Ahemaiti Rexiti, Zhang Tienan, Liu Yusheng, Yi Li, Wang Zonglei, Lu Enguo, Wu Yong, Ruan Qinrong, Li Jun

(22 assistants/other members) camel masters, drivers, and reporters

Itinerary: Sep. 28: Departure of the Chinese advance team; Oct. 3: Arrival in Minfeng driving along the desert highway just before opening; Oct. 8: Arrival at the stupa, setting up a BC, departure of the Japanese advance team, meetings with SACH, China and the Xinjiang Cultural Agency, attendance at the 40th anniversary of the Xinjiang Uyghur Autonomous Region, a welcome party, the architectural survey group conducting the research of dwelling sites in Hotan and Kapakeasican until Oct. 16; Oct. 5–8: Departure of the Japanese team, a Japan-China meeting in Urumqi, a welcome party sponsored by the Hotan Regional Office, arrival in Minfeng; Oct. 9: The Chinese team's desert vehicle didn't come back, so a part of the Japanese and Chinese teams left ahead for Kapakeasican; Oct. 10: All the members arriving at the ruins by desert vehicles, the plenary meeting, joining a camel team; Oct. 11–28: Dividing into an archaeological group, a distributional group, and a wood group to conduct research; Oct. 12: Discovery of the tomb of a king; Oct. 14: Opening a coffin and detecting valuable antiquities (Oct. 15: a part of members of both the Japanese and Chinese teams leaving home; Oct. 17: Inspecting the construction site for the Hotan Museum; Oct. 20: Reporting to the Xinjiang Autonomous Region, a return party by the Japanese team; Oct. 21: Reporting to SACH, China, a return party; Oct. 22: Leaving home); Oct. 29–Nov. 3: Leaving for home and arriving in Urumqi via Minfeng and Korla, a return party; Nov. 4–5: The Japanese team flying back home via Beijing, some members remaining for studying the opened coffins.

Investigation: Introducing the higher precision GPS to improve the accuracy of distributional research; the detailed excavation of 92B4 (N2); making a survey on 93A35 (N5) to excavate; the discovery of a lords' graveyard (No. 95MN1th) and excavating it for conservation, unearthed 6 coffins; continuing wood research and creation of pattern diagrams of dwelling sites; making a survey on the Kapakeasican village; collecting antiquities scattered in pieces on the ground; Donation of school supplies to elementary schools; Xinjiang Daily News accompanying us for reporting. (Xinjiang Daily News, Nov. 22, 1995; Xinjiang Newspaper World the Jan. edition, 1996)

People' Daily and Xinjiang Daily reporting as a valuable discovery, photo by Y. Kojima

On November 6 through 12, continuing research on site, both of the Japanese and Chinese teams studied each of the six opened coffins collected in the 1995 research at the Xinjiang Archaeological Institute together with Wang Jun and Wang Yarong who were dispatched by SACH, China. Besides a couple-mummy burial, we found lots of valuable antiquities such as silk brocades embroidered with the words, Wang Hou He Hum Qian Qiu Wang Sui Yi Zi Sun 王侯合昏千秋萬歲宜子孫 (Best wishes for the King's marriage) and Wu Xing Chu Dong Fang Li Zhong Guo 五星出東方利中国 (Five stars from the east beneficial to China).

Participants: Yue Feng, Wang Jun, Wang Binghua, Wang Yarong, Shabiti・Ahemaiti, Yu Zhiyong, Zhang Tienan, Liu Yusheng, Yi Li, Wang Zonglei, Lu Enguo, Wu Yong, Ruan Qinrong, Li Jun, Yasutaka Kojima, Shouzou Tanabe, Shin Yoshizaki, Sun Yuexin, Kazuki Sugimoto, Migifumi Sato

Vice-Director of SACH, China Yan Zhentang 閻振堂, Professors of Peking University Su Bay 宿白 and Yan Wending 嚴文明, a researcher at the Chinese Social Science Institute Xu Pingfang 徐苹芳, and others visited us for observation. Later on, some of these antiquities were designated as the first-class cultural assets (equivalent to national treasures).

In December, the discovery and the excavation of the lords' graveyard in the 1995 research were announced at a press conference in Beijing by SACH, China and the Xinjiang Cultural Agency with the participation of Director Zhang Deqin, Vice-Governor of the Xinjiang Wufuer Abudula 吾甫尔・阿不都拉, Su Bai, Yan Wenming, Secretary of the Xinjiang Cultural Agency Wang Zhongjun, Yue Feng, Wang Binghua, Shouzou Tanabe, Kodo Sanada, Sun Yuexin, and me. This discovery was widely reported within and outside China. (Xinjiang Daily News, Dec. 22 and 25, 1995, Jan. 2 and 30, 1996, Dec. 18, 1996; Mainichi Shimbun, Nihonkeizai Shimbun, and Tokyo Shimbun, Dec. 23, 1995; People's Daily, Dec. 25, 1995; Chinese Cultural Resources News, Jan. 14, 1996; Xinjiang Economics Journal, Jan. 29, 1996; Chunichi Shimbun, Sep. 30, 1996; Southern Weekly, Dec. 6, 1996; People's Daily for overseas, Dec. 16, 1996; People's Daily in electronic version, Sep. 9, 2009)

Investigating the opened coffin of couple burial (at the Xinjiang Archaeological Institute), photo by Y. Kojima

Silk brocade of 五星出東方利中国 designated as the national treasure of national treasures, photo by K. Sugimoto

5. Disclosure of achievements

In February 1996, the Niya ruins were selected as the 10 great archaeological new-discoveries in 1995 中国十大考古新発見（1995年）by the Chinese Cultural Resources News of SACH, China. (Chinese Cultural Resources News, Feb. 18, 1996) In April, the Xinjiang Autonomous Region notified time and again the prohibition of entry into the ancient ruins such as those of Niya and Loulan without its authorization after having been informed of unauthorized activities like archaeological researches, expeditions, and explorations, since the discovery of valuable, cultural assets was reported. On the other hand, the Japan-China joint research team which I led was allowed to enter these areas since we had already received the authorization of SACH, China. And it was so reported. (Wen Wei Pao, Ming Pao Daily News, Sing Pao, May 23, 1996; China Daily, May 24, 1996) In May, both of the Japanese and Chinese teams published research results from 1988 through 1993, titled, *Nicchu-Chunichi kyoudou Niya iseki gakujutsuchousa houkokusho* 『日中・中日共同ニヤ遺跡学術調査報告書』(The report of Japan-China joint scholarly research of the Niya ruins) (Vol. 1. Hozokan) thanks to the tremendous efforts of such people as: Taijun Inokuchi, Kodo Sanada, Kazutoshi Nagasawa, Fumitaka Yoneda, Takao Itoh, Toshio Asaoka, Sun Yuexin, Zhou Peiyan, Zheng Zhong, Masahide Furukawa, Toru Kaigara, Teruhiko Takahashi, Yousei Kouzuma, Toshitaka Hasuike, Tsutomu Saitou, Han Xiang, Yue Feng, Sheng Chunshou, Wang Binghua, Shabiti Ahemaiti, Yu Zhiyong, Ahemaiti Rexiti, Zhang Tienan, and Liu Yusheng, as well as the Grant-in-Aid for Publication of Scientific Research Results funded by the Educational Ministry (71005 Applicant: Taijun Inokuchi). (Yomiuri Shimbun, May 27, 1996; People's Daily for overseas edition, Jun. 12, 1996; Yomiuiri Shimbun, Jun. 18, 1996; Chunichi Shimbun, Oct. 19, 1996)

Its contents include: the congratulatory messages by ex-Prime Minister of Japan Toshiki Kaifu, Vice-Chairman of the NPC Tiemuere Dawamaiti, and Director of SACH China Zheng Deqin; the prefaces by Director-General of the Xinjiang Cultural Agency Maimaitizunong, Manager of the Assets Section of the Xinjiang Cultural Agency Han Xiang, President of Bukkyo University Kosyo Mizutani and me; the ruins' location and environments, the momentum and progression of researches, and the annual research records; the ruins' research of northern Niya; the survey research on the N2 dwelling site; the geographical survey surrounding the stupa; the analyses on collected tree species; the analyses on collected bronze and glasses; the memoir of the Niya ruins' research, the outline and building structure of N3, the view of Jing Jue Guo 精絶国; Kharosthi script materials and Buddhism;

Ex-Prime Minister Toshiki Kaifu (center), Representative Kosho Mizutani (far left), and others observing a mummy, photographer unknown the research on collected antiquities; and the research of residents relevant to today. This report constitutes of the six-page prefatory plates, the 32-page content and others, the 410-page main text, and the 60-page figures (A4 size). It is written both in Japanese and Chinese, along with the English summary.

In June, I retired from the president of the company which I myself had founded on the occasion of the 30th anniversary. While I had expanded the company successfully enough to have it be listed three years before, I thought that the company could not be expected to develop further with the traditional and conventional mode of thinking at the time of a drastic paradigm shift. This resulted in affording me the opportunity to spend far more time working for projects in Xinjiang than ever before when I had to accumulate vacation days to take a leave from work. (Nihonkeizai Shimbun, Yomiuri Shimbun, Asahi Shimbun, Mainichi Shimbun, Chunichi Shimbun, Chubukeizai Shimbun, Apr. 27, 1996 upon the announcement of my retirement; Yomiuri Shimbun Jun. 18, 1996)

In August, Honorary Chairman Toshiki Kaifu, Representative Kosyo Mizutani, Secretary General Shinkou Nakai (later to be the President), Sun Yuexin and I visited Urumqi and Beijing to ask Secretary of the Xinjiang Committee of the CCP Wang Lequan, Governor of the Xinjiang Autonomous Region Abulaiti Abudurexiti and Vice-Director of SACH, China Zheng Bai to further support the joint research as well as to cooperate for the symposium and the cultural heritage exhibition to slate at Bukkyo University in 1997. We received their acceptances. (Xinjiang Daily News, Aug. 20 and 21, 1996; The memorandum of agreement among Bukkyo University, the Academic Research Organization for the Niya ruins, Bukkyo University, and the Xinjiang Cultural Heritage Administration Bureau on Mar. 18, 1997) In the same month, Secretary of the Xinjiang Cultural Agency Wang Zhongjun 王中俊 and I signed the detailed memorandum of agreement on the 1996 research.

The research and the photo shootings of antiquities in 1996 were focused on the lords' coffin and the fabrics.

Schedule: August 19 through August 25
Participants: Takao Itoh, Teruhiko Takahashi, Yousei Kouzuma, Kazuki Sugimoto, Kazuko Sakamoto

Excavation under the dust thrown up (93A35 = N5), photo by Y. Kojima

In September, I introduced the Niya ruins' research to State Counselor Li Teiying 李鉄映 and Vice-Premier Wu Bangguo 呉邦国 when they visited Urumqi. I was surprised to hear, "Thank you very much, an old friend of Chinese people." from Li Tieying in Japanese. From the research in 1996, we started creating topographic maps with the participation of a special GPS engineer employing the large GPS. We also started making a survey on dwelling sites

Collecting refuse left by past explorers in Loulan, photo by Yang Xincai

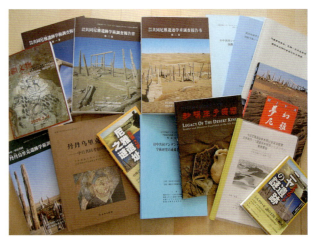

Releasing the results through reports and symposiums: Investigation reports on the Niya ruins and the Dandanoilik ruins and the symposium presentation summaries, etc. in 1995–2010, photo by Y. Kojima

and surrounding remains of production facilities along with excavating Buddhist temples to detect murals. We discovered ruins and relics estimated to be aged 3,000 years in the area 40 km north of the Niya ruins. (People's Daily on Dec. 14, 1996) A circle-structured mount was discovered and antiquities scattered in pieces on the ground were collected in the southern district of the Niya ruins. Besides field research, we studied woods and silk fabrics detected in 1995. At the same time, we visited the Loulan ruins and collected approximately 100 kg garbage left by past explorers. (The Memorandum between the Xinjiang Cultural Heritage Administration Bureau and Yasutaka Kojima on Jan. 29, 1994; Xinjiang Daily News, Nov. 27, 1996)

1996 research (the eighth research)

Schedule: October 2 through November 6

Participants (58 in total): (17 Japanese members) Yasutaka Kojima, Shouzou Tanabe, Kodo Sanada, Keiji Yoshida, Kiyomi Tanaka, Shin Yoshizaki, Tomoko Kondou, Jinichi Yonekawa, Minao Nakajima, Kazuki Sugimoto, Kenji Uchida, Gosuke Onoda, Yoshifumi Ichikawa, Satomi Kato, Hirokazu Kotegawa, Kazutaka Yoshikawa, Koichi Inamasu

(18 Chinese members) Yue Feng, Wang Binghua, Shabiti Ahemaiti, Wang Jinkui, Yu Zhiyong, Yisilafeier Ysufu, Ahemaiti Rexiti, Zhang Tienan, Liu Yusheng, Yi Li, Wang Zonglei, Lu Enguo, Wu Yong, Ruan Qinrong, Zhao Jing, Xing Kaiding, Zhang Shuchun, Adili Mamuti

(23 assistants) camel masters and drivers

Itinerary: Oct. 2–8: Departure of the Chinese advance team (Oct. 4: Arrival in Minfeng; Oct. 8: Setting up a BC near 93A35 (N5)); Oct. 3–4: Departure of the Japanese advance team, meetings, including

Shinkou Nakai, with SACH, China regarding the symposium and the cultural heritage exhibition and then meetings with the Xinjiang Autonomous Region and the Xinjiang Cultural Agency on the same subject, a welcome party by the Xinjiang Autonomous Region; Oct. 4–8: Departure of the Japanese team, Japan-China joint meetings in Urumqi, arrival in Minfeng via Luenthai; Oct. 9: Waiting for desert vehicles' return from the ruins; Oct. 10: Arriving at the Niya ruins by desert vehicle, the plenary meeting, joining a camel team; Oct. 11–28: Dividing into an archaeological group, a distributional group, and a topographic mapping group to conduct research (Oct. 13: Discovering ruins when researching distribution in the north area, a team-member incurring injury caused by a restive camel en route to home; Oct. 15: sending him to a hospital in Korla by desert vehicle; Oct. 17: Some members of both Japanese and Chinese teams heading for Loulan; Oct. 20: Arriving in Urumqi via Karla to report to the Xinjiang Autonomous Region; Oct. 24: Leaving for Lola; Oct. 29: Arriving in Lola; Nov. 2: Going back to Urumqi to join the Niya team): Oct. 29–Nov. 3: The main Japanese and Chinese teams leaving for home and arriving in Urumqi via Minfeng and Luenthai, studying at the Xinjiang Archaeological Institute, a return party by the Japanese side; Nov. 4–5: The Japanese team flying back home via Beijing; Nov. 5–6: The Japanese team leader reporting to SACH, China, hosting a return party, and returning home.

Investigation: Continuing distribution research and creation of pattern diagrams of dwelling sites; starting to create topography by introducing the large GPS and to make a survey on dwelling sites 93A10 (N13) and 93A9 (N14), as well as the remains of surrounding production facilities; excavating the Buddhist temples of 93A35 (N5) and 93A36 (N6) to detect murals; discovering ruins and antiquities when conducting research in the northern area; discovering a circle-structured mount at the south end of the Niya ruins; collecting antiquities scattered in pieces on the ground.

In November, Honorary Chairman Kaifu and I had a conference with Director of SACH, China Zhang Wenbin 張文彬 and agreed with him to further enhance the joint conservation and research projects as well as hold a symposium and an antiquities' exhibition. (Xinhua Daily Telegram, Nov. 15, 1996; Chinese Cultural Resources News, Dec. 1, 1996) In the same month, the whole Niya ruins site was upgraded and designated as the conservation unit of "the national significant relics" by the State Council. (Chinese Cultural Resources News, Dec. 29, 1996) In December, I reported the research results to Secretary of the Xinjiang Committee of the CCP Wang Lequan 王楽泉. (Xinjiang Daily News, Dec. 10, 1996) In the same month, the Academic Research Organization for the Niya ruins, Bukkyo University, held a press conference about the results of the prior research, where

Besides Sankei Shimbun (Dec. 6, 1996) as shown here, the announcement by the Niya Organization, Bukkyo University, was widely covered by other newspapers like Yomiuri, Asahi, Nikkei, Chunichi, and Kyoto, photo by Y. Kojima

leader of the scholarly group of the Japanese team Shouzou Tanabe referred to the silk brocade 五星 (Five stars) as a present from the Chinese Dynasty when a buried couple were married. (Yomiuri Shimbun, Asahi Shimbun, Nihonkeizai Shimbun, Sankei Shimbun, Chunichi Shimbun, Kyoto Shimbun, Dec. 6, 1996; Newsweek, Jan. 1, 1997)

In March 1997, the Xinjiang Autonomous Region's decision to separate the Assets Section from the Xinjiang Cultural Agency resulted in establishing the Administration Office of the Xinjiang Autonomous Government for Relics to manage the whole field of a relics administration (abbreviation: the Relics Bureau of the Xinjiang Uyghur Autonomous Government or the Xinjiang Cultural Heritage Administration Bureau). This Xinjiang Cultural Heritage Administration Bureau has become a Chinese representative office for the World Cultural Heritage afterward. On 22nd of the same month, Yue Feng and I signed the detailed memorandum of agreement after 1997, which was revised on May 27 and September 1, in the presence of Vice-Secretary of the Xinjiang Committee of the CCP Keyoumu Bawudong 克尤木·巴吾東 and Vice-Governor of the Xinjiang Mijiti Nasier 米吉提·納斯尔. (Xinjiang Daily News, Mar. 23, 1997) In May, the memorandum of agreement on the antiquities exhibition as mentioned below was concluded between Vice-Director of the Xinjiang Cultural Assets Bureau Aierken Mijiti 艾尔肯·米吉提 and Kodo Sanada 真田康道, along with me.

The relic research and photo-shootings in 1997 were conducted as follows.

Schedule: Aug. 3–11: (Participants) Shouzou Tanabe, Keiji Yoshida, Shin Yoshizaki, Teruhiko Takahashi, Kazuki Sugimoto, Tomoko Kondou, Yoshifumi Ichikawa, Satomi Kato, Hirokazu Kotegawa
Sep. 6–11: (Participants) Kodo Sanada, Tadashi Inoue

In September, the Symposium on the Japan-China Joint Academic Research Organization of the Niya Ruins and the Unearthed Antiquities Exhibition were held at Bukkyo University to commemorate the establishment of its new library (sponsored by Bukkyo University, the Xinjiang Cultural Heritage Administration Bureau and the Academic Research Organization for the Niya ruins, Bukkyo

Symposium to commemorate the establishment of Bukkyo University's new library, photo by Y. Kojima

Former Prime Minister Kaifu observing the antiquities exhibition to commemorate the establishment of Bukkyo University's new library, photo by Bukkyo University

University). Greetings and presentations were made by people, including Honorary Chairmen of Toshiki Kaifu, Cultural Counselor of the Chinese Embassy Zhang Baozhi, Kosyo Mizutani, Koji Takahashi, Shinkou Nakai, Professor of Bukkyo University Kenji Sugimoto, Maimaiti Zunong, Manager of the Archaeological Administering Section of SACH, China, Song Xinchao (later to be the Deputy Chief and currently being the Bureau Vice-Director), Xu Pingfang, a researcher at the Chinese Social Science Institute Meng Fanren, Assistant Professor of Peking University Lin Meicun (currently Professor), Director of the Kashiwara Archaeological Institute Yasutaka Higuchi, and Professor of Kyushu University Akihiko Akamatsu. Besides them, staff members of both Japanese and Chinese teams such as Kazutoshi Nagasawa, Shouzou Tanabe, Tadashi Inoue, Kodo Sanada, Takao Itoh, Sun Yuexin, Toshitaka Hasuike, Yue Fang, Wang Bighua, Shabiti Ahemaiti, Yu Zhiyong, Zhang Tienan and I followed suit. 500 people or so in total attended the ceremony. (Kyoto Shimbun, Sep. 10, 18, and 23, 1997; Mainichi Shimbun, Sep. 12 and 23, 1997; Sankei Shimbun, Sep. 17, 1997; Nagoya Times, Sep. 22, 1997; Yomiuiri Shimbun, Sep. 23, 1997; Bukkyo University Bulletin No. 285, Nov. 1, 1997) The Chinese delegates met with Honorary Chairman Toshiki Kaifu and Speaker of the House of Representatives Souichirou Itou.

The Exhibition of Recent Archaeological Discoveries in China was held at the National Museum of Chinese History from September through December and the silk brocades such as Wu Xing Chu Dong Fang Li Zhong Guo 五星出東方利中国 and Wang Hou He Hum Qian Qiu Wang Sui Yi Zi Sun 王侯合昏千秋萬歲宜子孫, detected both by the Japanese and Chinese teams were also exhibited. (Chinese Cultural Resources News, Oct. 3, 1997)

We discovered a graveyard in the northern tip of the Niya ruins during the research in 1997. We tidied it up to excavate along with the one discovered in 1995. We also conducted research on the southern mount and a geological survey.

1997 research (the ninth research)
Schedule: October 2 through November 5
Participants (45 in total) **:** (17 Japanese members) Yasutaka Kojima, Shouzou Tanabe, Kodo Sanada, Shiro Ishida, Sun Yuexin, Shin Yoshizaki,

Toshitaka Hasuike, Tomoko Kondou, Jinichi Yonekawa, Kazuki Sugimoto, Kenji Uchida, Gosuke Onoda, Yoshifumi Ichikawa, Satomi Kato, Hirokazu Kotegawa, Koichi Inamasu, Kazuo Kurita (14 members from China) Yue Feng, Yu Zhiyong, Zhang Yuzhong, Ahemaiti Rexiti, Yang Yiyong, Zhang Tienan, Wu Yong, Liu Yusheng, Yi Li, Wang Zonglei, Ruan Qinrong, Nijiati Rouzi, Gong Guoqiang, Liu Hongling

(14 assistants) camel masters and drivers

Itinerary: Oct. 2–8: Departure of the Chinese advance team (Oct. 4: Arrival in Minfeng; Oct. 7: Arrival at the stupa and the set-up of a BC); Oct. 3: Departure of the Japanese advance team, meetings with the SACH, China; Oct. 4–8: Departure of the Japanese main team to join the Japanese advance team in Beijing, Japan-China joint meetings in Urumqi, a welcome party, arrival in Minfeng via Luenthai, a welcome party by the Governor of Minfeng; Oct. 9: Arrival at the ruins by desert vehicle, a plenary meeting, joining with a camel team; Oct. 10–28: Dividing into an archaeological group, a distributional group, a topographic mapping group, and a geometrical group to conduct research (Oct. 17: Some members of both Japanese and Chinese teams heading home; Oct. 21: Returning to Japan; Oct. 17: The team leaders of both Japan and China heading for Minfeng to welcome visitors to the Niya ruins; Oct. 19: Returning to the ruins; Oct. 22: The leaders of both Japan and China and the visitors heading home while the Chinese leader visiting southern part of Xinjiang, including Loulan; Oct. 24: The Japanese visitors arriving in Urumqi via Luenthai, reporting to the Xinjiang Autonomous Region, a return party; Oct. 27: Reporting to SACH, China, and a meeting to discuss projects after 1998 on, a welcome and farewell party; Oct. 28: Return to Japan; Oct. 28: Some members of the Japanese and Chinese parties heading for Minfeng in advance); Oct. 29–Nov. 3: Heading home, visiting each ruin in Turpan via Minfeng, organizing equipment and studying antiquities at the Xinjiang Archaeological Institute, sharing information with the French team, observing the antiquities of the Kara-dong ruins, reporting to the Xinjiang Autonomous Region, a return party; Nov. 4–5: The Japanese team visiting the Exhibition of Archaeological Discoveries in China in Beijing and flying back to Japan.

Investigation: Continuing distributional research and creation of topological maps; discovering a graveyard at the north edge of the ruins and tidying it up to excavate along with the graveyard (No. 95MN1 tomb) discovered in 1995; making a survey on production facilities surrounding 93A10 (N13) and 93A9 (N14), as well as the sites surrounding 93A35 (N5) and 93A36 (N6); conducting research on the southern mount; conducting geological research; collecting antiquities scattered in pieces on the ground; a visit by Special Adviser of the Academic Research Organization for the Niya ruins, Bukkyo University, Mrs. Eiin Yasuda to see the research on site, along with Ms. Reiko Kiyota

While the memorandum of agreement from 1997 on had already been signed, we decided to terminate field research for the moment after a series of discussions with SACH, China, and both Japanese and Chinese sides agreed to focus on research and publications of reports. The Japanese team presented all the equipment, such as survey instruments at the time when research was terminated in 1997.

From April through October 1998, the Exhibition of Valuable Archaeological Relics on the Silk Road was held at the Shanghai Museum where a number of antiquities collected through our researches were displayed and received great response. (Chinese Cultural Resources News, Feb. 8, 1998 and Jan. 27, 1999) Vice-Governor of the Xinjiang Maimaitiming Zhakeer 買買提明・扎克尔 and members of both the Japanese and Chinese teams attended the opening ceremony. In June, a group headed by Governor of the Xinjiang Abulaiti Abudurexiti阿不来提・阿不都熱西提 visited Japan at the invitation of the Japan-China Friendship Association and me. They met Honorary Chairman Toshiki Kaifu, Foreign Minister Keizou Obuchi 小渕恵三 (later to be the Prime Minister), Ikuo Hirayama and Kosyo Mizutani, which helped enhance even further cultural and economic interactions between Xinjiang and Japan. (Reports of Benevolent Sinophilia of 2001) In December, I met with Mayor of Urumqi Nuer Baikeli 努尔・白克力 (later to be the Governor of the Xinjiang Autonomous Region) to consult about the foundation of Educational Support for Children. (Urumqi Evening News, Dec. 24, 1998) I will refer to this hereinafter.

In July 1999, I met with Governor of the Xinjiang Autonomous Region Abulaiti Abudurexiti to inform him of how preparations for compiling the secondary report had been implemented. (Xinjiang Daily News, Jul. 4, 1999) In November, both the Japanese and Chinese teams held a debrief session at the Shijo Center of Bukkyo University with attendance of about 100 people, including Kodo Sanada, Sun Yuexin, Secretary of the Xinjiang Cultural Agency Xu Huatian 徐華田, Deputy Chief of the Foreign Affairs Office of the Xinjiang Government Liu Xiaoqing 劉曉慶, Yidilisi Abuduresule, Yu Xhiyong, and me. In December, I submitted my view on "the development project of the Bogda Shan and its surroundings" to Secretary of Urumqi City Yang Gang 楊剛 (later to be the Standing Vice-Governor of the Xinjiang Gorvernment) for his reference, taking the example of Mt. Fuji. (Urumqi Evening News, Dec. 23, 1999) In the same month I also individually talked with Secretary of the Xinjiang Committee of the CCP Wang Lequan and Governor of the Xinjiang Government Abulaiti Abudurexiti who kindly gave us high marks for research of the Niya ruins. (Xinjiang Evening News, Dec. 24, 1999)

In January 2000, both the Japanese and Chinese teams published *Nicchu-*

Chunichi kyoudou Niya iseki gakujutsuchousa houkokusho『日中・中日共同ニヤ遺跡学術調査報告書』(The report of Japan-China joint academic research of the Niya ruins) (Vol. 2. Nakamura Printing) which recorded the results of the researches conducted up until 1997. This could never been brought to publication without the contributions of those people, including Kosyo Mizutani, Shouzou Tanabe, Kodo Sanada, Toshio Asaoka, Shin Yoshizaki, Takao Itoh, Hitoshi Yonenobu, Teruhiko Takahashi, Yoshifumi Ichikawa, Gosuke Onoda, Tomoko Kondou, Koichi Inamasu, Kazuko Sakamoto, Toshitaka Hasuike, Kazuki Sugimoto, Migifumi Sato, Sun Yuexin, Zhou Peiyan, Yue Feng, Wang Binghua, Shabiti Ahemaiti, Yu Zhiyong, Zhang Tienan, Liu Yusheng, Ruan Qiurong, Wang Zonglei, Wu Yong, Yang Yiyong, Gong Guoqiang, Lin Meicun, Wang Shouchun, Meng Fanren, and Yang Yichou. (Chinese Cultural Resources News, Apr. 9, 2000)

Its contents include: the congratulatory messages by ex-Prime Minister of Japan Toshiki Kaifu, Governor of the Xinjiang Government Abulaiti Abudurexiti and Director of SACH, China, Zhang Wenbin followed by the prefaces by Chief of the Xinjiang Cultural Heritage Administration Bureau Yue Feng, President of Bukkyo University Kosyo Mizutani and me, detailing such subjects as the ruins' location and environments, historical context, research transition, a researching organization, the results of distributional and excavation research, the verification of collected antiquities, and challenges for the future. It constitutes of the four-page prefatory plates, the 22-page contents, the main texts of 412 pages (Japanese) and 356 pages (Chinese), the 107-page figures (A4 size). It is written in Japanese and Chinese, along with the English summary. As appendices, the list of the GPS measuring values in distributional research of the Niya ruins and the distribution chart of the Niya ruins are attached therein, along with their CDs. It weighs as much as 3.7 kg as a whole.

In February, we had a meeting to discuss the following symposium at the Xinjiang Archaeological Institute. We asked Governor of the Xinjiang Autonomous Region Abulaiti Abudurexiti to support this project and proposed to hold the International Conference of Silk Road Cities in the 21st Century (the tentative name) in order to foster internationalization of Xinjiang by making the most use of its key word of Silk Road. (Xinjiang Daily News, Feb. 23, 2000)

In March, the Symposium on Japan-China Joint Scholarly Research of the Niya Ruins and the ceremony to celebrate the publication of the report (Vol. 2) (hosted by the Xinjiang Cultural Agency, the Foreign Affairs Office of the Xinjiang Government, the Xinjiang Cultural Heritage Administration Bureau, the Academic Research Organization for the Niya ruins, Bukkyo University, and the Xinjiang Archaeological Institute) were taken place at World Plaza Hotel in Urumqi with attendance of approximately 150 people from Japan and China, including Vice-Governor of the Xinjiang Government Maimaitiming Zhakeer, Director-General of the Xinjiang Cultural Agency Zunong Kutiluke 祖農・庫提魯克, Shouzou Tanabe, Kodo Sanada, Shin Yoshizaki, Takao Itoh, Sun Yuexin, Zhou Peiyan, Tadashi Inoue, Ken Kirihata, Gosuke Onoda, Yoshifumi Ichikawa, Toshitaka Hasuike, Koichi Kitsudo, Xu Huatian, Manager at the Foreign

Affairs Office of the Xinjiang Government Nixiang Yibulayin, Hang Xiang, Yue Feng, Wang Binghua, Yidilisi Abuduresule, Yu Zhiyong, Zhang Yuzhong, Yang Lin, Meng Fanren, and Lin Meicun, along with a staff member of the Xinjiang Museum Li Yuchun who conducted research of the Niya ruins in 1959, Director of the Xinjiang National Museum of Chinese History Yu Weichao 俞偉超 who is the foremost authority of Chinese archaeology, Chief at SACH, China Yang Zhijun, and Vice-Director of the China National Silk Museum Zhao Feng. (Xinjiang Daily News and Chenbao News, Mar. 21, 2000; People's Daily and Urumqi Evening News, Mar. 23, 2000; Xinjiang Economics, Mar. 24, 2000; Chinese Cultural Resources News, Apr. 9, 2000)

International symposium in Urumqi, photo by Yang Xincai

In October, the Exhibition of the Relics of a Prince in the Desert on the Silk Road, or specifically the exhibition of antiquities detected by the Niya researching team, was held at the China National Silk Museum in Hangzhou in which I myself participated and made a presentation on the outline of the Niya research. In December, I had a discussion with Governor of the Xinjiang Government Abulaiti Abudurexiti about the development of human resources. (Xinjiang Daily News, Dec. 19, 2000) The inauguration ceremony of the website to conserve Chinese historical, cultural heritages 中国歴史文化遺産保護网 was held at the People's Congress Hall in the presence of Vice-Chairman of the NPC Tiemuer Dawamaiti 鉄木尓・達瓦買提 in order to raise awareness of cultural assets' conservation.

Various Chinese newspapers reporting the Urumqi symposium (a part), photo by Y. Kojima

In February 2001, in response to a request from the Chinese side, Kosyo Mizutani and I visited Taiwan to meet Vice-Governor of the Kuomintang Wu Boxiong 呉伯雄 (later to be the Governor) and Venerable Master Hsing Yun 星雲 to discuss cross-strait cultural exchanges, such as launching an exhibition of the Niya ruins' antiquities. They agreed to cooperate for this project.

Director Yu Weichao, a leading archaeological authority in China also participated, photo by Yang Xincai

In March, the Niya research was selected as one of the Chinese 100 greatest discoveries in the 20th century 中国20世紀考古大発見 100 by SACH, China and the magazine called Archaeology. (Chinese Cultural Resources News, Apr. 4, 2001) In April, as the invitation application for Lin Meicun 林梅村 (submitted by Kodo Sanada) was approved thanks to great efforts made by those concerned, he was to conduct research in Japan on the subject related to Kharosthi documents at Bukkyo University until January the following year as a recipient of the invitation fellowships sponsored by Japan Society for Science Development. In March, I had talks with Secretary of the Xinjiang Committee of the CCP Wang Lequan. He expressed further support and a high hope for our activities. (Xinjiang Daily News, Apr. 7, 2001) In May, I conveyed the Taiwan's message to the Chinese side on their willingness of cooperation at the Diaoyutai Guest House, along with Kosyo Mizutani and Assistant Professor of Bukkyo University Seijun Inaoka. As being referred to later, though the exhibition of the Silk Road antiquities was held in Taiwan several years later, we have yet to be informed of whether or not our prior action had somehow made for this exhibition.

In June, having been esteemed for my long-time contribution to Xinjiang, the 20th Anniversary of Our Japanese Friend, Mr. Yasutaka Kojima's Visit to Xinjiang 日本友人小島康誉氏新疆来訪20周年記念大会 proposed by Governor of the Xinjiang Abulaiti Abudurexiti was launched at the People's Theater in Urumqi with attendance of about 800 people, including Governor Abulaiti Abudurexiti 阿不来提·阿不都熱西提, Japanese Minister Nobuyuki Sugimoto 杉本信行, Vice-Governor of the Xinjiang Simayi Tieliwaerdi 司馬義·鉄尓瓦力地 (later to be Governor), Director of Public Relations of the Xinjiang Committee of the CCP Wu Dunfu 呉敦夫, Manager of the Chinese Cultural Ministry Yin Zhiliang, delegates of both Japanese and Chinese, and local people. The outstanding performance award was presented to me by the Chinese Cultural Ministry. [21] (Asahi Shimbun, Jun. 19, 2001; Xinjiang Daily News, Xinjiang Economics, Xinjiang Urban Report, Urumqi Evening News, and Asia Times, Jun. 21, 2001; Chunichi Shimbun, Jul. 6, 2001;

photo by Yang Xincai

人民剧场充满了欢乐的气氛。

The 20th anniversary of Mr. Kojima's visit to Xinjiang hosted by the Xinjiang Government included a convention, a photo-exhibition, a memorial magazine issuance, a tree-planting ceremony, etc.

Japan and China, Jul. 15, 2001 and Oct. 5, 2002) Minister Nobuyuki Sugimoto said in his speech, "I've been working here in China for more than 10 years. I am surprised and pleased to learn that Xinjiang is the place with such a friendly atmosphere. That's because of having experienced no war with Japan and thanks to Mr. Kojima's activities as well." In my talks with Secretary of the Xinjiang Committee of the CCP Wang Lequan, he kindly expressed, "I highly appreciate your contributions and anticipate your further efforts until the occasion of 30th or 40th anniversary." In addition to the ceremony, various commemorating events were taken place, such as the grand reception, the commemorative photo exhibition, the tree-planting ceremony, the publication of the memorial magazine titled 外国友人中国情−小岛康誉与新疆 (A foreign friend's attachment to China as symbolized by Yasutaka Kojima in Xinjiang) and a memorial show. Japanese Ambassador Koreshige Anami 阿南惟茂 and his wife hosted a celebration party at their official residence. In December, I exchanged views on the development of human resources at the meetings with Secretary Wang Lequan and Governor Abulaiti Abudurexiti on a separate occasion. (Xinjiang Daily News, Dec. 20 and 21, 2001)

In the same month, I released a joint publication with the Archives Bureau of the Xinjiang Uyghur Autonomous Region as one of the related projects. As the first shot of a series, *Kindai gaikoku tankenka Shinkyou kouko touan shiryou* 『近代外国探検家新疆考古档案史料』 (The archaeological evidence of modern, foreign explorers in Xinjiang) was published by Xinjiang Fine Arts Photography Publishing House particularly focused on Stein, Hedin, Pelliot, Mannerheim, and Otani. I will refer to the joint publication hereinafter. I also had a meeting with Director of the Joint Front Division of the Chinese Communist Party Wang Zhaoguo 王兆国 to report the Niya ruins' research.

Though a huge amount of collected antiquities had been stored at the Xinjiang Archaeological Institute, its building had been not only insufficiently equipped but so boxy. Therefore, in 2001, it was expanded with the aid of the Japanese Government. Meanwhile, I donated an elevator to lift antiquities. As a result, the facilities were well-equipped and research environments were improved. It goes without saying that even a single piece of antiquities has never been brought back to Japan. (Yet, some staff members brought back sand of the desert just for memory.) In the same month, 「新疆ニヤ集落遺跡考古学研究」 (The archaeological study on the Niya village ruins in Xinjiang) written by Yu Zhiyong 于志勇, an archaeological leader of the Chinese team, was selected as the Significant Research Agenda by SACH, China. (Chinese Cultural Resources News, Dec. 21, 2001)

In January 2002, the silk brocade of Wu Xing Chu Dong Fang Li Zhong Guo 五星出東方利中国 was selected by SACH, China as one of the 64 prohibited antiquities from being exhibited abroad among Chinese immeasurable antiquities. This is tantamount to be selected as "the national treasure among national treasures", as being so valuable as to prevent it from being deteriorated by exhibiting abroad. (Chinese Cultural Resources News, Jan. 30, 2002) From August through December the same year, the Silk Road: the Exhibition of Silk and Gold hosted by NHK, the Japan-China Friendship Association and the Xinjiang Cultural Heritage Administration Bureau was held at the Tokyo National Museum and the Osaka Historical Museum where a number of antiquities detected by the research team, such as the silk brocade *Wang Hou He Hum Qian Qiu Wang Sui Yi Zi Sun* 王侯合昏千秋萬歳宜子孫. This exhibition received an enthusiastic public response. Vice-Governor of the Xinjiang Maimaitiming Zhakeer attended the exhibition and talked with Honorary Chairman Toshiki Kaifu at the exhibition in Tokyo. I accompanied the Vice-Governor on his visits to Tokyo, Sapporo, Otaru and Nara. Furthermore, Financial Minister Masajuro Shiokawa 塩川正十郎 who had long offered invaluable support for me kindly visited the exhibition in Osaka.

In July and August in a row, I guided cultural visitors to have meetings with Central Politburo Committee Member and the Xinjiang Committee of the CCP (doubled from 2002) Wang Lequan and Governor of the Xinjiang Abulaiti Abudurexiti to ask them for further support. (Xinjiang Daily News, Jul. 8 and Aug. 23, 2002) In September, I acted as intermediary for Tokai Television to shoot a reporting program in Xinjiang and partially accompanied that shooting (traveler: Hidetaka Yoshioka) the following year. (Xinjiang Daily News, Sep. 19, 2002 and Sep. 23, 2003)

In October, we made a survey of the Dandanoilik ruins. I will refer to this research hereinafter. In November, in order to have many people understand our research and studies, *Sirukuroudo Niya iseki no nazo* 『シルクロード・ニヤ遺跡の謎』 (The mysteries of the Niya ruins on the Silk Road) that employs a high number of photographs in its content was published by Toho Shuppan, thanks to valuable supports offered by people such as Kosyo Mizutani, Shinkou Nakai, Taijun Inokuchi, Shouzou Tanabe, Kodo Sanada, Eiin Yasuda, Junkei Yasuda, Toshio Asaoka, Takao Itoh, Sun Yuexin, Shin Yoshizaki, Teruhiko Takahashi, Toshitaka Hasuike, Ken Kirihata, Kazuki Sugimoto, Yu Weichao, Liu Yusheng, Sheng Chunshou, Lin Meicun, Yidilisi Abuduresule, Yu Shiyong, and Zhao Feng. (Nagoya Times, Nov. 18, 2002)

Its contents include: Loulan Kingdom and the Niya ruins; desert archaeology; the two legendary Kings of Jing Jue 精絶王; Niya and Xuanzang Sanzang; exploratory history of the Niya ruins; promotion of cultural interchanges; the archaeological perspective of the Niya ruins; search for relics remained on the bank of Niya River; kinds of trees and their ages, characteristics of the ruins; estimated ways of living of local people in those days; Kharosthi documents; monks going through encroaching sands; the Niya ruins from the perspectives of the mirror and money; the clarification of unearthed silk brocades; excavation; what made the research of the Niya ruins succeed?; and the primary research.

In January 2003, I presented a lecture on researches both on the Niya and the Dandanoilik ruins at the Chinese Historical Museum. Then, Secretary of the Xinjiang Cultural Agency Lu Jiachuan 呂家伝, Bureau Director Shen Chunshou, Vice-Director of the Xinjiang Archaeological Institute Zhang Yuzhong, Sun Yuexin, and I had a meeting with the Beijing side at the Diaoyutai.

In October 2004, we set foot on the Niya ruins to observe how each remain had undergone changes. It was the first visit in seven years for the Japanese team. I was surprised to see a limited, paved road built for petroleum development which leads to Kapakeasican from the Desert Highway. Though there was not much change made in each ruin, we found some looting traces. In the meantime, the restoration of the partially eroded stupa was underway according to the scheme to conserve the stupa in the Niya ruins proposed by the Xinjiang Cultural Heritage Administration Bureau, the Xinjiang Relics Conservation Center, and the Xinjiang Archaeological Institute. The reporters of NHK also accompanied us for featuring *The New Silk Road*.

In January 2005, we published 『絲綢之路·尼雅遺址之謎』(the Chinese version of the mysteries of the Niya ruins on the Silk Road 『シルクロード・ニヤ遺跡の謎』) with the supports of Sun Yuexin and Zhou Peiyan. (Xinjiang Daily News, Jan. 30, 2005) Also, *The New Silk Road* was televised for almost a year as the commemorative program featured to celebrate the 80th anniversary since NHK had first launched broadcasting. The Niya and the Dandanoilik ruins were introduced in some parts of this program. Apart from it, from April through October the New Silk Road Exhibition (hosted by NHK, Sankei Shimbun and others) was held at those places like the Edo-Tokyo Museum, the Hyogo Prefectural Museum of Art, and the Okayama Digital Museum where silk brocades and murals detected by the Niya and the Dandanoilik teams, respectively, were displayed. Due to Japan-China relations having been cooled down by the Yasukuni 靖国 issue, Chinese Ambassador to Japan Wang Yi's 王毅 attendance at the opening ceremony called for a state of high alert at the time of the Tokyo exhibition. From December through March of the following year, the Great Exhibition of Treasures on the Silk Road in Xinjiang was taken place in Hong Kong where Kharosthi wood slips and silk brocades detected by our team were displayed.

In 2006, in order to publicize the achievements of the research after Vol. 2, the discussion with the Chinese side was initiated to prepare for reporting Vol. 3. As a part of collecting research materials, we received the return of used equipment, such as tents, the GPS, and livingware from the Chinese side. In August, former Financial Minister Masajuro Shiokawa and I visited the Office of the Prime Minister and met Prime Minister Junichiro Koizumi 小泉純一郎 to report the outline of the research and presented him with a silk-brocade shield of *Wu Xing Chu Dong Fang Li Zhong Guo* 五星出東方利中国. (Covered by various newspapers, Aug. 25, 2008)

In October 2007, the Japan-China joint team summarized the achievements of their research following the 2nd volume of *Nicchu-Chunichi kyoudou Niya iseki gakujutsuchousa houkokusho*『日中・中日共同ニヤ遺跡学術調査報告書』(The report of Japan-China joint scholarly research of the Niya ruins, Vol. 3. Shinyousha) with untiring efforts of those people and organizations, such as Toshio Asaoka, Yoshika Ando, Kiyomi Tanaka, Shin Yoshizaki, Yoshifumi Ichikawa, Ken Kirihata, Shiro Ishida, Akio Katayama, Nobuhiko Kitano, Sun Yuexin, Zhou Peiyan, Sheng Chunshou, Yu Xhiyong, Zhang Tienan, Ruan Qiurong, Wu Yong, Qi Xiaoshan, Jia Yingyi, Lin Meicun, Wang Chen, Wei Si, Nijiati Rouzi, Lin Yixian, Qian Wei,

Cui Jianfeng, the Hotan Museum, and the Minfeng Relics Administration. This report was released as a related publication of the development project (FY 2003–FY 2007) of the MEXT's Open Research Center. (Asahi Shimbun, May 9, 2008)

Its contents include: the prefaces by President of Bukkyo University Ryuzen Fukuhara, Director of the Xinjiang Cultural Heritage Administration Bureau of the Xinjiang Uyghur Autonomous Region Sheng Chunshou and me followed by the investigation overview; the outline of the graveyard research; the research of unearthed antiquities of the Niya ruins stored in the Niya Relics Hall and the Hotan Museum; the analysis of unearthed glasses of the Niya ruins; the research and study of N6 and N14; the study of murals; the study of Kharosthi; the study of silk brocades, the topological and geological study, the research of furnace remains, the study of Zuicho Tachibana of the Otani Exploring team; significant discoveries; the study of *Wu Xing Chu Dong Fang Li Zhong Guo* 五星出東方利中国; the study of Buddhist temples' remains; the study of burial system. It constitutes of the two-page prefatory plates, the 16-page contents, the main texts of 353 pages, the 41-page figures (A4 size), which is written in Japanese along with the English summary. The Chinese version was decided to be published later.

The great mentors like Shouzou Tanabe 田辺昭三, Li Yuchun 李遇春, and Yu Weichao 俞偉超 who had made tremendous contributions to the scholarly research of the Niya ruins passed away before this book was released. In remembrance of these three mentors' virtues, we placed their feasts of reason on the Niya ruins in this report and offered it to their spirits. Without knowing when, the song *Hana* (flowers) has become our team song, which had always been conducted by nobody but Mr. Big Tanabe. I'm still missing his big belly.

The events afterward will be referred to in the chapter of Dandanoilik.

6. The organization for research and its achievements

The Niya research mentioned hereinbefore was led by me, Yasutaka Kojima 小島康誉 (ever since 1988) from Japan and Han Xiang 韓翔 (1988 through 1994), Yue Feng 岳峰 (1995 through 2001), and Sheng Chunshou 盛春寿 (from 2001 on) from China. The scholarly team was headed by Taijun Inokuchi 井ノ口泰淳 (1990 through 1994) and Shouzou Tanabe 田辺昭三 (1995 through 2006) from Japan, and Wang Binghua 王炳華 (1991 through 1996) and Yu Zhiyong 于志勇 (from 1997 on) along with Kodo Sanada 真田康道 as a deputy head (from 1990 on).

Since the scope of studies extends over a wide range of fields, a number of researchers from various institutions participated in this project as being mentioned hereinafter. Specialized fields include the administration of foreign affairs, the management of cultural assets, international cooperation, archaeology, Buddhist studies, philology of the Western Regions, history of East-West interactions, architecture, geography, geology, ligneous science, history of Buddhist arts, dyeing study, photography and survey. People in these fields had made their best efforts, which resulted in the following achievements.

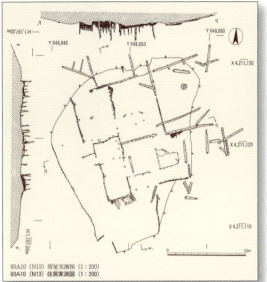

[Picture left] Excavation of remains leading to destruction to be kept to a minimum (93A35 = N5), photo by Kodo Sanada
[Picture right] Remains surveying chart (93A10 = N13)

○ Discoveries of about 250 relics, such as stupa, temples, graveyards, dwelling sites, production facilities, mounting, stables, orchards, reservoirs, tree-lined streets, construction materials and sites of dispersed remains followed by registering their latitude-longitude locations via GPS to create the distributional diagram of those relics.
○ Creation of surrounding topological charts via large GPS to clarify the whole picture of the Niya ruins.
○ Discoveries of much older relics and remains about 40 km north of the Niya ruins to verify living quarters moving south.
○ Making a survey on dwelling sites of relevant cities to identify the structure of ruined residences.
○ Excavating some residences to clarify the ways of living.
○ Making a survey on some groups of dwelling sites and production facilities to clarify urban structure.
○ Excavating to research temples and detecting murals to get a clue to identify Buddhism in the Western Regions.
○ Discovery of a lords' graveyard and detecting national-treasure class of many antiquities to clarify a close relationship in terms of politics, economics and culture between Jing Jue Guo 精絶国 and Chinese Dynasties in those days.
○ Excavating various gravesites that offered new insight into burying methods
○ Measuring post materials by means of C14, which gave us a lead to define ruin's age.
○ Detecting loads of valuable cultural assets, including Kharosthi and Chinese wood strips to gain new insight.
○ Deciphering documents in Kharosthi and in Chinese to gain new insight.
○ Detecting the supposedly fossils of neohipparion that offered us new insight in terms of geological formation in the area of the Niya ruins.

Couple-burial mummies assumed as King and Queen of Jing Jue

Kharosthi wood strip

Various accessories

Arrows and vows of burial goods within the couple-burial coffin, all the four photos by K. Sugimoto

7. Brief summary and future initiatives

You might assume after having read my paper so far that research had proceeded without any trouble. Actually, however, it entailed lots of troubles.

First of all, the fact that the ruins locate in the uninhabited area about 100 km inside the Taklamakan desert has made it difficult just to reach and bring something there. For example, if 60 or so people camp out for three weeks, we have to bring in massive amounts of food as well as investigating equipment, including 6 tons of water. Furthermore, the scale of the ruins is expansive as mentioned above. Aerial survey is limited, and it is disturbing to detect remains in such conditions as a series of tamarix banks and sand dunes. The surface temperature goes up over 70 centigrade in summer and plunge to 50 centigrade below zero in winter. In the spring, sand storm blows hard enough to limit a researching period on site weatherwise. While research was conducted during the period of a stable weather condition such as October through November, a temperature difference within a day comes close to 40 degrees. The investigating fields extend to so many areas that we are required to have quite a number of researchers involve in, which has made it complicate to coordinate their activities. In addition, the social system, investigating methodologies, and a lifestyle differ between Japan and China. And it requires huge amounts of money. The same goes with the research of the Dandanoilik ruins.

In retrospect, I would say what great achievements we have made under the demanding conditions as stated above. It may well be understandable for people who have experienced collaborative research overseas under very severe state control, particularly in China, and to say nothing of the extraordinarily vast desert.

It has become one of the most successful as well as the largest scale, collaborative research between Japan and China. Before researching, we must take it as a cardinal rule that the sovereignty of the Niya ruins lies in China, reflecting on the lesson of the Western Regions' explorations conducted in the past. When we see the Niya research from the centennial perspective, being based on the basic principle that the Japan-China joint scholarly research of the Niya ruins 『日中・中日共同ニヤ遺跡学術調査』 should be viewed as the initial phase of research, we have tried to keep excavations leading to destruction to a minimum. Instead, we focused on distributional research, shootings and surveying in each ruin and collecting antiquities scattered in pieces on the ground. Furthermore, we have considered this project, not just as scholarly activities, but as the activities leading to local development, such as having local people engaged in assisting excavation surveys so as to help them get education and cash income, naturally bringing all the garbage back, using propane gas and coal having been brought in all the way instead of using deadwood on site as a source of fuel.

In summing up the historical transition of the Niya research, the first phase is the discovery of the ruins and exporting antiquities by foreign explorers such as Stein's team in the early 20th century. The second phase is a desperate research by the team of the Xinjiang Museum without even enough food, conducted immediately after the establishment of the Xinjiang Uyghur Autonomous Region. And the third one is a large-scale research conducted by the Japan-China joint team during the period of reform and door-opening. This collaboration research between Japan and China was the largest in size and lasted the longest period as well. It has garnered distinguished achievements. And what's more, the publication of reports is still going on.

It is an extremely rare case even seen in the world scene that such valuable and sizable relics with a grove of pillars have survived two thousand years or so. Furthermore, tens of thousand dried-up poplar trees remaining here and there could be viewed as great natural relics essential for restoration of ancient environments. It is our mutual responsibility to conserve the Niya ruins which are one of the greatest cultural assets in China and can be said as the world cultural heritage shared by mankind. Thus, I am firmly resolved to be involved in it as much as I can. We also must enhance conservation and research of unearthed antiquities. The results of these activities should be made in public through reports and international symposiums from now on. I would like to possibly conduct those incomplete researches, such as supplementary distributional research (we can expect to discover much more antiquities), northern ruins' research (we can verify living quarters moving south caused by desertification along with possible discoveries of many remains), and southern mount's research (we can trace its role and age).

It is quite regrettable for me that Deputy Leader of the scholarly team Kodo Sanada withdrew due to sickness and retired from Professor at Bukkyo University. I pray for his recovery. Because of my insufficient faculty, I have failed to fully take over Professor Sanada's task, my scholarly review is incomplete, and records and photographs have been scattered among various members of the team. Unfortunately, since advancement of the Academic Research Organization for the Niya ruins, Bukkyo University, from a research workshop to a formal institution was passed over, I am anxious about how our achievements will be succeeded by the future generation.

Every single relic detected in the Niya ruins is stored at the Xinjiang Archaeological Institute. The development of science and technology will shed light on these relics to bring about new insights in 50 or 100 years' time. The field so-called "Niya-Silk Road studies " will be further fostered from now onward.

Notes:
………

(14) M. Aurel Stein, *Serindia* (Vol. I), Oxford, 1921, p.242; Han Xiang, Wang Binghua, et al., eds., the preface of 『尼雅考古資料』(The archaeological evidence of the Niya ruins), the Xinjiang Printing Agency of Social Science for School Graduates, 1988; Lin Meicun, 『絲綢之路散記』 (The random notes of the Silk Road), People's Fine Arts Publishing House 2004, p.66; and others. The Niya ruins site is a part of Minfeng County in the Hotan Prefecture as the administrative district.

(15) Since it is a vast area, it entails an extremely hard work to make distributional investigations, surveys, and excavations of remains surviving in small, large dunes and tamarix banks as well as a place where an aerial survey is restricted. It is stated in the Aurel Stein's *Innermost Asia* 『中央アジア踏査記』(Junnosuke Sawazaki, Trans.). Hakusuisha Printing, 1984, p.98, "What has been found out in the subsequent investigations is that the area where antiquities scattered around covers over 22 kms from north to south and about 7 kms from west to east."

(16) The hypothesis that the ancient Western Regions' Southern Route connects such ancient ruins as Niya, Dandanoilik, and Rawaq seems to be the accepted view. But this theory has not been proven. The team members and I have doubts about this hypothesis.

(17) M. Aurel Stein, *Ancient Khotan*. (Vols. 1–2) Oxford, 1907; *Serindia*. 1921; *Innermost Asia*. 1928

(18) Akio Katayama, *Otani tankentai dainiji taiin Tachibana Zuichou no seiikinandou tousa* 『大谷探検隊第2次隊員橘瑞超の西域南道踏査』(The survey of the Western Regions' Southern Route by Zuicho Tachibana who was the member of the Otani exploration team) in *Nicchu-Chunichi kyoudou Niya iseki gakujutsuchosa houkokusho* 『日中・中日共同ニヤ遺跡学術調査報告書』(第三巻) (The report of the Japan-China joint scholarly research of the Niya ruins, Vol. 3), Shinyousha Printing Co., Ltd., 2007, pp. 226-228. Mr. Katayama, well-known for his elaborate research on the Otani exploration team, says in this paper citing the records and the diaries of both Zuicho Tachibana and Eizaburo Nomura, and 『近代外国探険家新疆考古档案史料』(The archaeological evidences of modern, foreign explorers in Xinjiang) edited by the Archaeological Center of the Xinjiang Uygur Autonomous Region and the Academic Research Organization for the Niya ruins, Bukkyo University, as well as The Times on Feb. 3, 1910, "It is certainly said that they visited Imam-Jafaul-Sodick-Mazar, but it should be next to impossible to travel to and from the Niya ruins itinerarywise, but, indeed, we cannot definitely negate the possibility. A conclusion has yet to come."

(19) The Xinjiang Museum,「新疆民豊県北大沙漠中古遺址墓葬区東漢合葬墓清理簡報」(The brief report on how to tidy up a couple-mummy burial of the old graveyard in the great northern desert of Minfeng in Xinjiang) in 『尼雅考古資料』(The archaeological evidence of the Niya ruins), The Youth Printing Agency of Social Science, 1988, pp. 6-9

(20) The excavation certificate which was addressed to me with the letterhead of SACH, China specifies in Chinese, affixing the seal of Director Zhang Deqin in red, "We are pleased to inform you on the occasion to finalize your research on the Niya ruins that those divisions concerned with the Chinese Government have already ratified the application you have submitted to research and excavate the Niya ruins in the same manner as a collaboration with the Xinjiang Cultural Heritage Administration Bureau. We would like to ensure that research activities will be smoothly conducted by abiding the following points: concluding the basic consultation agreement in unison with the representatives of the Xinjiang Cultural Agency; defining specific plans along with each special institution; discussing investigations, excavation methods, subjects, expenses, protection, and safety; organizing the China-Japan joint excavation and research team; signing a consultation agreement annually; preparing a procedural application; reporting its activities. While the Xinjiang region is one of our most important archaeological districts, such as the Niya ruins, natural environments cause extreme hardship due to its location in the desert. I take it great pride in you and your team members for having made such tremendous contributions to activities including the Xinjiang archaeological research and protection of cultural assets for a long time. I am humbled by delegating SACH, China to pray for further, greater achievements to be attained through proceeding with the China-Japan collaborative research project. For your information, you can refer to this certificate in *Kindai gaikoku tankenka Shinkyou kouko touan shiryou* 『近代外国探検家新疆考古档案史料』(The archaeological evidences of modern, foreign explorers in Xinjiang) p.36 as mentioned in the above note (18).

(21) As they say, it is an extremely rare case to hold a conference such as for awarding a foreigner in China. Besides the publication of 『外国友人中国情・小島康誉与新疆』(A foreign friend's attachment to China as symbolized by Yasutaka Kojima in Xinjiang), the photo exhibition, the tree-planting event, the lectures along with a great banquet were taken place in the commemorative ceremony. I was the 11th person to receive the outstanding performance award. I myself hosted the return banquet for the 20th anniversary of Yasutaka Kojima's visit to Xinjiang to express my appreciation to previous leaders, senior staff members, and friends in the whole variety of fields of Xinjiang. In 2011, the 30th anniversary of Yasutaka Kojima's visit to Xinjiang was held.

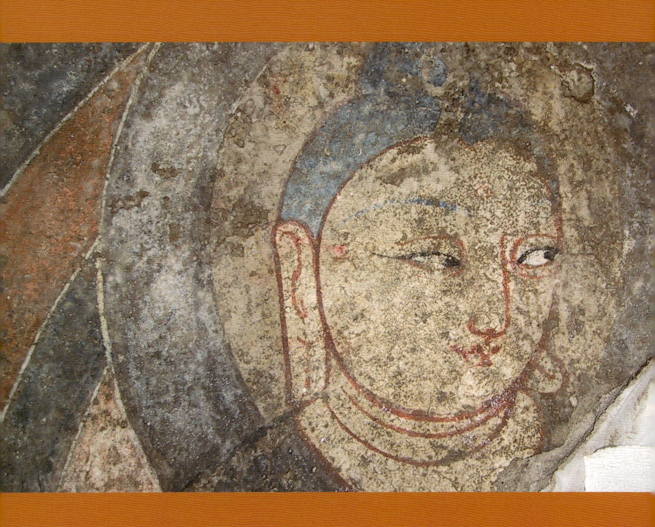

IV. The Japan-China Joint Scholarly Research of The Dandanoilik Ruins and the Outline

―日中共同ダンダンウイリク遺跡学術調査とその概要―

Taking a rest to avoid the harsh glare of the sun on our way to the Dandanoilik ruins (2006), photo by Y. Kojima

The mural buried back for conservation after excavation and research (2006), photo by Y. Kojima

IV. The Japan-China Joint Scholarly Research of The Dandanoilik Ruins and the Outline

1. The transition of research

The Dandanoilik 丹丹烏里克 ruins were discovered by Swedish explorer and geographer Sven Hedin in January 1896. Stein, being inspired by this discovery, conducted a large-scale excavation in December 1900, and collected a huge amount of murals and others, including the painting on wooden panel depicting the legend of the princess who hid silkworm eggs in her headdress to smuggle them out of China to the Kingdom of Khotan 桑種西漸伝説. In this way, the legend which had been described in 『大唐西域記』 (The great Tang records on the Western Regions) was verified. He, then, headed east to find the Niya ruins and conducted a large-scale excavation to collect a great amount of valuable remains.

Sven Hedin who discovered the Dandanoilik ruins, reprinted from 近代外国探検家新疆考古档案史料 (The archaeological archives of Xinjiang by modern foreign explorers)

Back in London, he released its outline through the preliminary report and others, which is supposed to have given a chance to form the Otani exploration team headed by Rev. Kozui Otani 大谷光瑞 who had stayed in London for study at that time.

Thus, the Dandanoilik ruins have become well-known as the starting point of Silk Road studies. In 1905 American geographer Huntington made a survey, and in 1928 a member of the German Trinkler's team Bosshart, a Swiss botanist, explored there as well.[22] Since then, there had no known where it is about. However, in 1996 and 1997, the staff of the Xinjiang Archaeological Institute that accompanied an oil exploration team rediscovered the ruins and the location was clarified. Based on this information, a Swiss named Baumer made an illegal survey in 1988.[23] As seen above, while explorers and archaeologists across the world have shown interests, a full-fledged research was not conducted because of its location of lying far deep within the great desert, as well as of being an unopened city.

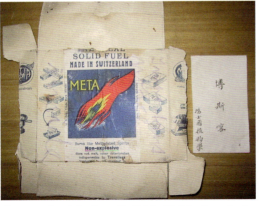

Name card and the box of solid fuel left in the ruins by Bosshart, photo by Y. Kojima

Newspapers left by Bosshart, photo by Y. Kojima

The ruins locate in the area at 37 degrees and 46 minutes northern latitude and 81 degrees and 4 minutes eastern longitude where 70 or so remains, such as temples and dwellings, were distributed in an area stretching for around 2 km from east to west and around 10 km from north to south (including the surrounding area). Stein estimated from collected remains that the ruins had been discarded around 8th century. For your information, the Niya ruins situate about 145 km east of the Dandanoilik ruins. Even far more remains will be discovered in the course of the future research. It is more or less 1,250 meters above sea level. The ruins' name means an ivory house. The elephant-headed Ganesha statutes were included among enormous amounts of antiquities excavated by Stein. When so called treasure hunters were rampant in the Western Regions' Southern Route, they had probably brought out these statutes long before his excavation, because of which the ruins' site came to be called as an ivory house (Dandanoilik). It is spelled in several different ways either in Chinese, Japanese, or English. It was referred to as Jiexie 傑謝 in the era of the Tang Dynasty.

The Japan-China joint scholarly research of the Dandanoilik ruins (organized by the Academic Research Organization for the Niya ruins, Bukkyo University, the Xinjiang Cultural Heritage Administration Bureau and the Xinjiang Archaeological Institute, and subsidized by the Religious Culture Research Institute of Bukkyo University) was initiated by the wish of Junkei Yasuda who was then a Ph.D. student at Nara Women's University and researching Xuanzang Sanzang's return journey from India. Her wish was made come true based on the memoranda of agreement on the research of ruins in the Western Regions' Southern Route including the ruins in Niya and Dandanoilik signed by Japan and China on July 19 and November 14, 1988 as referred to hereinbefore.

2. The discovery of "Mona Lisa of the Western Regions"

The Taklamakan Desert covers the area about 90% as large as that of Japan. The survey in the vast desert entails extreme hardships. There is little difference from the one 100 years ago. It is literally "exploration." We drove northward along the Keriya River from Yutian于田 (renamed in 1959 from Keriya) a small city in the Western Regions' Southern Route which is currently called the national route 315. Even 4WD vehicles were frequently stuck in the rough dirt road. It took us about six hours to cover around 120 km. At the small village called Bakkakuegiri 米薩来, we switched our ride to camels. It was really hard work to load massive amounts of equipment and food on camels, for they had not been trained as such any more because the development of truck transportation had reduced camel caravans. Thus, it took three hours to prepare for leaving. Yet, it was a magnificent view that 41-camel's team was crossing the affluent Keriya River.

We advanced across a number of megadunes toward the ruins' location positioned by the Xinjiang Archaeological Institute via GPS in 1996. On the second day, too, we headed off for farther westward. As camels always make a point to detour dunes, their walking distance usually increases 1.5 times more than when going straight. It's getting drastically cold when the sun sets into the horizon of

The 1st caravan: Far from the romantic song "Tsukino sabakuwo (Desert in moonlight)", a long ride on a camel was like torture

Desert poplar strongly surviving even in the desert (the Dandanoilik ruins west)

Column members which have been proven to show high processing levels

As if suddenly an inhabitant to pop up and say, "Hello" (CD-7 = D7), all the four photos by Y. Kojima

the great desert. Notwithstanding, we advanced even after dark due to the limited itinerary. It hurts all over your body when you keep on riding a camel. On the third day, we finally reached the east edge of the ruins after 14:00. The whole members cheered because of the joy of arrival and the relief of a no more camel ride. We covered approximately 50 km in terms of a camel distance. On October 30, 2002, it was the first Japanese visit there officially authorized by the Xinjiang Government.

With little time to enjoy our arrival at our targeting destination, we started to conduct an introductory distributional research breaking into several groups. Remains were surviving here and there between the dunes of the boundless desert. Some remains are big, others small. When observing their architectural structures, I heard a loud glad cry in front. A member of the Chinese team found an exposed mural. We found the depicted Buddha's face slightly appearing on the surface of the ground maybe being exposed due to fickle gusty wind. We proceeded with an immediate excavation for conservation under the directives of Bureau Director Sheng Chunshou 盛春寿 and Vice-Director of the Xinjiang Archaeological Institute Zhang Yuzhong 張玉忠. The east side wall of a temple fell outward. With careful removal of sand, murals appeared one after another. I unintentionally joined my hands in prayer with the pleasure of seeing the divine face of the Buddha that appeared after having been buried for a thousand and several hundred years.

We were all so impressed with a curious coincidence because this preliminary survey originally had been scheduled in the previous year but postponed on the recommendation of the Xinjiang Government just before departure due to the battle in Afghanistan. Should it have been conducted in 2001, we might not have been blessed with the opportunity to see this Buddha. We practiced informal Buddhist memorial service and chanted *Hannyashingyou* 般若心経 (Heart Sutra) which sounded like having echoed all around there after the lapse of a thousand and hundred years. Having failed to fully prepare for excavation at that time, the

[Picture above] Mural depicting Buddha also referred to as Mona Lisa of the Western Regions 西域のモナリザ (a part, at the Xinjiang Archaeological Institute), photo by Y. Kojima
[Picture below] Once discovered a mural, emergency trial excavation for conservation (CD-4 = D1), photo by Y. Kojima

team of the Xinjiang Archaeological Institute headed by Zhang Yuzhong urgently positioned themselves, left Urumqi on 11th of the following month to excavate there for a couple of weeks, and arrived back on December 5. It was a serious challenge to carry a large mural excavated deep inside the great desert without damage all the way to the Institution in Urumqi about 1,400 km away. Taking a look at a part of the mural where Buddha is depicted, we spontaneously exclaimed by seeing its eyes and smile, "Mona Lisa of the Western Regions 西域のモナリザ."

2002 research (the first research and the preliminary survey)
Schedule: October 25 through November 9
Participants (31 in total): (8 Japanese members) Yasutaka Kojima, Junkei Yasuda, Zenzaburo Kishida, Teruko Kishida, Reiko Kiyota, Kazuo Nakatsukuri, Kazuyuki Takada, Yoko Takada
(7 Chinese members) Sheng Chunshou, Zhang Yuzhong, Li Jun, Tong Wenkang, Zhang Tienan, Tuohuti Tulahong, Maiti Kasimu
(16 assistants) camel masters and drivers
Itinerary: Oct. 25–27: Departure of the Japanese team, a welcome party

Immediately after mural discovery, photo by Y. Kojima

Upon urgent excavation, murals unearthed one after another, photo by Y. Kojima

Butts of small Buddha statutes and murals, photo by Y. Kojima

Man sustaining Buddha statue, photo by Y. Kojima

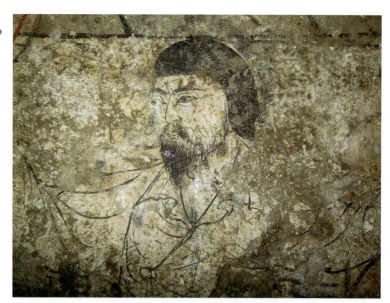

Murals brought in the Xinjiang Archaeological Institute and unpacked, photo by Y. Kojima

Unpacked small Buddha statues, photo by Y. Kojima

hosted by the Xinjiang Government (Xinjiang Daily News, Oct. 26, 2002), Japan-China joint meetings in Urumqi, arrival in Yutian via Minfeng through the desert highway dropping by Korla, preparations, donation such as personal computers to the Relics Department of Yutian city; Oct. 28: Leaving Yutian by truck and 4WD, 6 vehicles in total, switching a ride to camels at Bakkakuegiri to advance into the Taklamakan Desert; Oct. 30: Finally reaching the east edge of the ruins in the afternoon, confirming the outline of the ruins, discovery of murals, excavating partially for conservation; Oct. 31: Leaving in the afternoon; Nov. 2: Arrival in Yutian; Nov. 4: Arrival in Urumqi taking the reverse route, meeting to discuss the excavation of murals by the Chinese team. Return party hosted by the Japanese team; Nov. 6: the Japanese team leaving for home, meanwhile, the leader of the Japanese team released the outline of the Niya ruins' research at the Symposium in Hangzhou, reported the discovery of murals to Vice-Chairman of the National Committee of the Chinese People's Political Consultative Conference Abulaiti Abudurexiti 阿不来提·阿不都熱西提 in Beijing, visited Director Yu Weichao 俞偉超 being hospitalized, and left for Japan on 9th. (Xinjiang Daily News, Nov. 8, 2002)

Investigation: Grasping of the ruins' outline; registration via GPS; discovery of murals and a trial excavation; and collection of relics scattered on the surface of the ground

In December, I reported the discovery of the mural to Vice-Chairman of the NPC Tiemuer Dawamaiti 鉄木尓·達瓦買提, along with expressing my appreciation to his long-standing support.

3. Initiating conservation of the mural and a full-scale research

In January 2003, the project of research and studies of the ruins was authorized as a related part of the Japan-China joint scholarly research of the Niya ruins at the conference of the Academic Research Organization for the Niya ruins, Bukkyo University. Because it was evaluated that the mural was extremely distinguished in contents (abundant Buddhas, Buddhist saints, prayers, and animals), quantity (such a scale as large as about 10 squire meters) and quality (with highly sophisticated, expressive faculties) and thus "the ruin was essential for studies of not only the Western Regions' Buddhism but ancient Buddhism painting history of Asia." In the same month, we received a response of acceptance on the above-mentioned policy from the Xinjiang Cultural Heritage Administration Bureau.

In April, we started the preliminary research of the mural at the Xinjiang Archaeological Institute together with its staff members, including Zhang Yuzhong and Li Wenying. Professor of Kyoto University of Art and Design Tadashi Inoue (former professor of Bukkyo University) admired the mural stating, "Its contents are rich and it is one of the finest Western Regions' mural masterpieces. Exactly

During the SARS outbreak, only 7 passengers being on board, photo by Y. Kojima

as being said in a literature, I'm just feeling like watching "*Youhitsu kinkei nishite kuttetsu banshi no gotoshi* 用筆緊勁にして屈鉄盤絲の如し (The brushstrokes are emphatically contrasted, what with some parts being as powerful as an iron wire and other parts being as fine as a thin thread)." I reported about conservation and studies of the ruins to Governor of the Xinjiang Simayi Tieliwaerdi 司馬義・鉄力瓦尓地. (Xinjiang Daily Newspaper, May 1, 2003) After researching, Tadashi Inoue 井上正, Yoshika Ando 安藤佳香, and Professor of Otemae University Ken Kirihata 切畑健 visited Turpan to watch the grottoes' murals, too. At that time, the SARS scare was running rampant in China and passengers from Osaka to Beijing were four Japanese of us and three Chinese going home. Beijing Airport was quiet and empty.

Schedule: April 25 through May 6
Participants: Yasutaka Kojima, Tadashi Inoue, Yoshika Ando, Ken Kirihata

In July, I urged Member of the Politburo Standing Committee and Secretary of the Xinjiang Committee of the CCP Wang Lequan 王楽泉 for further support. (Xinjiang Daily News, Jul. 14, 2003) From July through August, a party headed by Bureau Director Sheng Chunshou visited Japan to have a meeting. On September 22, Deputy Director of the Xinjiang Cultural Heritage Administration Bureau Aierken Mijiti 艾尓肯・米吉提 and I singed the memorandum of agreement on conservation and studies and received a formal approval from SACH, China, in October. After I had talks with Aierken Mijiti and Zhang Yuzhong in December, I brought home a fraction of the mural under the approval of the Chinese side, and analyzed it with the cooperation of Nara National Research Institute for Cultural Properties. In the same month, I expressed appreciation to Deputy Director of SACH, China Song Xinchao 宋新潮 for approving conservation and studies of the mural and asked for his further cooperation in the future. Also, being requested by NHK (Japan Broadcasting Corporation), I made a request to Bureau Director Sheng Chunshou for cooperating to shoot The New Silk Road 新シルクロード as well as to display antiquities of the ruins both in Niya and Dandanoilik at the New Silk Road antiquities exhibition.

In January 2004, I expressed my gratitude to former Finance Minister Masajuro Shiokawa for all his assistance and guidance since the establishment of the Japan-China Friendship Association to Restore and Conserve the Kizil Grottoes, such as the Educational Ministry's subsidy for the scientific research of the Niya ruins through hosting a many-thanks party for his hard work at the time when he retired from politics. So many people attended the party, including Presidency of Yakushiji Temple Eiin Yasuda and his wife.

In February, Kodo Sanada, Tadashi Inoue, and I had talks with Lin Meicun 林

梅村 and people related with Chinese Central Television's *The New Silk Road* who were invited by NHK. In the same month, although the authorization of shooting The New Silk Road was discussed among NHK, Chinese Central Television, the Foreign Affairs Office of the Xinjiang Government, the Xinjiang Cultural Heritage Administration Bureau, and me in Urumqi, it ended up with only signing the conference minutes because ulterior motives among them were conflicting with each other. In March, Tadashi Inoue, Yoshika Ando, Ken Kirihata, Sun Yuexin, the leading authority of cultural assets' conservation Iwataro Oka 岡岩太郎, the president of Bokkodo, Head of Art Preservation Services Yoshikazu Tsujimoto, 辻本与志一 and I from Japan developed a draft for conservation and studies at the Xinjiang Archaeological Institute together with Professor of Peking University Ma Shichang 馬世長, Professor of Chinese National Museum Tie Fude 鉄付徳, researching staffers of the Kuqi Grottoes Institution Liu Yongqui and He Lin from China, and both sides agreed to preserve the murals in a flexible way of thinking as well as by using sophisticated technology. Then I met with Vice-Governor of Xinjiang Kurexi Maihesuti 庫熱西·買合蘇提. (Xinjiang Daily News, Mar. 12 and Nov. 10, 2004 and Apr. 5, 2005; Xinjiang Economic, Mar. 12, 2004)

Meeting on a preserving policy among Japanese and Chinese members, photo by Tong Wenkang

In the same month, although the shooting negotiation for The New Silk Road was facing a deadlock, I tried to persuade all the concerned parties to compromise for the sake of my birthday celebration, which led to signing the memorandum of agreement. (Xinjiang Daily News, Xinjiang Economics, and Xinjiang Urban Daily, Jun. 14, 2004) In April, the negotiation of the Silk Road Exhibition was accelerated. In May, Aierken Mijiti, Zhang Yuzhong, Tie Fude, Tadashi Inoue, Professor of Kokushikan University Masaaki Sawada 沢田正昭 (the former Head of the Center for Archaeological Operations at Nara National Research Institute for Cultural Properties and Professor of Tsukuba University), Yoshikazu Tsujimoto, Sun Yuexin, and I attended the council consisting of six members of the specialist committee for SACH, China, such as Wang Danhua 王丹華 and Pan Lu 潘路 at University of Science and Technology of Beijing, and explained the original plan for conservation. This council reviews whether or not the project meets appropriately and scientifically the requirements imposed by

Xinjiang Daily reporting the conservation start, photo by Y. Kojima

SACH, China. And it was authorized. Based on this authorization, we started to prepare materials and chemicals. Some parts of them were offered from Iwataro Oka and Yoshikazu Tsujimoto free of charge.

In October, Vice-Governor of the Xinjiang Kurexi Maihesuti and Bureau Director Sheng Chunshou who were invited to Japan by NHK and me signed a final agreement with NHK for the New Silk Road Exhibition. The members of the party had talks with President of Bukkyo University Kosyo Mizutani, Shinkou Nakai, and Kodo Sanada and agreed to further cooperate for research of the Dandanoilik ruins and murals' conservation. Also in Nara, they met Governor of Nara Prefecture Zenya Kakimoto, President of Nara Women's University Kenji Kume, and Presidency of Yakushiji Temple Eiin Yasuda. In the same month, we ventured the second research to register 26 remains via GPS such as series of remains in the southern part where Stein had excavated valuable remains and created those pattern diagrams, and verified the said remains as those of the ancient Buddhist city so-called "the Buddhist sacred site." Revisiting the Niya ruins, we registered three tombs in the northern area which were considered to be unregistered.

2004 research (the 2nd research)
Schedule: October 10 through October 27
Participants (34 in total): (5 Japanese members) Yasutaka Kojima, Toshio Asaoka, Yoshika Ando, Sun Yuexin, Ken Kondou
(5 Chinese members) Zhang Yuzhong, Li Jun, Tie Fude, Tong Wenkang, Maiti Kasimu
(24 assistants/other members) camel masters, drivers, a cook, and reporters
Itinerary: Oct. 10–11: Departure of the Japanese team, a welcome party by the Xinjiang Cultural Assets Bureau, Japan-China joint meetings in Urumqi, the address of Vice-Governor of the Xinjiang Kurexi Maihesuti to offer cooperation, various preparations, arrival in Hotan; Oct. 12: Arrival in Yutien, joining together with the Chinese advance team; Oct. 13–15: Departure by 6 4WDs, cooked engine causing a fire, having lost water, switching a ride to 37 camels at Bakkakuegiri to advance into the desert; Oct. 15: Arrival at the ruins in the afternoon to set a BC in the north-eastern edge of the ruins; Oct. 15–16: Investigations; Oct. 17–19: Leaving for home, switching a ride to 5 4WDs at Bakkakuegiri, causing breakdown of cars one after another, reaching Yutian accordingly, the team leader's last arrival at 3:30 am on 19th, after organizing various things, leaving for Minfeng; Oct. 20: Visiting the Niya ruins by 4 desert vehicles, donating school supplies for the children of Kapakeasican, setting up a BC near the stupa; Oct. 21–22: Investigations; Oct. 23: Starting homeward, arrival in Hotan via Minfeng; Oct. 24: Visiting the Shanpula ruins, organizing equipment, arrival in Urumqi;

Mural conservation: First testing and then actual practice, photo by Y. Kojima

Reproduction by a specialist who reproduced the Japanese national treasure 源氏物語絵巻 (Illustrated handscroll of the Tale of Genji), photo by Y. Kojima

Oct. 25: The Japan-China joint meeting and study of the mural, a return party by the Japanese team; Oct. 26–27: The Japanese team returning home via Beijing.

Investigation: Registering 25 buildings' remains like temples and one orchard, creation of remains' pattern diagrams, collection of antiquities scattered on the surface of the ground, and besides researching, being accompanied by the reporters of NHK and Chinese Central Television for producing The New Silk Road.

In November of that year, fully preparing every necessary arrangement, we started conserving treatments for the mural making use of both sides' techniques along with Zhang Yuzhong, Tie Fude, Nijiati Rouzi, Liu Yong, and He Lin. Head of Roppou Arts Chisako Tomizawa 富沢千砂子 reproduced it. Iwataro Oka suggested saying, "Xinjiang specialists have techniques extremely high. It's better not to completely remove stein. Leave rugged surface, so that we can recall the elegance of over thousand years ago." Zhang Yuzhong and Tie Fude also agreed.

Schedule: November 6 through November 14

Participants: Yasutaka Kojima, Iwataro Oka, Yoshikazu Tsujimoto, Chisako Tomizawa, Sun Yuexin, Ryouko Kamei

In December, the basic authorization to exhibit mummies at the New Silk Road Exhibition was finally obtained, which had long been prohibited from showing outside China since the Loulan Exhibition. In addition to work for research, conservation, and studies, I had to be involved in the negotiations of The New Silk Road, TV program and the New Silk Road Exhibition which made me visit China 14 times in 2004.

In January 2005, both parties confirmed development of conserving treatments and also conducted the studies.

Schedule: January 28 through February 6
Participants: Yasutaka Kojima, Tadashi Inoue, Yoshika Ando

[Picture above] Mural before restoration, photo by Y. Kojima
[Picture upper right] Removing extraneous matter by volatile chemical which causes a headache, photo Y. Kojoma
[Picture lower right] Proceeding in restoring while discussing, photo by Zhang Yuzhong

Mural stained with much extraneous matter before restoring treatments, photo by Y. Kojima

Mural after completion of restoring treatments (a part), photo by Y. Kojima

Mural after completion of restoring treatments, photo by Y. Kojima

Yoshika Ando made the following comment: Tessenbyou 鉄線描, or wire-line drawing, seen in the newly discovered mural which makes me feel like the origin of the old wall paintings of the Horyuji Temple's Golden Pavilion 法隆寺金堂, reminds me of the style of Yu-chi Yi-seng 尉遅乙僧, the distinguished painter with the royal roots of Hotan. The movement of vividly shining eyes appeals deeply into the eyes and heart of worshippers. It is not too much to say that this is the emergence of the world-class masterpiece. Then Bureau Director Sheng, Li Jun, Sun Yuexin, and I went straight to the Xiaohe ruins 小河墓遺跡 and visited members of the excavation team there for encouragement. I was told that this was the first step to the ruins as a foreigner officially authorized by the Xinjiang Cultural Heritage Administration Bureau.

4. Releasing achievements

The conservation-treated four murals including "Mona Lisa of the Western Regions" and a flower-brocaded pouch, etc., detected by the Niya team were open to public at the New Silk Road Exhibition held in Tokyo, Kobe, and Okayama from April through December 2005. Mummies were also exhibited for the first time since "A Beauty in Loulan." (Sankei Shimbun, Aug. 11, 2005) Yoshika Ando conducted research during the time of a displaying preparation at the above-mentioned sites in April and August. From January through December in that year, The New Silk Road was frequently televised by NHK to introduce the murals and a part of discoveries made in the previous year.

In June, Division Chief of the Foreign Affairs Office of the Xinjiang Government Liu Xiaoqing kindly guided Junkei Yasuda, Kazuo Okada and me to research the Bedel Pass where Xuanzang Sanzang 玄奘三蔵 was hypothetically thought to have crossed. In August, the International Symposium on Japan-China Joint Scholarly Research Project of the Dandanoilik Ruins was convened at the Shijo Center of Bukkyo University, in which addresses or presentations were delivered for 200 audiences or so by such people as President of Bukkyo University Ryuzen Fukuhara, Shinkou Nakai, Kenji Sugimoto, Yoshika Ando, Toshio Asaoka, Iwataro Oka, Sun Yuexin, Lu Jiachuan, Deputy Secretary of the Xinjiang Autonomous Region Arifu Zhuorebaike, Li Jun, Zhang Yuzhong, Tie Fude, Rong Xinjiang, and me. In the meantime, the photo exhibitions were also held at the Religious Culture Research Institute of Bukkyo University as well as at this Shijo Center to introduce the outline of the project. This exhibition also traveled the NHK Kobe broadcasting station and the Digital Museum of Okayama city. On September 25, Zhang Yuzhong and I signed the memorandum of agreement for the Japan-China joint research for 2005 and 2006.

International symposium held at the Bukkyo University Shijo Center, photo by Y. Kojima

Japan-China joint studies on murals after completion of conservation treatments, photo by Y. Kojima

Exhibition of murals at 新シルクロード展 (New Silk Road exhibition) based on the rule of the earliest release of information, photo by Y. Kojima

In October, I had talks with Governor of the Xinjiang Simayi Tieliwaerdi to express my celebration for the 50th anniversary of the Xinjiang Uyghur Autonomous Region and kindly asked him further support for conservation and research. The group of Japanese cultural visitors guided by me enjoyed the photo exhibition to commemorate the 50th anniversary. (Xinjiang Daily News, Oct. 2, 2005) From October through December, we conducted the third research covering the area roughly 12 km from north to south and 5 km from east to west. While we additionally registered about 60 sites such as a circular remain, we made a survey on 7,487 points to create topographic charts. These were great achievements. After completing research, we observed statues and murals at Damagou Temple and attended the opening ceremony of the Hotan Museum which took 10 years to complete since I had first funded to build it.

2005 research (the 3rd research)
Schedule: October 7 through November 1
Participants (24 in total): (5 Japanese members) Yasutaka Kojima, Toshio Asaoka, Tetsuya Inui, Hiroshi Okuyama, Tomomi Murakami (6 Chinese members) Zhang Yuzhong, Liu Guorui, Tong Wenkang, Alifujiang Niyazi, Lu Zongyi, Li Dong
(13 assistants) camel masters, drivers, and a cook
Itinerary: Oct. 7–8: Departure of the Japanese team, Japan-China joint meetings in Urumqi, a welcome party by the Xinjiang Cultural Heritage Administration Bureau, various preparations, arrival in Hotan; Oct. 9–12: Leaving for Yutien, switching a ride to 40 camels at Bakkakuegiri, arrival at the ruins; Oct. 13–24: Investigations; Oct. 25–28: Overnight stays at Bakkakuegiri and Yutian on our way back, visiting Damagou Temple, arrival in Hotan, a welcome party by the Hotan Government; Oct. 29–30: After attending the opening ceremony of the Hotan Museum, leaving for Urumqi, the joint meeting at the Xinjiang Archaeological Institute, a welcome and farewell party by the Xinjiang Government; Oct. 30–Nov. 1: The

Japanese team returning home via Beijing.

Investigation: Registering 55 sites in total, such as 15 architectural remains including temples and others like collapsed buildings, kilns, orchards, and places with scattered antiquities; surveying the northern part of the ruins and finding a building remain like a temple and a place with scattered antiquities, and registering them; making a survey on each remain; collecting antiquities scattered in pieces on the ground; Liu Guorui, some members, and I went back from the ruins to Bakkakuegiri on foot to check out our level of tiredness.

After completing research, I guided Professor of Nara Women's University Kazuhisa Ideta, Junkei Yasuda, and others through the Xiaohe ruins. Then, I reported to Member of the Politburo Standing Committee and Secretary of the Xinjiang Committee of the CCP Wang Lequan about research and studies and proposed to proceed with further conservation. (Xinjiang Daily News,

Light wave surveying by a survey engineer, photo by Y. Kojima

The 2005 team working in collaboration, photo by a Chinese member

Walking back as leading camels, photo by Y. Kojima

Many a relic surviving in the area of Damagou Temple, photo by Y. Kojima

Guiding Professor Kazuhisa Ideta and others to the Xiaohe ruins, photo by a Chinese member

Nov. 7, 2005) In December, Yoshika Ando and I conducted research of the mural at the Xinjiang Archaeological Institute.

In January 2006, I delivered a lecture on the importance of conservation and research of cultural assets for 100 or so senior staff members of the Xinjiang Government. I will refer to this kind of public relations' activities hereinafter. In March, a party headed by Governor of the Xinjiang Simayi Tieliwaerdi was invited to Japan by NHK and me to visit such places as Tokyo, Nagoya, and Nara. From May onward, the workshop of the Academic Research Organization for the Niya ruins, Bukkyo University, led by Yoshika Ando started. In June,

Providing financial cooperation for building the Damagou Temple Museum as well, photo by Y. Kojima

partly because of the achievements made by our team, the Dandanoilik ruins were promoted to the Chinese Cultural Assets of Important Protection by SACH, China. (Guang Ming Daily, Jun. 10, 2006) In July, since the conserving treatments of the entire mural had been completed, the committee for examining completion of protection gathered at the Xinjiang Archaeological Institute with the participation of Iwataro Oka, Masaaki Sawada, and I as well as specialist-committee members for SACH, China Pan Lu and Ma Jiayu, Bureau Director Sheng Chunshou, Tie Fude, Zhang Yuzhong and Liu Guorui, and the said treatments were certified. As a supplementary opinion, it was recommended that color of unity should be made on the frame of the mural. Thus, the certification was submitted to SACH, China. (Chinese Cultural Resources News, Aug. 4, 2006) I met with Governor of the Xinjiang Autonomous Region Simayi Teiliwaerdi to report our achievements. (Xinjiang Daily News, Jul. 24, 2006)

During the period from October through December, the fourth research was conducted. We failed to find the Rawak stupa and D17 in the northern part, as described in the Stein's report through distributional research. Yet, we newly discovered collapsed buildings, kilns, and a site with scattered antiquities, all of which were registered. In addition to them, we registered another 20 or so sites,

Recording by a digital camera, photo by Y. Kojima

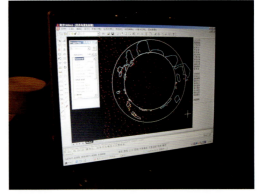

Measuring actual dimensions of antiquities and scanning them into PC (CD-30), photo by Y. Kojima

such as remains and sites with antiquities scattered in pieces on the ground. Under the official authorization of SACH, China (the 106th issue, 2006), the Chinese team excavated several remains with the assistance of the Japanese team. We also confirmed the conditions of the temple remain and shot a mural abundant with contents and buried it back for conservation. We complemented the points which had been transferred by movement of dunes and made a survey on these excavated remains. All of these investigations have added up to the conclusion that the whole picture of the ruins was assumed to verify as "the Buddhist sacred site" in the Western Regions.

2006 research (the 4th research)

Schedule: October 9 through November 8

Participants (19 in total): (5 Japanese members) Yasutaka Kojima, Toshio Asaoka, Tetsuya Inui, Hiroshi Okuyama, Mayuko Takeshita
(7 Chinese members) Zhang Yuzhong, Ruan Qiurong, Tong Wenkang, Alifujiang Niyazi, Maiti Kasimu, Lu Zongyi, Han Shanfeng
(7 assistants) camel masters, drivers, and a cook

Itinerary: Oct. 9–11: Departure of the Japanese team, a welcome party by the Xinjiang Government, Japan-China joint meetings in Urumqi, arriving in Hotan; Oct. 12: Arrival in Yutien; Oct. 13: Departure by 4WD, switching a ride to two desert vehicles on the way to reach straight to the ruins, the set-up of a BC; Oct. 14–Nov. 1: Dividing into a distributional group, an excavating group, and a surveying group to conduct research work sometimes over using camels; Nov. 2: Starting homeward, arrival in Yutian by desert vehicle; Nov. 3: Reporting to the Secretary of Qira County, arrival in Hotan; Nov. 4–5: Organizing various things, a welcome and farewell party by the Hotan Government, arrival in Urumqi at 2 am of 5th, a welcome and farewell party by Director of the Public Relations Division of the Xinjiang Committee of the CCP Li Yi 李屹; Nov. 6–8: The Japanese team returning home via Beijing.

Excavation under the scorching sun, photo by Y. Kojima

Carrying heavy sand with young people under the scorching sun, photographer unknown

Investigation: Distributional research including the northern part, researching excavation of several remains, making a survey on each ruin, and collecting antiquities scattered on the surface of the ground.

In March 2007, Yoshika Ando and I had a meeting with Bureau Director Sheng Chunshou, Yu Zhiyong, Zhang Yuzhong, and others at the Xinjiang Archaeological Institute to discuss the third volume of the Niya ruins' report and the Dandanoilik ruins' report. After studying the mural, we conducted research on the mural in Damagou Temple in Qira County and also visited the Rawaq ruins. In the same month, we measured the actual dimensions of about 100 unearthed antiquities in the Dandanoilik ruins.

Itinerary: March 13 through March 23
Participants: Toshio Asaoka and Mika Hagiwara

In the same month, a party headed by Sheng Chunshou and Yu Zhiyong was invited to Japan by the Academic Research Organization for the Niya ruins, Bukkyo University and concluded the agreement with Ryuzen Fukuhara and me to hold symposiums at Bukkyo University in November 2007 and in Peking University in 2008 respectively. The party and I paid a courtesy call on UNESCO Goodwill Ambassador Ikuo Hirayama 平山郁夫 (in charge of cultural assets conservation) at home and received a valuable suggestion as to the application for the Silk Road to the World Heritage Committee.

In April, I met the representative of four professors at a certain Japanese university and research institute who had undertaken an unauthorized investigation to make a survey in Xinjiang. They were sentenced to pay a fine and to have their equipment and materials confiscated. The representative and I visited the Foreign Affairs Office of the Xinjiang Government, the Xinjiang Survey Bureau, and the Xinjiang Cultural Assets Bureau. I acted as intermediary for their apology. The Xinjiang authority stated that it is an absolute must to be authorized to work on research and this kind of unpleasant conduct should not be repeated. The relevant verdict was handed down to the representative of the four people. Their real names were reported in the newspapers. (Xinjiang Daily News, Apr. 28, 2007; Yomiuri Shimbun and Kyoto Shimbun, May 10, 2007; Yangtse Evening News, Jun. 20, 2007) In June, Member of the Politburo Standing Committee and Secretary of the Xinjiang Committee of the CCP Wang Lequan expressed his great appreciation for our activities when I had talks with him. (Xinjiang Daily News, Jun. 20, 2007) Then, I had discussion about the report and the symposium with the Xinjiang members, along with Toshio Asaoka. In August, I attended an opening ceremony of the Damagou Temple's Museum together with a group of cultural visitors and donated a construction fund.

In November, the International Symposium on the Japan-China collaborative scholarly research in the Silk Road was held at the Shijo Center of Bukkyo University. The addresses and presentations were made by people, such as Ryuzen Fukuhara, Kenji Sugimoto, Professor of Bukkyo University Toru Yagi, Yoshika Ando, Toshio Asaoka, Professor of Tokai University Akio Katayama, Sun Yuexin, Zhou Peiyan, Aierken Mijiti, Zhang Yuzhong, Yu Zhiyong, Ruan Qiurong, Rong Xinjiang, Leader of the Xinjiang team at the Archaeological Institute of the Chinese Social Science Academy Wu Xinhua, and me. (Chugainippou, Nov. 20, 2007) Meanwhile, the achievements of research, studies and conservation were compiled in *Nicchu-Chunichi kyoudou Dandanuiriku isekichousa gakujutsu houkokusho*『日中・中日共同ダンダンウイリク遺跡調査学術報告書』(The report of the Japan-China/China-Japan joint scholarly research of the Dandanoilik ruins) (a Japanese version) thanks to the supports of Toshio Asaoka, Yoshika Ando, Iwataro Oka, Masaaki Sawada, Mayuko Takeshita, Junkei Yasuda, Sun Yuexin, Zhou Peiyan, Tetsuya Inui, Hiroshi Okuyama, Sheng Chunshou, Zhang Yuzhong, Rong Xinjiang, Tong Wenkang, Lu Zongyi, Liu Guorui, Gulibiya, Alifujiang Niyazi, Qu Tao, Ruan Qiurong, and Wu Xinhua, and it was published by Shinyosha as a related publication of the development project (FY2003–FY2007) of the MEXT's Open Research Center. (Asahi Shimbun, May 9, 2008) After the symposium, I guided the Chinese delegates to the Kyushu National Museum and other places.

The contents of the report include: the prefaces by President of Bukkyo University Ryuzen Fukuhara, Director of the Xinjiang Cultural Heritage Administration Bureau of the Xinjiang Uyghur Autonomous Region Sheng Chunshou, and me followed by the research outline; the location and natural environments; the historical context; the research history; the methods of distributional research and their transition; the research methodologies; the ruins and the outline of antiquities; the achievements of excavation research; the mural's conservation; related studies; the report of the excavation research of Damagou Temple. This article constitutes of the two-page prefatory plates, the 22-page contents, the main texts of 345 pages, the 58-page figures (A4 size), which is written in Japanese along with the English summary. The distributional map of the ruins and topographic charts are attached herewith.

In December, after Japan-China joint conference in Urumqi, followed by discussion with people from Peking University in Beijing, the Xinjiang team put forth a proposal to Peking University for "The International Symposium on Niya and Dandanoilik - the Western Regions in the Ages of Han and Tang from the archaeological perspective."

In April 2008, I met with Governor of the Xinjiang Juer Baikeli 努尔·白克力 for celebrating him assuming the position of Governor who had supported me one way or another since his Urumqi Mayor's day. I also reported to him about the researches of both Niya and Dandanoilik and presented the reports. Governor Juer Baikeli said to me, "You are a living witness of 30-year reform and door-opening in Xinjiang," which led me to publish a book as detailed below. (Xinjiang Daily News, Apr. 17, 2008; Xinmin Evening News, Jan. 12, 2009) In November, the Retrospective Convention of Xinjiang Friendship with Foreign Countries to Commemorate the 30th Anniversary of the Reform and Door-Opening Policies was held in Urumqi under the sponsorship of the Foreign Affairs Office of the Xinjiang Government. I delivered a talk on my activities for international cooperation to conduct research and presented a photo book titled 見証新疆変迁 (Witnessing the transition of Xinjiang), which was published by Xinjiang Fine Arts Photography Publishing Houser, to about 200 attendees from China and overseas, such as the Association of Japanese Autonomous Internationalization and delegates from neighboring nations. (Xinjiang Daily News, Nov. 21 and Dec. 2, 2008)

Asahi Shimbun covering the publication of the report underlining a long-standing trust relationship and its significance, photo by Y. Kojima

The above-mentioned symposium was not approved partly due to the Beijing Olympics that year, yet both sides agreed to continue their efforts.

From December 2008 through March 2009, the Great Exhibition of the Xinjiang Cultural Heritage on the Legendary Silk Road was held at the National Historical Museum in Taipei, showing lots of valuable cultural assets including the brocade of Wang Hou He Hum Qian Qiu Wang Sui Yi Zi Sun 王侯合昏千秋萬歲宜子孫 and "Mona Lisa in the Western Regions."

In June 2009, I was asked to attend some shooting scenes of The Mystery of Master Sanzang Set under Seal (Traveler: Koji Yakusho) in Xinjiang, such as the Astana tombs, the Xinjiang Museum, and the Bedel Pass, which was broadcast by Tokyo Television. Because I helped them receive the shooting authorization. (The memorandum of agreement on filming, Mar. 26, 2009) As the Bedel Pass is on the border with Kyrgyzstan under the military control, it was the first time that the Japanese television was allowed to shoot.

In June, the above-mentioned symposium submitted to the Chinese Educational Department (equivalent to the Japanese Ministry of Education, Culture, Sports, Science and Technology) after having been authorized by Peking University finally garnered the government's approval and we started its preparations. In the same month I had talks with Standing Vice-Governor of the Xinjiang

Autonomous Region Yang Gang 楊剛 to express appreciation for his long-standing support. Secretary of the Foreign Affairs Office of the Xinjiang Autonomous Region Wu Xian 呉憲 and Deputy Manager Kongduozi Yusufu 孔多孜·玉素甫 (currently Counselor for the Chinese Embassy in Tokyo), Director Kang Xiuying 康秀英, and I launched a PR campaign called 新疆改革開放成就広報万里行 (the long journey to celebrate the achievements of the reform and door-opening policies in Xinjiang) by using the 2nd volume of 見証新疆変迁 (Witnessing the transition of Xinjiang) published in the previous month and visited eight cities, including Urumqi, Turpan, Altay, Aksu, and Hotan. (Xinjiang Daily News, Jun. 12 and 16, 2009) Originally we were scheduled to visit 15 cities, though, due to various reasons, we moved up the plan and on the day when I returned to Japan, the Urumqi 7-5 Violent Incident broke out. From July through December of the following year, the Exhibition of Civilizations across the Ages of Qin, Han and Rome was held in Beijing and Rome, Italy, in which the brocade of the Niya ruins was displayed.

In September, I visited Urumqi to be informed of the post-riot situation and met with Vice-Governor of the Xinjiang Autonomous Region Tieliwaerdi Abudurexiti to express him my sincere condolences and sympathy for the victims and their families. I was told that the situation was stabilized and then set out on a tour of downtown Urumqi. (Xinjiang Daily News and Xinjiang Economics, Sep. 4, 2009) Since large-scale demonstrations were held from that day and lasted for several days, tight security measures were enforced. On my way back, I made a presentation on how Xinjiang has developed, as well as on my activities for international cooperation, such as both researches in Niya and Dandanoilik, by showing films at the reception of the International Symposium on Soft Power and Governmental Communication at Tsinghua University 清華大学. As just after the large-scale demonstrations following the riot, it gave them a huge impact. On this occasion, I received the outstanding contribution award for international affairs. (www.people.com.cn, Nov. 3, 2009; www.chinanews.com, Nov. 9, 2009; Tencent News, Mar. 26, 2010) In the same month I visited Oxford University and the British Museum to research Stein's related materials (the diary and correspondences written by Stein himself) and obtained some of their photocopies.

On November 21 and 22, the International Symposium on Niya and Dandanoilik in the Western Regions in the Ages of Han and Tang from the Archaeological perspective was held at Peking University 北京大学 (hosted by the Archaeological Institute of Peking University, the Xinjiang Cultural Heritage Administration Bureau, the Archaeological Research Center of Peking University, Bukkyo University, and the Archaeological Institute of the Chinese Social Science Academy). It was a great success with the attendance of 100 or so researchers of various fields including 18 people from Japan who made addresses, presentations and vigorous discussions for two days Those who attended were: President of Bukkyo University Nobuyuki Yamagiwa 山極伸之, Head of faculty of literature at Bukkyo University Kenji Nakahara, Yoshika Ando, Toshio Asaoka, Shin Yoshizaki, Iwataro Oka, Takao Itoh, Keiji Yoshida, Sun Yuexin, Zhou Peiyan, Kiyomi Tanaka,

Yoshifumi Ichikawa, Chisako Tomizawa, and Kimie Matsumura; and from China: Vice-Secretary of Peking University Wu Zhipan, Vice-Director of SACH, China Tong Mingkang, Vice-Director of the Archaeological Institute of Peking University Sun Hua, Deputy Head of the Archaeological Institute of the Chinese Social Science Academy Bai Yunxiang, Bureau Director Sheng Chunshou, Lin Meicun, Ron Xinjiang, Professor of Chinese People's University Wang Zijin, Vice-President of Tsinghua University Li Xiguang, Wu Xinhua, Tie Fude, Professor of Jilin University Zhu Hong, Professor of Chinese People's University Wei Jian, Director of the Xinjiang Archaeological Institute Wang Weidong, Yu Zhiyong, Zhang Yuzhong, Zhang Teinan, Li Jun, and Gan Wei.[24]

President Nobuyuki Yamagiwa delivered an opening address, along with Vice-Secretary Wu Zhipan 呉志攀, Deputy Director Tong Mingkang 童明康, and Bureau Director Shen Chunshou, and stated, "I am so grateful to see the achievements made by the researches of Niya and Dandanoilik together with relevant institutions under the authorization of SACH, China. Bukkyo University commemorates the 100th anniversary in 2012. I would like to continue to boost exchanges with universities in the world and make my utmost efforts to develop the world cultures and enhance human welfare."

At the closing ceremony, Bureau Director Sheng stated, "Xinjiang is a tough place comparing with inlands, or urban areas. The conditions for research on site are severer and there is a problem with the treatment of people working here into the bargain, which have often incurred loss of valuable human resources. I want people in Xinjiang to hang in here and people in urban areas to stick up for Xinjiang." In response to his statement, I said, "I'm very pleased with a whole variety of presentations released by prominent specialists from both Japan and China. It was almost next to impossible to start a collaborative work in Xinjiang two decades back. The achievements earned by the undertakings over 20 years for research, studies, and conservation were so great, and yet at the same time

[Picture left] Two-day session with earnest presentations and discussions, photo by Y. Kojima
[Picture right] Some of Japanese attendees at the symposium, photo by Y. Kojima
Both of them at Peking University, the venue of "The International Academic Symposium of Niya and Dandanoilik - the Western Regions in the Ages of Han and Tang"

it was also a great achievement to have been able to offer subjects of research to a number of people. This should go on much longer. And I shall keep on doing what I can." Meanwhile, 丹丹烏里克遺址－中日共同考察研究報告 (The report on the China-Japan joint studies and research on the Dandanoilik ruins) was published by Cultural Relics Press. Although this is the Chinese version of the same book published in Japanese in 2007, there were some missing parts (those of Mayuko Takeshita and me) and some additions.

The progress of the symposium was widely reported apart from Chinese Cultural Resources News. (Chinese Cultural Resources News, Nov. 25, 2009; One-page feature, Xinjiang Daily News, Dec. 9, 2009) The Japanese participants accompanied by Sheng Chunshou could visit the closed part of the National Palace Museum through the kind offices of Standing Vice-Director of the National Palace Museum Li Ji 李季 who was a member of the Niya team as well. In December, Sheng Chunshou, Wang Weidong, Yu Zhiyong, Zhang Yuzhong, Li Jun, Gan Wei and I reviewed the symposium in Urumqi to confirm its success. We also agreed to publish the official collection of theses and hold a symposium again.

In March 2010, we published *Kan Tou Seiiki koko–Dandanuiriku kokusai gakujutsu shinpojium happyo youshi youyaku shiryoushu* 『漢唐西域考古－ニヤ・ダンダンウイリク国際学術シンポジウム発表要旨要約資料集』 (The information packet of summaries for the international scholarly symposium on Niya and Dandanoilik in the Western Regions in the ages of the Han and the Tan dynasties from the archaeological perspective) in which the purport of the presentations at the above-mentioned symposium including relevant publicity was translated into Japanese with the supports of Toshio Asaoka, Sun Yuexin and Zhou Peiyan. From this March through December, the exhibition of Secrets of the Silk Road was held in Santa Ana and Huston in the US showing the silk brocade *Wang Hou He Hum Qian Qiu Wang Sui Yi Zi Sun* 王侯合昏千秋萬歲宜子孫 and others. In May, I was bestowed the title of People's Friendship Messenger 人民友好使者 from the Chinese People's Association for Friendship with Foreign Countries in honor of my international cooperation and undertakings such as the projects for conservation and research of cultural heritages. (The Chinese People's Association for Friendship with Foreign Countries, electronic edition and www.ts.cn, May 22, 2010; www.china.org.cn. and www.chinanews.com, May 24, 2010; Youth Journalist May edition; www.people.com.cn, Japanese version, Jul. 5, 2010)

In June, my humble efforts for conservation and research of cultural heritages were highly evaluated and I was selected as 薪火相伝－中国文化遺産保護年度傑出人物 (Endless cultural inheritance—the distinguished person of the year for conservation of the Chinese cultural heritages), along with ex gratia payment. (China Culture Relics Protection Foundation, electronic edition, Jun. 13, 2010; www.chinanews.com, Jun. 17, 2010; www.people.com.cn, Jun. 18, 2010; World Journal, Jun. 22 and 29, 2010; Xinmin Evening News, Japanese version, Jun. 28, 2010; Japan and China, Jul. 5, 2010; Xinjiang Daily News, Sep. 6, 2010) At the red-carpet presentation ceremony held in Wuxi, Director of SACH, China Shan Qixiang 單霽翔 said after memorial shooting with the leaders related to the

[Picture left] Talks with Head of Xinjiang Zhang Chunxian, photo by the Xinjiang Government
[Picture right] Xinjiang Daily News reporting the statement that Secretary Zhang praised me highly, photo by Y. Kojima

Chinese cultural assets seating in the front row and the recipients standing in the rear row, "Let's shoot again with the recipients in the front row. Use this photo for a public release." I was very impressed with such leadership credentials as the Head of the vast Chinese cultural heritages who had written lots of conservation-related books and frequently lectured around the world.

In August, I had talks with Secretary of the Xinjiang Committee of the CCP Zhang Chunxian 張春賢, or the Head of Xinjiang. He told me, "I appreciate you so highly that you are the first foreigner I have met at the Xinjiang CCP Committee since I assumed this position at the end of April. As I will support you in the future, too, please don't hesitate to tell me whatever proposals you might have." So, I suggested, "Would you please further promote cultural conservation because it will lead to an increase in economic activities." Then I presented him with the research reports of both Niya and Dandanoilik. I also informed him of Japanese Ambassador to China Uichiroh Niwa's 丹羽宇一郎 readiness to visit Xinjiang and invited the Secretary to visit Japan to launch the public information campaign of a New Xinjiang. (www.cpcnews.cn, Xinjiang Daily News, www.ts.cn, and www.xjtvs.com.cn, Aug. 14, 2010; www.xinhuanet.com, Aug. 15, 2010; www.gov.cn, Aug. 17, 2010)

In December 2010, Director of the Xinjiang Cultural Heritage Administration Bureau Sheng Chunshou, Director of the Xinjiang Archaeological Institute Wang Weidong, Yidilisi Abuduresule, Yu Zhiyong, Zhang Yuzhong, and I had a meeting at the Xinjiang Archaeological Institute and agreed to strive for issuing the Chinese version of *Nicchu-Chunichi kyoudou Niya iseki gakujutsu chousa houkokusho*『日中・中日共同ニヤ遺跡学術調査報告書』(第三巻) (The report of the Japan-China joint scholarly research of the Niya ruins, Vol. 3) by October 2011, whose publication had been delayed due to congested schedules on the Chinese side, as well as to further the study of unearthed antiquities in Niya and Dandanoilik. On my way back, when I delivered a lecture on the hardship and significance of mutual understanding through a so-called 29-year public diplomacy at the International Transfer Study Center of Tsinghua University, many delicate and sensitive questions were raised in the midst of strained relations between Japan and China since the clashing incident of a fishing boat off the coast of the Senkaku islands. I tried to explain that mutual understanding is, indeed, quite difficult between countries with different systems and cultures, so that it is all the more imperative for both of us to exert efforts to enhance mutual understanding. As Director Li Xiguang 李希光 made a proposition to hold the photo exhibition, From Gandhara to Niya, in April 2011, as one of the 100th anniversary's events of its foundation (those related with Gandhara having been offered by the Pakistan Embassy), we reached a basic agreement on this proposal.

In the same month, the Exhibition of the Silk Road and Dunhuang was held in Seoul, Korea, displaying the Kharosthi documents, murals, bows, and arrows unearthed in the Niya ruins, and the murals found in the Dandanoilik ruins, all of which had been excavated by the Japan-China joint team. I visited there, too.

In March 2011, I released a thesis titled *Shinkyou deno sekaiteki bunkaisan hogo kenkyu Jigyou to kokusaikyoryoku no igi—Kijiru, Niya, Dandanuiriku*『新疆での世界的文化遺産保護研究事業と国際協力の意義−キジル・ニヤ・ダンダンウイリク−』(The projects to conserve and research world-class cultural heritages in Xinjiang, China, and the significance of international cooperation—Kizil, Niya, and Dandanoilik) in *Bukkyodaigaku Shukyoubunka Myujiamu Kenkyu Kiyo*『佛教大学宗教文化ミュージアム研究紀要』(The research bulletin of the Bukkyo University Museum of Religious Culture, No. 7) which summarized my longstanding projects for conservation and studies of cultural heritages beginning with cooperation to restore and conserve the Kizil grottoes followed by the researches of the Niya ruins and then the Dandanoilik ruins.

In April 2011, the above-mentioned exhibition From Gandhara to Niya was held as scheduled and about 100 people attended the opening ceremony. The attendees include a Pakistani Ambassador, Vice-Director of SACH, China, Song Xinchao 宋新潮, Vice-Director of the Xinjiang Public Relations Division Hou Hanmin 侯漢敏, Director of the Xinjiang Cultural Heritage Administration Bureau Sheng Chunshou, Director of the Xinjiang Archaeological Institute at the Xinjiang Cultural Heritage Administration Bureau Wang Weidong 王衛東, Vice-Director Yu Zhiyong 于志勇, Mr. Sun and Mrs. Zhou 孫周夫妻, Doctor Zhao Xinli, and me.

[Picture left] Opening ceremony of the photo-exhibition, From Gandhara to Niya
[Picture right] Explaining research status to the Pakistani Ambassador and Director of SACH, China Song Xinchao
Above two photos by Zhao Xinli

In September 2012, there were so many anti-Japan demonstrations in China due to the issue of nationalization of the Senkaku islands by the Japanese Government. Some of them went on rampages to destroy Japanese companies' offices and the relations between two countries cooled down at once. In the following month, the international symposium on the archaeological perspective of the Western Regions in the Han dynasty and its culture was held in Urumqi with the participation of Toshio Asaoka, Takao Itoh, Kiyomi Tanaka, Sun Yuexin, Zhou Peiyan, and me. We also made presentations on our studies and researches of Niya and Dandanoilik. Though the Foreign Affairs Office of the Xinjiang Autonomous Region urged us to postpone our visit, we dared to participate in it considering the necessity of mutual understanding. There was a series of flight cancellations and some of Japanese prospective participants canceled their attendance. I made a presentation on the conservation and research of the Western Regions' cultural heritages and the significance of international cooperation in order to emphasize it all the more at this very moment.

In November 2012, I was invited by the British Museum to make a speech at the international conference on archaeology of the southern Taklamakan: Hedin and Stein's legacy and new explorations under the title of the Japan-China joint research of Niya and Dandanoilik—my life-long mission for conservation and research of world-class cultural heritages.

In February 2013, the exhibition of the legend of the Western Regions in China and the Silk Road was held in Nagasaki, Japan, displaying a number of relics detected by the Japan-China joint scholarly research team of the Niya ruins.

In March 2013, *Shinkyou deno sekaiteki bunkaisan hogokenkyujigyo to kokusaikyoryoku no igi—Kijiru Niya Dandanuiriku*『新疆での世界的文化遺産保護研究事業と国際協力の意義−キジル・ニヤ・ダンダンウイリクー』(The projects to conserve and research world-class cultural heritages in Xinjiang, China, and the significance of international cooperation—Kizil,, Niya, and Dandanoilik) was published by the Bukkyo University Museum of Religious Culture in book form.

In November the same year, in response to this publication, the international symposium on the conservation and research of world-class cultural heritages on the Silk Road in Xinjiang and international cooperation was held at the Bukkyo University Museum of Religious Culture. Addresses and presentations were made by such attendees as Shunzo Onoda 小野田俊蔵, Yoshika Ando, Toshio Asaoka, Shin Yoshizaki, Zhang Yuzhong, Wu Yong, Tian Xiaohong, Jiao Jian, and me. Later, many of those who had participated in the researches in Niya and Dandanoilik enjoyed renewing old friendships at the reception. A photo exhibition was also held. The Xinjiang group visited Kyoto, Osaka and Kobe.

In January 2014, thanks to full cooperation offered by staff-member Toshio Asaoka, we completed organizing and digitizing a huge amount of photos relevant to the ruins of Niya and Dandanoilik. A copy of the data was presented to Director of the Xinjiang Archaeological Institute Yu Zhiyoug.

The Stein's reports were very helpful for our researches in the ruins of Niya and Dandanoilik. Besides that, as I also took an interest in his whole life spent abroad for explorations, I released a thesis titled as *Sutain daiyonji Shinkyou tanken to sono tenmatsu*「スタイン第四次新疆探検とその顛末」(The whole story of the Stein's fourth expedition to Xinjiang in Central Asia) in *Bukkyodaigaku Shukyou Myujiamu Kenkyukiyou*『佛教大学宗教文化ミュージアム研究紀要』(The Research Bulletin of the Bukkyo University Museum of Religious Culture, No. 10) in March 2014. I reviewed his achievements based on Stein's Diary, the British official documents relevant to Stein, and the historical archives of the Stein's explorations stored in the Bodleian Library of Oxford University, the British Museum and the Xinjiang Archives Center, respectively. The English summary is attached at the end of this thesis.

In May 2014, I paid respect at the tomb of Taoist Wang Yuanlu 王圓籙 in Dunhuang who had been fooled into handing over huge amounts of relics by Stein's skillful talks. Whereas it thrust Stein into prominence, Wang ended his life in having been despised and called a traitor or a crass. Because, while I was writing the above-mentioned thesis, I happened to discover the day when Stein crossed a pass from China to then British Imperial India after his fourth humiliating, unsuccessful expedition to Xinjiang was precisely the day when Taoist Wang passed away. I felt some very mysterious favor and resentment. Though I would like to visit the tomb of Stein in Kabul, I would wait and see for a while as the Japanese Government issued travel restrictions to Kabul and evacuation recommendations.

I directly visited Xinjiang from there to have a meeting with people like Director of the Xinjiang Archaeological Institute Yu Zhiyong and found that the delayed report of Niya to be compiled by the Chinese team would be published by the end of that year. We also talked about matters related to the Silk Road to be registered on the World Heritage list and I was informed of the attendance of Director Sheng Chunshou at the UNESCO's World Heritage Committee in Doha, Qatar as a member of the Chinese delegate.

In June of that year, Silk Roads: the Routes Network of Chang'an Tianshan Corridor, the Kizil grottoes included, were designated as the World Cultural Heritage as referred to before. In September, I revisited Xinjiang to appreciate the efforts made by Bureau Director Sheng Chunshou and others for the designation of the World Cultural Heritage. Bureau Director Sheng asked me to make a presentation at the Beijing Forum 2014 to be held at Peking University in November on the projects to conserve and research world-class cultural heritages in which I have been involved in Xinjiang. He also put forth a plan that Xinjiang Television Network wishes to cover a story when I pay a visit again to the six ruins in Xinjiang that have been listed as the World Cultural Heritage. I was told that this was as part of preparations for the 60th anniversary of Xinjiang Uyghur Autonomous Region in 2015. Director Yu Zhiyong informed me that the Niya report would be published by next spring even though it lagged behind schedule.

As of September 2014, thanks to vigorous exertion by Yu Zhiyong, the Xinjiang Archaeological Institute published 新疆文物 (Cultural Relics of Xinjiang, the 2014 3Q–4Q issue), which featured relics detected by the Japan-China joint research team of the Niya ruins.

From October through November in the same year, thanks to Bureau Director Sheng's kind arrangement, I could visit six World Heritage sites again, such as the Kizil grottoes, the ancient cities of Gaochang, Jiao River, and Beiting, the Kizilgaha Beacon, and the Subash Buddhist Temple Ruins, to celebrate and encourage staff members. I reunited there with those who had earned the Kojima awards for outstanding performances for Xinjiang culture and relics, through which I have tried to foster human resources. We all shared the joy of winning the World Heritage designation. After that, I went straight to the 11th Beijing forum held at the Diaoyutai State Guesthouse and Peking University to make a presentation titled "The Silk Road in Xinjiang and me: the roads for culture, economics, politics, and cooperation and was met with a warm reception. (Peking University News, electronic edition, Nov. 15, 2014) In December, I was invited to the international symposium on Kharosthi at School of Foreign Languages, Peking University and gave a presentation on Japan-China joint research of the Niya ruins where many Kharosthi wood strips had been detected. Chinese, American and German researchers who listened to my Power Point presentation were unduly impressed, what with such a large-scale survey having been conducted in an unknown desert. Then, I visited the Niya ruins along with these people to observe alterations of the ruins and found out that there were some damages incurred by nature and human. I stressed them the difficulties to conserve large-scale ruins in a vast desert. That's my 10th visit to the Niya ruins. (Xinjiang News, Dec. 23, 2014; Xinjiang News, electronic edition, Dec. 25, 2014; Xinjiang News, Jan. 15, 2015)

In October 2015, Chief of the Xinjiang Cultural Heritage Administration Bureau Gan Wei and I drove into the Niya ruins to photograph how it had been changed. It was my 11th visit there. Main relics such as a pagoda were undergoing conserving treatments to prepare to apply for World Heritage status. I donated a small-sized desert vehicle of Polaris for patrolmen to boost conservation.

5. The organization for investigations and its achievements

The investigations mentioned hereinbefore were led by me from Japan and Sheng Chunshou and Zhang Yuzhong from China, and I was assisted by Toshio Asaoka.

Since the scope of studies extends over a wide range of fields, a number of researchers from various organizations participated in this project as being referred to below. Specialized fields include the management of cultural assets, international cooperation, archaeology, architectonics, the history of Buddhist art, conservation of cultural assets, reproduction, and survey. People in these fields had made tireless efforts, which have resulted in the following achievements:

○ Confirming about 70 relics, such as temples, dwelling sites, circular castle walls, fireplaces, kilns, orchards, and about 30 sites of dispersed remains followed by registering their latitude-longitude locations via GPS to create the distributional diagram of those relics

- Creation of the surrounding topological chart of each remain via light wave survey
- Discovering a large quantity of national-treasure class murals and urgently excavating them for preservation and conducting conservation and research
- Collecting many remains such as coppers to start research
- Under the authorization of SACH, China, the Chinese team conducted a trial excavation of several temples' remains to confirm their conditions and to shoot the murals, which were backfilled for preservation.

6. Summary and future initiatives

As we have seen, the fundamental research of the ruins as "the Buddhist sacred site" in the Western Regions has been completed. Yet, in fact, there are still so many challenges we have to tackle with. I would like to proceed with further research on unearthed antiquities of the ruins in Niya and Dandanoilik. Its results should be open to public through reports and symposiums. This paper is a record by letters, yet electronic data of photographs and others are now being introduced with the help of Toshio Asaoka and other members.

On top of that, while I have lots of challenging items coming up to my brain, it is quite a demanding load for me aged over 70 years old. For example, a comprehensive study on the murals of grottoes at Damagou Temple, Kizil, and Kumutula in the area of Kuqa; eastward and westward advance of Buddhism; ages of rise and fall; the formation of deserts; history of explorations to the Western Regions; the validity of a theory to identify different "Yumi Kingdoms" as Dandanoilik and the validity of a theory to identify the ancient Western Regions' Southern Route as connecting Niya and Dandanoilik. I would like to anticipate that people within and without Japan would work through these challenges.

Every single antiquity collected by the Japan-China joint team is stored in the Xinjiang Archaeological Institute. The development of scientific technology will definitely bring about new insights in coming 50 or 100 years.

Notes:

(22) While we were conducting an excavation in 2002, we discovered the English note of Bosshart who made a survey on this site in 1928, saying, "To the poor fellow who believed to find something here we leave these papers with our kindest regards. E. Trinkler, W. Bosshart. 25-3-28." This was written on his business card in Chinese characters (博斯喀・瑞士国植物学, or Bosshart, Swiss botanist). We also found the paper *Neue Zürcher Zeitung* of that time, the outer case of solid fuel, and others. I also actually saw it at the Xinjiang Archaeological Institute to find an interesting part of history. The details were written down along with several photos by Rong Xinjiang in *Dandanuiriku no koukogakutekichousa to kenkyu* (1869–2002)「ダンダンウイリウクの考古学的調査と研究」（1896〜2002年）(The archaeological research and studies on Dandanoilik 1896-2002) in *Nicchu-Chunichi kyoudou Dandanuiriku iseki gakujutsuchousa houkokusho*『日中・中日共同ダンダンウイリク遺跡学術調査報告書』(The report of the Japan-China joint scholarly research of the Dandanoilik ruins), Shinyousha, 2007, pp. 51–52.

(23) Christoph Baumer, *Die Sudliche Seidenstrabe*, Mainz am Rhein: von Zabem, 2002. Baumer intruded and excavated without an official permission and brought back remains. They had various kinds of troubles with the authority in conducting research. They self-proclaimed as the Sino-Swiss Expedition 1988 which consisted of nine members, namely four Swiss and five other members, including Uyghur camel masters and Han travel agents. Presumably, he somehow recognized that he received an excavating permission and so he said in his report and published it. I have heard that some part of the remains were returned in deference to protests by the Xinjiang side. Rong Xinjiang described the context in detail as mentioned in the above note (22), or the archaeological research and studies on Dandanoilik (1896–2002) on pp. 50-51 stating that we must point out this kind of arbitrary excavation is illegal and causes serious problems in terms of conserving important buried cultural assets located in the Silk Road.

(24) The Xinjiang Archaeological Institute and others, eds. 『漢唐西域考古－尼雅・丹丹烏里克国際学術研討会会議論文提要』(The archaeology of the Western Regions in the ages of the Han and the Tang dynasties – the summary of discussed documents at the international scholarly conference on the Niya and the Dandanoilik ruins), 2009. As referred to in the above note (7), due to communication with outside being shut down after the Urumqi riots, it was so difficult for the symposium office in Xinjiang to communicate with researchers in Europe and the U.S. that they had only one participant from there.

V. Related Projects and the Outline
―関連事業とその概要―

V. Related Projects and the Outline

Besides investigations, conservation and research which are directly associated with cultural assets, I have developed the following activities. I would say that those activities should get to be relatively powerful synergy to help boost investigations, conservation and research themselves.

1. The presentation of the Yasutaka Kojima Awards for outstanding performances for Xinjiang cultures and relics

Human resources are the ultimate source to perform investigations, conservation and research of cultural heritages. In considering the significance of nurturing those performance capabilities, the Foreign Affairs Office of the Xinjiang Autonomous Region, the Xinjiang Cultural Agency, the Xinjiang Cultural Heritage Administration Bureau and I founded the Kojima awards for outstanding performances for Xinjiang cultures and relics in 1999 and presented 20 awards each year for people as well as organizations to serve as powerful encouragement. (The memorandum of agreement between the Xinjiang Cultural Agency and Yasutaka Kojima, Jul. 3, 1999; Chinese Cultural Resources News, Aug, 1, 1999 and Jan. 17, 2001; Xinjiang Daily News, Dec. 22, 1999, Dec. 20, 2000, Dec. 19, 2001, Dec. 25, 2002, Dec. 17, 2004, Dec. 20, 2005, Dec. 20, 2006, Dec. 19, 2007, Nov. 19, 2008, Dec. 6, 2009, and Dec. 3, 2010; Urumqi Evening News, Dec. 25, 1999; Xinjiang Economics, Dec. 24, 2002; China News, electronic edition, Dec. 2, 2010) The ceremony of awards presentation has been taken place magnificently every year with attendance of big-time statespersons, such as then Vice-Governor of the Xinjiang Autonomous Region like Kurexi Maihesuti 庫熱西·買合斯提, Tieliwaerdi Abudurexiti 鉄力瓦尔迪·阿不都熱西提, or Aierken Tuniyazi 艾尔肯·吐尼亜孜; then

Yasutaka Kojima award ceremony of the outstanding performances for Xinjiang cultures and relics where many people moved to tears, photo by Yang Xincai

Happy future for youths shouldering the world tomorrow. Commemorative photo after the award ceremony of Kojima Scholarship to Xinjiang University, photo by Yang Xincai

Secretary of the Cultural Agency like Lu Jiachuan 呂家伝 or Han Ziyong 韓子勇； the then Director-General of the Xinjiang Cultural Agency like Zunong Kutiluke 祖農·庫提魯克, Abulikezi Abudureyimu 阿不力孜·阿不都熱依木, or Muhetaer Maihesuti 穆合塔尔·買合蘇提; then Bureau Director of the Xinjiang Cultural Heritage Administration Bureau like Yue Feng 岳峰 or Sheng Chunshou 盛春寿; then senior staff members of the Xinjiang Autonomous Region like Liu Yusheng 劉宇生, Liu Xiaoqing, Kang Xiuying, or Mubarak Mukit. These rewards have been received by people active in the front lines, such as not only administrators and researchers of cultural heritages but successors to traditional songs and dances and even a security guard for the Niya ruins. Their achievements were shown on the screen, which these people found very stimulating. A total sum of 300 awards, including people and organizations, was presented thus far. I was advised of this award's idea from Zhang Yuzhong and founded it. The term of this agreement was valid until 2013. While we tried to extend it from that year on, the agreement is presently suspended because we are not in such a mood because of being in the midst of chill relations between Japan and China after 2012. Apart from this, I established a specialist development program within the Chinese Cultural Relics Protection Foundation which annually has given two researchers the opportunity to study at the Japanese institutions for five years from 1993. (The memorandum of agreement between SACH, China and Yasutaka Kojima, Jun. 18, 1993)

2. Operation of the website to conserve Chinese historical, cultural heritages

In the middle of increasing destruction of environments caused by an economic boom, I launched the website to conserve Chinese historical, cultural heritages (www.wenbao.net) in order to raise conservation awareness of Chinese cultural heritages in 2000 with the support of Sun Yuexin and Zhou Peiyan. It is now being operated as a network purely for public interest and being highly valued. (China Daily, Mar. 12, 2004) This network has been funded by Sun Yuexin, Zhou Peiyan, and me along with our friends' contribution.

Opening ceremony of the website with attendance of Vice-Chairman of NPC Tiemuer Dawamaiti, photo by Zhou Peiyan

3. Publication of historical archives

In order to provide those researchers with historical records hard to access, I have helped publish historical materials stored in the Archives Center of the Xinjiang Uyghur Autonomous Region since 2001. They include: 『近代外国探検家新疆考古档案史料』(The archaeological evidence of modern, foreign explorers in Xinjiang);『中瑞西北科学考察档案史料』(The archives of Chinese-Swedish

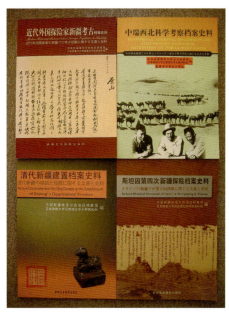

Publication of historical archives, photo by Y. Kojima

scientific studies on Northwest China); 『斯坦因第四次新疆探検档案史料』 (The archives of the Stein's fourth expedition to Xinjiang); and 『清代新疆建置档案史料』 (The archives of Xinjiang province in the Qing Dynasty). (Xinjiang Daily News, Dec. 19, 2000, Jan. 23, 2006, and Nov. 30, 2010; Chinese Archive Report, May 17 and 31, 2004) For your information, some parts of them are cited from those of the Second Chinese Historical Archives Center. I wrote the following papers during the course of my researching these archives: *Sutain daiyonji Shinkyou tanken to sono tenmatsu* 『スタイン第四次新疆探検とその顛末』 (The whole story of the Stein's fourth expedition to Xinjiang in Central Asia) and *Hedin in kansuru to anshiryou no jakkan no shoukai* 『ヘディンに関する档案史料の若干の紹介』 (The Introduction of some relevant archives on Hedin).

The above-mentioned three sections are related to conservation and research of cultural assets.

4. Provision of the Yasutaka Kojima Scholarship for Xinjiang University

Human resources are a basis for everything. I have granted scholarships for nurturing undergraduate students and graduate students at Xinjiang University, one of the major universities in China, as the Kojima Scholarship Program for Xinjiang University since 1986. (The memorandum of agreement between Xinjiang University and Yasutaka Kojima, Jul. 16, 1986; Xinjiang Daily News, Oct. 12, 1994, Jan. 7, 1999, Jan. 10, 2001, Dec. 25, 2002, Dec. 16, 2004, Dec. 21, 2005, Dec. 19, 2006, Dec. 19, 2007, Nov. 19, 2008, Dec. 6, 2009, and Dec. 3, 2010; Xinjiang Education Report, Mar. 16, 1996; Urumqi Evening News, Jan. 12, 1999 and Dec. 24, 2000; Xinjiang Economics, Jan. 21, 1999 and Dec. 20, 2005; www.ts.cn, Dec. 2, 2010) The annual award ceremony has been held with attendance of such leaders as then Vice-Governor of the Xinjiang Autonomous Region like Liu Yi 劉怡 or Kurexi Maihesuti 庫熱西·買合斯提 ; then presidents of the university like Akemu Jiapaer 阿克木·加帕尔, Yibulayin Halike 伊布拉音·哈力克, Azhati Sulidan 阿扎提·蘇里旦, Aniwaer Amuti 安尼瓦尔·阿木提 or Taxifulati Teyibai 塔西甫拉提·特依拝 (a doctorate of engineering at Tokyo University of Science); then senior staff members of the Xinjiang Autonomous Region like Liu Yusheng, Liu Xiaoqing, Kang Xiuying, or Mubarak Mukit. This ceremony has been taken as a very treasured occasion for awarded students. This scholarship was the first of this kind in Xinjiang and had value equivalent to a year-long cost of living at the time. Nowadays, however, as the ways of living have improved and so many scholarships are available, this scholarship symbolizes the well-deserved honor. For example, whenever President Aniwaer would address, "Let's learn the Kojima spirit," clapping never stopped and I was overwhelmed by floods of students asking for my autograph after the ceremony in any given year. About 4,300 students have received the scholarships in sum total, many of whom have become leaders or executives in various fields in Xinjiang, such as the president of Xinjiang University. The agreement term is valid until 2015 as of today. Some businesses supported this program at one time.

5. Construction of Kibo, or Hope, Elementary Schools

Japan-China Friendship Hope Elementary School of Kuqa, photo by Yang Xincai

For improvement of learning environments, I funded the construction of five Japan-China Friendship Hope Elementary Schools in the backcountry with the supports of the Foreign Affairs Office of the Xinjiang Autonomous Region and the Xinjiang Youth Development Foundation from 1998. (Bayinguoleng News, Jul. 9, 2003; Xinjiang Daily News, Jul. 11, 22, and 25, 2003, Oct. 2, 2005, Sep. 4, 2009; Asia Times, Aug. 7, 2003; Xinjiang Economics, Sep. 4, 2009) We have always kept it in mind to take the balance of various races, such as Han, Uyghur, and Mongol, due to its characteristics as a pluralistic region. Some parts of funds were contributed by Chosaku Ueoka, Takayuki Kitano, Tu Shanxiang, Sachiko Endoh, Eiin Yasuda, and another friends of mine.

6. Provision of educational support for grade-schoolers in areas along the Silk Road

Donation of education allowance and school supplies for underprivileged children, photo by Y. Kojima

Despite rapid economic growth, there still are many households that can't afford to buy school supplies in poor areas. In order to enhance learning environments there, we have provided poor children with scholarships in concert with the Urumqi City Government since 1999. (The Agreement of a Memorandum between the Urumqi City Government and Yasutaka Kojima, Jul. 1, 1999; Urumqi Evening News, Dec. 23, 1999, Jul. 16, 2000, Dec. 21, 2001, Jul. 7, 2003, Apr. 16, 2008, and Mar. 5, 2009; Xinjiang Urban Report, Dec. 23, 1999; Xinjiang Daily News, Jul. 7, 2003; www.chinanews.com and www.163.com, Jul. 22, 2010) Recipients have come to 1,600 pupils. Some parts of the funds were contributed by my friends.

The above-mentioned three sections are related to the development programs of human resources.

7. Various contributions

Since 1982, various contributions have been made on a variety of occasions, including construction

Also providing the construction fund for the Hotan Museum, photo by T. Asaoka

of temples, learning equipment, construction of museums, communication tools, research facilities for cultural assets, welfare materials, books, photographic equipment, donations for disaster areas, computer equipment, and researches at several universities. (The Letter of Appreciation from the Xinjiang Cultural Agency, Aug. 12, 1991; Xinjiang Daily News, Apr. 11, 1996, Jul. 17 and 25, 2000, Jul. 8, 2002, Mar. 4, 2003, May 20 and Jun. 27, 2008, and Dec. 7, 2009; Xinjiang Economics, Jul. 25, 2000 and May 16, 2008; Urumqi Evening News, May 16, 2008) A part of them includes contributions from friends and acquaintances of mine.

8. Expedition of various delegates

In order to expand understandings of Xinjiang, I have dispatched a number of delegates in a whole variety of fields, including politics, administration, culture, economics, media, and sightseeing since 1988. (Xinjiang Daily News, Apr. 11, Aug. 27, and Sep. 2, 1996, Jun. 9, 1997, Jul. 17 and 25, 2000, Jul. 8, 2002, Mar. 4, 2003, May 20 and, Jun. 27, 2008, and Dec. 7, 2009; Urumqi Evening News, Aug. 29, 1999 and May 16, 2008; Xinjiang Economics, Jul. 25, 2000, May 16 and Jun. 25, 2008) As for the Urumqi Foreign Trade Fair, I have frequently sent delegates since it started and hosted the Japan-China joint concerts at the People's Hall where you can enjoy the performances of Chinese lute playing, Japanese dancing, shamisen, folksongs and piano from Japan together with the Xinjiang Symphony Orchestra and dancing groups. Some of them were collaborations with other groups.

Dispatch of the delegate of medium-sized companies, photo by a delegate member

9. Various lectures, photo-exhibitions, and publications

For the purpose of promoting mutual understanding, I have been engaged in activities, such as conservation and research of cultural assets, introduction of Xinjiang to Japan, and vice versa since 1989. (Xinjiang Daily News, Aug. 4, 1989, Jul. 2, 1999, Jul. 23, 2000, Mar. 26 and 27, 2002, Aug. 15, 2003, and Jan. 23, 2006; Urumqi Evening News, Aug. 4, 1989, Jul. 3 and Dec. 22, 1999; Yomiuri Shimbun, Oct. 3, 1995; www.chinanews.com and www.sohu.com, Jul. 19, 2010; The Cultural Division of People's Republic of China, electronic edition, Jul. 23, 2010; www.Xinhuanet.com, Aug. 9, 2010; Xinmin Evening News, Japanese edition, Aug. 16, 2010) In China, I have been associated with those organizations, including the Xinjiang Autonomous Region, the Xinjiang Production and Construction Corps, the Xinjiang Cultural Agency, the Xinjiang Cultural Heritage Administration

Bureau, the Xinjiang Museum, Xinjiang University, Xinjiang Normal University, Xinjiang University of Economics, the Urumqi City Government, Peking University, Tsinghua University, Nankai University, Tongji University, Tianjin Academy of Fine Arts, Dalian University, Beijing University of Technology, and the National Museum of China. I always conclude my speech in China, saying, "Try hard for yourself, for your hometown, for China and ultimately develop yourself good enough to work for the world." In Japan, as well, I held various events in such places as Jodo Buddhist Sect, Rinzai Buddhist Sect, Bukkyo University, Kyoto University, and Nara Women's University and

Delivering a lecture emphasizing the importance of conserving cultural assets and international cooperation at the Xinjiang Museum, photo by the Xinjiang Cultural Assets Bureau

delivered lectures at the New Silk Road Exhibition hosted by NHK, at the meeting of Namu, at the Duan Press, and other places. I have also been extensively associated with the photo exhibitions of Li Xueliang 李学亮 and publications, such as 『王恩茂日記』 (The diary of Wang Enmao in a Japanese version), 『鉄木尔・達瓦買提詩集』 (The poetry anthology of Tiemuer Dawamaiti in a Japanese version), *Shirukurodo no ten to sen* 『シルクロードの点と線』 (Points and lines on the Silk Road), and *Shirukurodo Shinkyou no tabi* 『シルクロード新疆の旅』 (The journey along the Silk Road in Xinjiang), along with releasing postcard sets to introduce Xinjiang for a fund-raising purpose.

10. Various intermediaries

Negotiations with other countries are somehow complicated one way or another. I have worked as an intermediary in response to requests from various fields, such as economics, education, and media, since 1990. They include: The comprehensive agreement between Itochu Corporation and the Xinjiang Autonomous Region; Promotion of collaborative arrangements between Nomura

Intermediary for TV Tokyo to receive an authorization to shoot its program, with an actor, Koji Yakusho, photo by the Xinjiang Government

Introducing Vice President of Itochu Corporation Tadayoshi Nakazawa (5th from the left) and others to the Xinjiang Government, photo by Y. Kojima

Securities Co., Ltd. and the Xinjiang Autonomous Region; The scholarly exchange agreement between Nara Women's University and Xinjiang University; The projects like utilization of natural energy and mountaineering between Shibaura Institute of Technology and Xinjiang Technology Academy; Association of sister-school relationship between Moriguchihigashi High School and Urumqi First Junior and Senior High School; The shooting contracts of such as NHK, Tokai Television, and TV Tokyo with the Foreign Affairs Office of the Xinjiang Autonomous Region and the Xinjiang Cultural Heritage Administration Bureau; The exhibition agreement between NHK and the Xinjiang Cultural Heritage Administration Bureau; The collaborative research agreement between the Research Institute for Humanity and Nature and the Xinjiang Archaeological Institute. (Nihonkeizai Shimbun, Jul. 27, 1993, Sep. 2, 1994, and Apr. 24, 1995; Xinjiang Daily News, Sep. 2 and 3, 1994, Dec. 26, 1995, Apr. 13, 1996, Jul. 28, 1997, and Mar. 27, 2002; Urumqi Evening News, Dec. 26, 1995 and Jul. 27, 1997; Nikkankougyou Shimbun, Nov. 11, 1997; Asahi Shimbun, Mainichi Shimbun, and Nara Shimbun, Apr. 2, 2002; Yomiuri Shimbun, Apr. 4, 2002; www.chinanews.com, May 12, 2010; www.china org.cn, May 14, 2010)

As being referred to before, I worked as an intermediary of an apology for Japanese professors arrested for illegal survey. Even for this kind of intermediary work, I paid out of my own pocket, such as airfares, various expenses, and declined to receive any honorarium. It was because of a volunteer work, unlikely a business work.

11. The invitations of various delegates

As the old proverb says, "Seeing is believing," since 1993 I have invited lots of delegates headed by the three-generation Chairmen of the Xinjiang Autonomous Region, the Secretaries or Mayors of Urumqi City and those who worked on politics, administration, culture, economics, education, and so on, whereby they will better understand Japan. And I have found it very effective and relevant. (Naranichinichi Shimbun, Apr. 23, 1995; People's Daily, electronic edition in Japanese, Aug. 4, 2008) Some of these invitations were made jointly with other institutions.

The above 5 sections were related to the promotion of mutual understanding.

Inviting a group headed by Governor of the Xinjiang Simayi Tieliwaerdi, a photographer unknown

VI. The Significance of International Cooperation
―国際協力の意義―

VI. The Significance of International Cooperation

1. Essentiality of international cooperation

There are about 200 nations across the world, yet the number of races is more than that. Each of them has its own history, system, institutions, culture, language, etc. And as its national interest differs from each other, people crash each other insisting on conflicting ideas. Mutual understanding is almost next to impossible to achieve. That's the very reason why effort is need to achieve mutual understanding. Furthermore, Japan is in a position to contribute to and lead the world in a variety of fields, such as not only investigations, conservation, and research of cultural heritages and development of human resources to which I have long committed myself, but also poverty, medical care, environments, population, gender, culture, education, research, natural resources, science, industries, agriculture, fishing industries, economics, politics, and conflicts as one of the top-level nations in the world. International cooperation is essential to enhance mutual understanding and contribution to various fields (including not only finance but human resources and technology). On the level of businesses and individuals as well as nations, coexistence, shared education, and recycling-oriented activities are crucial issues to be dealt with.

The 21st century is, in other words, the century of international cooperation. This underlies the fact that civilization has drastically developed and mutual dependency among nations has increasingly deepened. 7.3 billion people in the world today have come to share a common destiny. On March 11, 2011, the Great East Japan Earthquake occurred. Staggering disasters were instantly reported all over the world. Over 130 countries, including our allied America, various regions and organizations lent us a helping hand. Many of these countries explicitly expressed that they would do it in return for contributions Japan has ever offered them. Radioactive substances were carried by an air current to cover the earth, which has given enormous impacts on the nuclear policy of each country. And many foreigners left Japan. And what's worse, due to the shortage of Japanese-made components, production lines were terminated in various nations. All of this underlies just how the world shares a common destiny. For myself, I brought food produced in Fukushima on my visit to China just after the great disaster to appeal their safety.

International cooperation was beginning to emerge around the middle of the 20th century. When I first visited Xinjiang in 1982, I had a low level of awareness regarding international cooperation. In making the said various contributions, the thought of "public diplomacy" has gradually come to my mind.

Inviting a group of youth delegates from Xinjiang, a photographer unknown

To continue international contributions has really made me realize that I am influenced by the power of a nation. As a marine superpower our ancestors had been active on the international scene any number of times before. Regrettably, however, Japan has now become rather introverted because of going through a spell of post-war experiences and 20 or so years of various recent stagnations which had been presumably originated in the DNA of national isolation ingrained during the Edo era. I am one of those who wish that an increasing number of people will get to be extroverted and work actively in the world to improve people's living standards, which will definitely help the existence and prosperity of Japan itself as well. The reason why I have long referred to the facts as they are in this thesis is to give references in any way to people practicing international cooperation. We Japanese tend to think it a virtue to hide our contributions. It is not so in the world. I am wondering to what extent valuable contributions Japan and Japanese people have made internationally have been informed to the people of the world. Even Japanese have scarcely been communicated. I'm a firm believer in winning the world confidence if Japan, its groups and its individuals should disseminate their contributions without hesitation.

We hold an advanced position in the field of international cooperation. Besides Official Development Assistance (ODA) financed by tax revenue, we have established the organizations and the frameworks, including the Japanese International Cooperation Agency (JICA), the Japan Bank for International Cooperation, Japan Overseas Cooperation Youth Volunteers and Japan Overseas Cooperation Senior Volunteers. They have developed international cooperation in many countries around the world and been highly appreciated by the people there. I'm very pleased to see a variety of NGOs, businesses, and individuals being actively committed to their own missions. International cooperation studies also seem to be being acknowledged.

For individuals, it can be a source of happiness to paint your life with your favorite color being full of originality while being away from a given concept, common sense, precedent, and image-consciousness.

International cooperation would be all the more required for Japan having entered a mature phase in order to sustain development. I would say that the 21st century needs those who are well aware of sharing a burden for practicing public diplomacy regardless of whether they are sightseers, business people, researchers, international students or general public, to say nothing of statespersons, government workers or diplomats.

International cooperation signifies activities not only to heighten the power of Japan and directly boost national interest, but to maintain peace, deter war, and contribute to peace of mind for all. International cooperation is one of the key elements for our nation to break through the recent chaos to attain further enhancement just like we had got through with the Meiji Restoration or the post-war period, isn't it? Whereas the standard definition of national strength is said to consist of such comprehensive powers as geopolitics, the scale (including sea), heritages, population, human resources, natural resources, politics, diplomacy, economics, military, culture, and public relations, I would like to introduce the notion of public diplomacy and international cooperation faculties. It is very regrettable that our ODA is shrinking. It should be increased. Naturally, it goes without saying that as times change, we need strategic responses.

2. Transcending such barriers as races, systems, cultures, ideologies, and languages

The language used in Japan is different from that of China. I have made international contributions crossing that language barrier. But come to think of it, I find now that both Japanese and Chinese teams have got through with barriers like races, systems, cultures, and ideologies as well. The first step is to mutually recognize other party's standpoint. The second one is to respect and appreciate mutually.

While attending the fourth international forum for research on the Japanese linguistics and culture among China, Japan, and Korea held at Dalian University in October 2010, I am now writing this part of my thesis. In the last month collision of a Chinese fishing boat with the Japanese patrol ship off the coast of the Senkaku Islands, as well as the nationalization of the Senkaku Islands in September 2012, led the relationship between Japan and China to a state of alert high enough to cause severe anti-Japan demonstrations in more than 100 cities in the latter case. Ever since 1972 when I crossed over an iron bridge between English Hong Kong and China under scrutiny by a solder with a bayonet sword of the People's Liberation Army, anti-Japan demonstrations have been carried out time and time again, which has cooled down relations between Japan and China on each and every occasion. Under such circumstances, the reason why I could continue solid, long-standing international cooperation is that I have had both of Japan and China clarify the significance, purpose, goal and among other things basic concept of each project in order to overcome enormous challenges. And I am blessed with diplomatic power and faculties as a person in my own way.

Let me take one example of how I have overcome barriers. When I met with Governor of the Xinjiang Nuer Baikeli 努尔·白克力 in April 2008, the governor said to me, "You are a living witness of 30-year reform and door-opening in Xinjiang." This unearned praise gave me a chance to publish『見証新疆変迁』(Witnessing the transition of Xinjiang). As I mentioned before, in November in the same year, I delivered a lecture at the retrospective convention of Xinjiang friendship with foreign countries to commemorate the 30th anniversary of the reform and door-opening policies sponsored by the Foreign Affairs Office of the Xinjiang Government and presented this book to 200 or so participants from China and overseas. It is filled with old photos which even the natives in

Governor Nuer Baikeli saying, "You are the living witness of Xinjiang development", photo by Yang Xincai

Xinjiang have never seen before, which garnered a solid reputation.

In May 2009, in response to such a great popularity, I published the 2nd volume of 『見証新疆変迁』 (Witnessing the transition of Xinjiang). During the period from June through July that year, using the book, I launched a PR campaign visiting 15 cities to celebrate the 30th anniversary of the reform and door-opening policies in Xinjiang (briefly called the Long Journey) along with the staff of the Foreign Affairs Office of the Xinjiang Autonomous Region in order to have the Xinjiang people realize through old photos how Xinjiang has developed. It started in Urumqi followed by Turpan, Aksu, Kashi, Altay, Shihezi, Karamay, and Hotan. The number of visiting cities was reduced to eight from the original schedule. On the very day when I came back home earlier, the Urumqi riot broke out.

While you might think that I need not to publicize the development of Xinjiang in Xinjiang, this activity would help the people there have confidence because a foreigner like me who has actually seen this development shows them through images. It would also surely promote understanding about Japan by letting them know there is a Japanese man like me. I firmly believe that international cooperation is fostered by breaking down barriers instead of getting introverted by creating walls around you.

3. Clarification of significance, purpose and goal

It is a crucial element for us to investigate, conserve and research ecology, environments, cultural heritages because it leads to protection of human beings. We have to take it as a due sense of responsibility. It is especially to be noted that conservation comes before research. Because research will advance as times go by but lost cultural assets will not return.[25]

Speaking of relations between Japan and China, the fact that the slogan of Japan-China Friendship 日中友好 is so frequently addressed signifies itself that the relations are yet to be matured. It is natural that countries all over the world should be friendly. Yet, it is somehow a sad thing that we have to chant Japan-China Friendship loudly. And there is any number of organizations bearing Japan-China Friendship as well. Based on Japan-China Friendship 日中友好, we must enter the second phase which I think you could call Japan-China Mutual Understanding 日中相互理

Publications explaining how Xinjiang has developed through the reform and opening policies for 30 years, photo by Yang Xincai

Introducing via images the great development of Xinjiang in 8 cities in Xinjiang, photo by the Xinjiang Government

Being asked for my autograph at any venue, photo by the Xinjiang Government

解, and then both nations should work together to advance to the third phase, Japan-China Collaboration 日中共同.

In the process of my activities thus far, both Japan and China have clarified the significance, purpose and goal of those activities in the form of a memorandum or a memorandum of agreement.

4. Clarification of a fundamental philosophy
　—Friendship, Collaboration, Safety, High Quality, and Frugality—

International activities entail conflicts. What's crucial is that we should have an original point to return to, which is the fundamental philosophy. The strategic mutually beneficial relationships are often referred to between the Governments of Japan and China. We, the Japan-China joint team, held out five spiritual principles, namely friendship, collaboration, safety, high quality and frugality, to proceed with archaeological work in a desert which has constituted a major part of our international cooperation in Xinjiang. It is not necessary to explain about friendship and collaboration. Activities in the desert also entail jeopardy. There is a record of the example leading to death. We have experienced the unexpected accidents time and again, such as emergency camping due to inability to trace a route, encountering sandstorms, concussion or fracture due to falling off a camel, sudden sickness and a vehicle fire. While it is routinely allowed to act on your own judgment, in an emergency it is the key point to maintain a unified chain of command to follow a leader's directive to secure safety.

As it was required to conduct conservation and research on a level high enough to correspond with a world-class cultural heritage, I have organized a team consisting of leading professionals both from Japan and China. Not being a professional, myself, but as the promoter of a project for investigations, conservation and research, I have had my heart set on this point.

From Japan, the team consists of: Taijun Inokuchi, Shouzou Tanabe, Kodo Sanada, Kazutoshi Nagasawa, Takara Horio, Fumitaka Yoneda, Masahide Furukawa, Toru Kaigara, Takao Itoh, Toshio Asaoka, Kiyomi Tanaka, Shin Yoshizaki, Tomoko Kondou, Sun Yuexin, Yousei Kouzuma, Jinichi Yonekawa, Minao Nakajima, Keiji Yoshida, Satomi Katoh, Teruhiko Takahashi, Gosuke Onoda, Yoshifumi Ichikawa, Toshitaka Hasuike, Kazuko Sakamoto, Kazuki Sugimoto, Migifumi Sato, Shiro Ishida, Kenji Uchida, Tadashi Inoue, Yoshika Ando, Ken Kirihata, Masaaki Sawada, Iwataro Oka, Yoshikazu Tsujimoto, Chisako Tomizawa, and others.

From China, they are: Han Xiang, Yue Feng, Sheng Chunshou, Li Jun, Wang Binghua, Yidilisi Abuduresule, Yu Zhiyong, Zhang Yuzhong, Liu Guorui, Zhang Tienan, Shabiti Ahemaiti, Ahemaiti Rexiti, Liu Yusheng, Tong Wenkang, Li Xiao, Liu Wenzhen, Liu Yusheng, Yi Li, Wu Yong, Ruan Qiurong, Wang Jingkui, Li Ji, Wang Jun, Yang Lin, Xu Pingfang, Lin Meicun, Wang Bangwei, Ren Shinan, Meng Fanren, Wang Yarong, Wu Xinhua, Qi Dongfang, Yang Jing, Yang Yichou, Wang Shouchun, Jing Ai, Liu Shuren, Tie Fude, Ma Shichang, Lu Zongyi, and others. I cannot thank them enough.

Having a Japan-China joint meeting every evening, photo by Y. Kojima

Standing up even at supper to relieve weariness (Niya, BC), photo by Y. Kojima

I have been mindful of frugality costwise and environmentwise, except for the cost to reduce friction for better interpersonal communication. While we have experienced a whole variety of collisions, large or small, both the Japanese and Chinese teams have returned to the fundamental principles to solve each issue, accordingly.

5. Getting through challenges

First of all, we had to overcome the differences in races, histories, systems, institutions, cultures, and languages. A large-scale survey in such an uninhabited area as the great desert has required us to bring in food and surveying equipment by desert vehicles and camels. The weather there limited the period of our investigations like only for a month in a year, or from October through November, which had cost us to spend a number of years for research. In respect of livelihood, we rose around the time the sun was rising (with the temperature occasionally going 15 degrees below zero Celsius), poured down the last-night leftover such as a bowl of mutton rice or rice porridge, headed for sites on foot or on a camel group by group to conduct distributional research, survey, excavation and studies. After washing a hard naan, sausage and an apple down with a little water and taking a rest under the scorching sun (with the temperature occasionally going over 30 degrees Celsius), we kept on working until evening and again had a bowl of mutton rice or mutton soup noodle (In the latter part of research, we could afford to bring in beer, soccer balls, cards and a radio). After that, we had a meeting, followed by measuring antiquities and sorting out materials each day, and huddled in small tents to sleep without shower for about three weeks. Sometimes you may be able to enjoy gazing at a sky full of stars by sleeping outside a tent, but it is impossible to endure without toughness of mental and physical strength as well as cooperativeness.

Since there was no organizing the experts of various fields with a sole university, a number of universities, research institutes and specialty businesses kindly participated in our projects. And this demanded a great deal of hard work for coordination. The large amount of funds is required to conduct investigations, conservations, researches, reports, and symposiums. Although a part of the funds for the Japanese team was provided by the subsidies from the Ministry of Education, Culture, Sports, Science and Technology and Bukkyo University, a large part of them was managed by my pocketbook and debt loan.

6. Power of diplomacy and faculty as a person

I've seen and heard lots about the cases where scholars and the media conducted investigations, research, and shooting without authorization. Or I was told that researchers and visitors had proceeded to the area of Loulan, Niya, and Dandanoilik without approval. As I referred to this in this paper and its notes, many of these people tried to allege, saying that they thought that their Chinese counterpart had acquired the authorization." Eventually, however, those people, their related institutions, and ultimately Japan were discredited. Unilateral action to bring out research achievements and photographed materials does not differ too much from that of having exported cultural assets at the beginning of the 20th century.

Both the Japanese team and the Chinese team would mutually pay due respect to the other party's sovereignty, regulations and culture. As mentioned earlier, we have received a written official authorization in each and every phase to implement our activities through a memorandum or a memorandum of agreement. Among other things, I have frequently read and thoroughly observed 中華人民共和国考古涉外工作管理弁法 (The guidelines for management of archaeological negotiation activities of the People's Republic of China) (So-called, the first order of SACH, China, ratified by the State Council on Dec. 31, 1990, effective on Feb. 22,1991).

Diplomacy is to shake hands to advocate, which I have actually put into practice. The reason why many political leaders who seem not to be associated with research have appeared in this paper is that China administers everything under the support and directives of the Communist Party. Therefore, as I find it essential to communicate with those leaders, I have dealt with this crucial matter seriously. Before meeting, I prepared sufficiently along with imagery rehearsal. I kept it in mind to be seen as confident over a smile face without seeing a memo. May it be poor, though, I tried to make myself understood in Chinese. I took a positive stance toward dinning with those people as well, because it is one of the most important scenes for diplomacy.

As for socializing with people, avoiding interacting superficially, temporarily and financially, I have always made a point to get in touch with them trying to get to their heart with such manners as faithfulness, appreciation, good fortune, obligation, and humanity. These kinds of attitudes as well as a solid and long-standing relationship have produced remarkable results, which added up to reliability. Not just talks and intelligence, but hearty communion is exactly what it takes. During my 33-year undertakings in Xinjiang, I have dealt with several generations of leaders in various positions. The four generations of Secretary of the Xinjiang Committee of the CCP, or the uppermost echelon, include Wang Enmao 王恩茂, Song Hanliang 宋漢良, Wang Lequan 王楽泉, and Zhang Chunxian 張

春賢. And the five generations of the Governor of the Xinjiang are Tiemuer Dawamaiti 鉄木尔·達瓦買提, Abulaiti Abudurexiti 阿不来提·阿不都熱西提, Simayi Tieliwaerdi 司馬義·鉄力瓦尔地, Nuer Baikeli 努尔·白克力, and Shohrat Zakir 雪克来提·扎克尔. The same goes with the Foreign Affairs Office, the Cultural Agency, the Xinjiang Cultural Heritage Administration Bureau, the Archaeological Institute, the Archives Center, Xinjiang University, the Government of Urumqi city, etc.

In spite of the changes in people as mentioned before, the reason why I have been able to keep a close contact with each person is that I have never negotiated ad hoc behind the curtain or fallen into a special relationship with anyone. Otherwise, my relationships with those organizations would have been severed after personnel reshuffles.

Sometimes negotiations were tough. Even then, I tried to deal with them with humor. For instance, while the China side mainly explained a project at a conference to discuss conservation of the Dandanoilik ruins, the atmosphere was not amicable in the morning session because quite a few participants had met for the first time. In the afternoon, my statement, punning on a word, that it is highly honorable to have Chairperson 王丹華 (Wang Danhua) review this project who is the Empress (or 王) of Dandanoilik (or 丹) in China (or 華) turned around the overall course of discussion.

Setting up the joint-team flag, the landmark of the BC, photo by Y. Kojima

Shaving a camel master's head, photo by a Japanese member

159

Notes:
....

(25) Various reasons can be considered for loss of cultural assets. For instance, long-time natural deterioration; an unintentional or intentional destruction because of construction of roads and cities; looting; fires; explorations and excavations (there are many cases even for a research purpose leading to deterioration and loss); ideological destruction (massive ravages by the Cultural Revolution and the explosion of the Bamiyan ruins by the Taliban); and wars. Speaking of intangible cultural assets, we can point out the absence of a successor. In spite of those losses, new cultural assets are being created one after another. At the time when I conversed with then-Chief Steward of Yakushiji Temple Eiin Yasuda in Nara on a newspaper project to commemorate having been listed, he said, "(Though some people say Yakushiji Temple has been dedicated to constructing buildings), we are determined to construct a national treasure in terms of a thousand years. We have restored the Golden Pavilion, the West Stupa followed by the Middle Gate, the Religious Seclusion, and the Xuanzang Sanzang Hall. We are currently building the Cloister and further would like to restore the Great Hall, the Bell Tower, and the Scripture House." I was impressed with his grand vision of building a national treasure in a thousand years.
(Chubukeizai Shimbun, May 21, 1993) These are just some of the examples.

Conclusion
With My Life Mission in Mind
おわりに－使命として

My life mission was initiated by the renovation of the Kizil grottoes, followed by the research of the Niya ruins and then the research of the Dandanoilik ruins as well as the conservation of their murals. Besides these undertakings, further enormous achievements in the related fields have been attained. I would like to express my hearty appreciation to those people and organizations that have long advised and cooperated with me on this occasion. Among other things, I'm deeply grateful to those members and their organizations who participated in conservation and research work in Urumqi as well as on-site investigation work under demanding conditions in the desert. As I have already noted the names of participated members on a yearly basis in this paper, I would like to offer my gratitude by way of noting the names of those organizations.

1995 Niya research team: Putting all our strength together (a part/at BC) photo by K. Sugimoto

The Japanese side: Bukkyo University, Ryukoku University, Kyoto University of Arts, the National Museum of Japanese History, the Nara National Research Institute of Cultural Properties, the Science and Technology Agency, Waseda University, Kyoto University, Kokugakuin University, Kansai University, Kansai Gaikokugo University, the Kyoto City Archaeological Research Institute, the Osaka City Cultural Properties Association, the Nagaokakyo City Archaeological Research Center, the Archaeological Institute of Kashiwara, the Ancient Orient Museum, the Ruins Investigation Committee of Rokko Mountains, Otemae University, Terao Corporation, Tsurukame Corporation, the Iida City Museum, Kokushikan University, Nara Women's University, Oka Bokkodo, Art Preservation Services, Roppou Art and Nara University.(Random order)

Surveying engineers, camel masters, and cooks, all together, Dandanoilik research team 2004 (a part/at BC), phot by China Central TV

The Chinese side: the Xinjiang Government, the Xinjiang Cultural Agency, the Xinjiang Cultural Heritage Administration Bureau, the Xinjiang Archaeological Institute, the Museum of the Xinjiang Uyghur Autonomous Region, the Relics

Though people think no water in a desert, some locations are abundant in ground water. Water flowed out into a hole dug by a petroleum exploring team, photo by Y. Kojima

The great desert which has prevented people from intruding protects the ruins(Roughly a halfway point between Bakkasuegiri and the Dandaoilik ruins), photo by Y. Kojima

Administration Center of the Hotan Region, SACH, China, Peking University, East China Normal University, the Chinese Academy of Sciences, the Chinese Academy of Social Sciences, the Chinese Relics Research Institute, the National Museum of China, the Kucha Grottoes Research Institute and Eastern China Petroleum Company. (Random order)

I would also like to render thanks for the fullest efforts exerted for me by the following people from Bukkyo University, including Kosyo Mizutani, Yuishin Itou, Koji Takahashi, Shinkou Nakai, Ryuzen Fukuhara, Nobuyuki Yamagiwa, Kodo Sanada, Kenji Sugimoto, Shunzo Onoda, Toru Yagi, Seiichi Monta, Yoshika Ando, Shozui Nishina, Hiroo Okita, Yoshihide Honjo, Takumi Umeda, Norio Tachi, Yoshinori Takai, Yoko Kohara, Ryuko Jyuge, Koken Honda, Ryokei Kume, Kimie Matsumura, Toshinari Obata, Shigehisa Tsuhara. And special thanks go to postdoctoral scholar Toshihiko Saito for advising me to get through this thesis, as well as Mr. Sun Yuexin and Mrs. Zhou Peiyan who long stayed in Japan for playing valuable parts for various negotiations. Last, but not least, my comrade, Satoko Kojima, who has supported me all the way through my humble international contributions both materially and mentally.

The projects to investigate, conserve, and research as mentioned above would have never been managed successfully without enormous passion, time, intelligence and funds offered by those people.

The celebration to commemorate the 30th anniversary of Mr. Yasutaka Kojima's visit to Xinjiang hosted by the Xinjiang Government, photo by Yang Xincai

The 30th anniversary round-table talks among people in the cultural relic world, photo by Yang Xincai

Japanese members meeting with Secretary Zhang Chunxian who was selected as one of the top 25 members of the Politburo Standing CCP Committee in Nov. 2012, photo by Yang Xincai

In July 2010, Japanese newly-appointed Ambassador to China Uichiro Niwa 丹羽宇一郎 addressed at the farewell and welcome reception in Tokyo that he would like to devote himself to building a new and promising relationship between Japan and China from the viewpoints of being friendly to Chinese while loving Japan 愛国親中 and friendly to Japanese while loving China 愛国親日, which garnered unanimous applause. I was extremely impressed with him for his commitment to embarking upon a new mission because he had already distinguished himself as the president and the chairman of Itochu Corporation. I also owed him a lot, such as addressing a farewell speech at the company funeral for my successor, President Kousaku Matsumoto. Immediately after his assignment in China, he faced such a tremendous challenge as the fishing boats' collision off the coast of the Senkaku Islands.

In September 2011, the 30th anniversary of Mr. Yasutaka Kojima's visit to Xinjiang 小島康誉氏新疆来訪30周年記念活動 was held with the sponsorship of the Xinjiang Autonomous Region as long as one week, which includes: the meeting with Secretary Zhang Chunxian, the commemorative reception, the commemorative ceremony, the commemorative round-table talks on the cultural relics world, the commemorative photo exhibition, the commemorative publication of 大愛無疆 (No boundary for love of humanity), the commemorative return banquet, and the renovation ceremony of the monument to commemorate a fund-raising

Vice-Governor of the Xinjiang Tieliwaerdi observing the 30th anniversary photo exhibition, photo by Yang Xincai

Singing "Kitagunino Haru (spring in the north land)" together by Japanese and Chinese to pray for Tohoku's reconstruction, photo by Yang Xincai

Tree-planting as one of the events of the 20th Anniversary of Mr. Kojima's visit hosted by the Xinjiang Government, photo by the Xinjiang Government

Putting a premium on specific action to foster mutual understanding, photo by Zhao Xinli

campaign for restoring the Kizil grottoes. This ceremony which followed suit the 20th anniversary was more than I could have hoped for as a citizen. Xinjiang Graphics featured the anniversary spanning 12 pages. (Xinjiang Graphics, Oct. 10, 2011)

In December 2012, at the welcome and farewell reception for the old and new ambassadors held in Tokyo Uichiro Niwa gave a speech as the former ambassador to China, "My term of office began with Senkaku 尖閣 and ended with Senkaku 尖閣. No country compromises in territory and sovereignty. We should be determined not to go to war. I hope that new ambassador Kitera will try his best, as the Japan-China relationship couldn't be worse." The new Ambassador Masato Kitera 木寺昌人 addressed, "My first mission is to improve relations with China. Even though we are facing various challenges, we must focus on fostering economic relations. I will also try my best to boost exchanges among the youth of both nations. And I will conduct diplomacy with persistent dialogues and a great deal of legwork." Chinese Ambassador to Japan Cheng Yonghua 程永華 stated in Japanese, "The ambassador is to work for securing and enhancing national interest. Indeed, both countries have got something that we cannot compromise, but we are neighboring nations and there is no way to move elsewhere. We must sustain strategic and mutually beneficial relationships corresponding to political reality."

In June 2013, the Japanese version of 大愛無疆 (No boundary for love of humanity) published to commemorate the 30th anniversary was also released. Chinese journalist Duan Yuezhong 段躍中 living in Japan who has been anxious about a deteriorating relationship between Japan and China brought it out thinking that now is the time to let not only Japanese and Chinese but people in the world know that there is a Japanese who has constantly devoted his life to mutual understanding between Japan and China for 30 years.

In February 2014, Duan Yuezhong and I visited former Ambassador Niwa to put forward a plan to hold the symposium of those who have practiced Japan-China interactions, as well as a photo exhibition. Mr. Niwa evaluated the plan so highly that he said he would inform relevant divisions about it.

In November of that year, the said 11th Beijing Forum was held and its opening ceremony was taken place at the Diaoyutai State Guesthouse where a Chinese Vice-Prime Minister, a French ex-Prime Minister, a Korean ex-Prime Minister, and an American Nobel Prize-winning economist delivered lectures. On that day, at the same venue a common awareness of improvement in a cold-war relation since Japan's nationalization of the Senkaku Islands 尖閣 of Okinawa Prefecture in September 2012 came to be shared in the meeting of senior government officials from Japan and China. I immediately referred to this development in my speech and expressed a hope that the summit talks of both nations would be realized in the near future. On the following day, this very summit of both nations actually came true, in an impassive mood, but the improvement of relations between Japan and China has taken one step forward.

Although it seems that I am regarded as belonging to the China-friendly group, it's natural that I basically value a spirit of patriotism as Japanese.

I really appreciate a curious coincidence. I have devoted the latter half of my life without regret both materially and spiritually to conservation and research of cultural heritages, the promotion of Japan-China mutual understanding, and development of human resources centering on the Xinjiang Uyghur Autonomous Region. And I'm determined to do my utmost for this life-long mission of mine in the future as well. Once I was asked by Vice-Director of Kyodo News Shigeki Wada of how he should describe such a person like me practicing a wide range of activities. My answer was a life-long volunteer for practicing international contributions and it was so reported in newspapers across Japan. Should people concerned extend to me further assistance and cooperation, I would be highly obliged to it.

Since my first visit to Xinjiang in 1982, I have been adopting an attitude of sincerity. While I might have offered quite a modest pleasure to the people of each race in Xinjiang, a far greater pleasure have been all mine. I am very proud of both members of the Japan and China teams who have accomplished such remarkable achievements.

In February 2015, Zhang Chunxian 張春賢, one of the 25 top echelons of the Politburo Standing Committee of the Chinese Communist Party, who also serves as Secretary of the Xinjiang Uyghur Autonomous Regional CCP Committee, wrote me a New Year's card saying he appreciates my efforts to conserve cultural assets and support for people's livelihood. I responded that I would like to publish a photo collection, produce a TV program, and support people's livelihood in order to commemorate the 60th anniversary of the Xinjiang Uyghur Autonomous Region slated for October 1, 2015.

In April of that year, I met with Chairman of the Xinjiang Uyghur Autonomous Region Shohrat Zakir 雪克来提·扎克尔 to put forth five proposals for the said commemoration, such as production of a TV program for Xinjiang public relations, extension and increase in the amount of scholarship for Xinjiang University, the publication of *Shinkyou sekai bunka isan zukan* 『新疆世界文化遺産図鑑』 (A guide to World Cultural Heritage sites in Xinjiang) alongside a set of post cards, and support for people's livelihood. His acceptance of my proposals started to make substantial progress. (Xinjiang Daily, April 8, 2015)

In August 2015, I started up producing the TV program for Xinjiang public relations and then in September, signed up for extension and increase in the amount of scholarship for Xinjiang University, and published *Shinkyou sekai bunka isan zukan* 『新疆世界文化遺産図鑑』 (A guide to World Cultural Heritage sites in Xinjiang) and a set of post cards, as well. On top of that, I offered an assistance to help improve people's livelihood, including installing well excavators and street lights, and the renovation of elementary schools during the period of September through October. In October 2015, I had a talk with Secretary of the Xinjiang Uyghur Autonomous Regional CCP Committee Zhang Chunxian 張春賢, who then applauded me for those initiatives. (Xinjiang Daily, October 16, 2015)

The sun rises and sets, flowers blossom and fall, the summer comes and the winter comes. Oh, having strayed around for three decades in Xinjiang to at times find enlightenment, I thank everything and anything.

> Bury my ashes in the Taklamakan Desert.
> With my hands clasped in prayer

Summary of the Timeline

時系列概要

Please refer to the summary of the timeline since the content of this book covers a whole variety of matters for a long period of time. This describes the condensed chronology of conservation and research of world-class cultural heritages and their related activities having collaborated with a number of people in Xinjiang.

1982: The first trip to the Xinjiang Uyghur Autonomous Region; commencing various donations

1986: The first visit to the Kizil grottoes; personally offering a restoring fund; initiating the Kojima Scholarship Awards for Xinjiang University

1987: The establishment of the Japan-China Friendship Association to Restore and Conserve the Kizil Grottoes

1988: The first provision of the fund by the Kizil Association; launching the Japan-China joint scholarly research of the Niya ruins; starting to dispatch various delegates

1989: The second provision of the fund by the Kizil Association; initiating various lectures, photo-exhibitions and publications

1990: The second research of the Niya ruins; starting to serve as a mediator

1991: The third research of the Niya ruins

1992: The fourth research of the Niya ruins; launching research in a large scale; receiving the first subsidy by the Ministry of Education, Culture, Sports, Science and Technology, Japan

1993: The fifth research of the Niya ruins; a reporting team of the Niya ruins dispatched by the NPC; broadcasting nationwide in Japan the TV program on the Kizil grottoes

1994: The sixth research of the Niya ruins; the establishment of the Academic Research Organization for the Niya ruins, Bukkyo University; Excavation being authorized by SACH, China;

1995: The seventh research of the Niya ruins; the discovery of a lords' graveyard; the excavation of a number of national-treasure-class antiquities such as *Wu Xing Chu Dong Fang Li Zhong Guo* 五星出東方利中国 and *Wang Hou He Hum Qian Qiu Wang Sui Yi Zi Sun* 王侯合昏千秋万歳宜子孫 which were selected as the 10 great archaeological new-discoveries in 1995; broadcasting nationwide in Japan the TV program on research of the Niya ruins; providing funds to build museums in Hoten and Minfeng

1996: The eighth research of the Niya ruins; the discovery of a mysterious castle wall in the southern area; the discovery of relics and antiquities about 3,000 years ago in the northern area; the publication of the 1st volume of *Niya chousa houkokusho*『ニヤ調査報告書』(The research report of the Niya ruins)

1997: The ninth research of the Niya ruins; the excavation of a large-sized temple; holding an antiquities exhibition as well as an international symposium at Bukkyo University; displaying antiquities found by the Niya ruins research in the exhibition held at the National Museum of Chinese History

1998: Holding an antiquities exhibition for six months at the Shanghai Museum; starting to build Kibo Elementary School

1999: The publication of the 2nd volume of *Niya chousa houkokusho* (The research report of the Niya ruins); initiating the Kojima Awards for outstanding performances for culture and relics in Xinjiang; commencing educational support for grade-schoolers in the area along the Silk Road

2000: Holding an antiquities exhibition as well as an international symposium in Urumqi; launching the website to conserve Chinese historical, cultural heritages

2001: Research of the Niya ruins is selected as the Chinese 100 greatest discoveries in the 20th century; commencing the publication of historical materials from various archives; the memorial event to commemorate the 20th anniversary of Mr. Kojima's visit to Xinjiang hosted by the Xinjiang Government

2002: The publication of *Niya iseki no nazo* 『ニヤ遺跡の謎』 (The mystery of the Niya ruins); displaying a number of antiquities of the Niya ruins at "The Silk Road Exhibition" sponsored by NHK; launching the Japan-China joint scholarly research of the Dandanoilik ruins; excavating national-treasure-class murals 西域のモナリザ

2003: Commencing studies of the murals excavated by research of the Dandanoilik ruins

2004: The second research of the Dandanoilik; starting to conserve the excavated murals; guiding the NHK reporting team to the Niya ruins and others

2005: The third research of the Dandanoilik; broadcasting nationwide the NHK program, The New Silk Road showing the researches of the ruins in Niya and Dandanoilik; displaying a number of murals having completed a preserving treatment

2006: The fourth research of the Dandanoilik ruins

2007: The publications of the 3rd volume of *Niya chousa houkokusho* (The research report of the Niya ruins) and *Dandanuiriku chousa houkokusho* 『ダンダンウイリク調査報告書』 (The research report of the Dandanoilik ruins); holding an international symposium at Bukkyo University

2008: Making a presentation at the event to commemorate the 30th anniversary of the reform and door-opening policies hosted by the Xinjiang Government

2009: Holding an international symposium at Peking University; the publication of the Chinese version of the report on research of the Dandanoilik ruins

2010: Addressing a symposium at the Kizil grottoes; the donation of a large commuting bus for the institution staffers

2011: Holding the photo exhibition, "From Gandhara to Niya" with Tsinghua University; the event to commemorate the 30th anniversary of Mr. Kojima's visit hosted by the Xinjiang Goverment

2012: Making a presentation at the international conference held in the British Library, as well as at the symposium in Urumqi

2013: The publication of *Shinkyou deno sekaiteki bunkaisan hogo kenkyu jigyou to kokusai kyoryoku no igi*『新疆での世界的文化遺産保護研究事業と国際協力の意義』(The projects to conserve and research world-class cultural heritages in Xinjiang, China, and the significance of international cooperation); holding the international symposium and the photo exhibition at Bukkyo University

2014: The designation of the Kizil grottoes as the World Heritage; visiting the six World Heritage sites in Xinjiang; making presentations at the Beijing Forum and at the Peking University international symposium; accompanying 20 Kharosthi researchers such as professors of Peking University and researchers from China, America, and Germany to visit the Niya ruins to appeal for preservation

2015: As the Xinjiang Autonomous Region marked the 60th anniversary of its establishment on October 1, 2015, I presented five mementoes to celebrate this significant occasion, such as the publication of *Shinkyou sekai bunkaisan zukan*『新疆世界文化遺産図鑑』(The pictorial guide to the world heritages sites in Xinjiang) along with the Xinjiang Cultural Assets Bureau, TV program production to introduce Xinjiang, presentations for improving people's livelihood like drilling agricultural wells, and extension of Kojima Scholarship to Xinjiang University.

References

参考文献

General

Xie Bin 謝彬. 1934. *Shinkyou jijou*『新疆事情』(The Xinjiang Affairs) [新疆遊記 (The Xinjiang Diary)]. (Investigation Division of Ministry of Foreign Affairs of Japan 日本外務省調査部, Trans.). Tokyo: Investigation Division of Foreign Affairs of Japan 外務省調査部.

Tsutomu Hino 日野強. 1909. *Irikiko*『伊犂紀行』(Iri Journal). Reprint, Tokyo: Fuyoshobo 芙蓉書房, 1973.

The publishing committee to commemorate Dr. Hisao Matsuda's seventieth birthday 松田壽雄博士古稀記念出版委員会, ed. 1975. *Touzaibunka kouryushi*『東西文化交流史』(History of cultural exchange between the east and the west). Tokyo: Yuzankaku 雄山閣.

Shinji Maejima 前嶋信次 and Kyusaku Kato 加藤九祚, eds. 1975. *Shirukurodo Jiten*『シルクロード事典』(Silk Road Dictionary). Tokyo: Fuyoshobo 芙蓉書房.

Takashi Okazaki 岡崎敬. 1980. *Zouho: Touzai Kousyou no Koukogaku*『増補・東西交渉の考古学』(An enlarged edition: Archaeology of the interactions between the east and the west). Tokyo: Heibonsha 平凡社.

The Institute of Ethnology, Xinjiang Social Science Academy 新疆社会科学院民族研究所, ed. 1980.『新疆簡史』(第 1 巻) (The outline of Xinjiang history). Vol. 1. Urumqi: People's Publishing House of Xinjiang 新疆人民出版社.

Hideaki Shio 塩英哲, Trans. and ed. 1983. *Seisen: Chugoku Chimei Jiten*『精選・中国地名辞典』(Concise Chinese Gazetteer). Tokyo: Ryoun Publishing House 凌雲出版.

Kazutoshi Nagasawa 長澤和俊. 1983. *Shirukurodo bunkashi*『シルクロード文化史』全 3 巻 (Cultural History of the Silk Road). 3 vols. Tokyo: Hakusuisha 白水社.

Genjou 玄奘 and Benki 弁機. 1984. *Genjousanzou no tabi–Daitouseiiki*『玄奘三蔵の旅－大唐西域記』全 2 巻 (The Xuanzang Sanzang's travel-The Great Tang Dynasty Record of the Western Regions). 2 vols. (Shinjou Mizutani 水谷真成, Trans.). Tokyo: Heibonsha 平凡社.

Namio Egami 江上波夫, ed. 1987. *Chuoajiashi*『中央アジア史』(History of Central Asia). Tokyo: Yamakawa Publishing House 山川出版社.

Tamio Kaneko 金子民雄. 2002. *Seiiki tanken no seiki*『西域探検の世紀』(The century of exploring the Western Regions). Tokyo: Iwanamishoten 岩波書店.

Liu Yusheng 劉宇生, Zhang Bin 張濱, and Liu Xiaoqing 劉曉慶, eds. 2003. *Shirukurodo no jujiro–Shinkyou Gairan*『シルクロードの十字路・新疆概覧』(The crossroad of the Silk Road–The outline of Xinjiang). (Akira Yamaguchi 山口昭 et al., Trans.). Tokyo: Bungeisha 文芸社.

Those related with the Kizil grottoes

Heibonsha 平凡社 & Chinese Relics Publishing House 中国文物出版社, eds. 1983–1985. *Chugoku sekkutsu Kijiru sekkutsu*『中国石窟キジル石窟』(The Kizil grottoes among the Chinese grottoes). 3 vols. Tokyo: Heibonsha 平凡社.

Kenyu Hori 堀賢雄. 1987. *Otani tankentai–Seiiki ryokou nikki*『大谷探検隊・西域旅行日記』 (The Otani Expeditions–The diary on the Western Regions). Tokyo: Hakusuisha 白水社.

The Japan-China Friendship Association to Restore and Conserve the Kizil Grottoes 日中友好キジル千仏洞修復保存協力会. 1987. *Nicchu yukou Kijiru senbutsudo shufuku hozon kyousankin no onegai*『日中友好キジル千仏洞修復保存協賛金のお願い』 (The fund-raising campaign by the Japan-China Friendship Association to Restore and Conserve the Kizil Grottoes). Nagoya

The Japan-China Friendship Association to Restore and Conserve the Kizil Grottoes 日中友好キジル千仏洞修復保存協力会. 1988. *Kijiru senbutsudo shufuku hozon bokin chukan houkoku*「キジル千仏洞修復保存募金中間報告」(The interim report of the fund-raising campaign to restore and conserve the Kizil grottoes). Nagoya

The Japan-China Friendship Association to Restore and Conserve the Kizil Grottoes 日中友好キジル千仏洞修復保存協力会. 1989. *Kijiru senbutsudo shufuku hozon bokin saishu houkoku*「キジル千仏洞修復保存募金最終報告」(The final report of the fund-raising campaign to restore and conserve the Kizil grottoes). Nagoya

The Tokyo National Museum 東京国立博物館 et al., eds. 1991. *Doitsu torufan tankentai–Seiiki bijutsuten*『ドイツ・トゥルファン探検隊・西域美術展』(The German expeditions to Turpan–The art exhibition of the Western Regions). Tokyo: The Asahi Shimbun 朝日新聞社.

Those related with the Niya ruins

Aurel M. Stein. 1933. *On Ancient Central-Asian Tracks*. London: Macmillan.

Otani tankentai 大谷探検隊 and Kazutoshi Nagasawa 長澤和俊, eds. 1966. *Shirukurodo Tanken*『シルクロード探検』(The Silk Road exploration) Tokyo: Hakusuisha 白水社.

Kazutoshi Nagasawa 長澤和俊. 1979. *Shirukuroudoshi kenkyu*『シルクロード史研究』(Studies of the Silk Road's history). Tokyo: Kokushokankokai 国書刊行会.

M. Aurel Stein. 1980. *Serindia* (reprinted edition). Delhi: Montilal Banarsidass. (Original work published by Oxford University 1921)

M. Aurel Stein. 1981. *Ancient Khotan* (reprinted edition). New Delhi: Cosmo Publications. (Original work published by Oxford University 1907)

M. Aurel Stein. 1981. *Innermost Asia* (reprinted edition). New Delhi: Cosmo Publications. (Original work published by Oxford University 1928)

Lu Yan 蘆燕. 1984.『絲路文物被盗記』(Theft stories on the Silk Road). Beijing: Xinhua Publishing House 新華出版社.

Han Xiang 韓翔, Wang Binghua 王炳華 et al., eds. 1988.『尼雅考古資料』(The archaeological evidence of the Niya ruins). Urumqi: Printing House for the Young Intelligentsia, the Xinjiang Social Science Academy 新疆社会科学院知青印刷庁.

The Japan-China scholarly research team of the Niya ruins 日中共同ニヤ遺跡学術調査隊, ed. 1996. *Chunichi-Nicchu kyoudou Niya iseki gakujutsuchousa houkokusho*『中日・日中共同ニヤ遺跡学術調査報告書』(The report of China-Japan/Japan-China joint scholarly research of the Niya ruins). Vol. 1 with an English summary. Kyoto: Hozokan 法蔵館.

The Japan-China scholarly research team of the Niya ruins 日中共同ニヤ遺跡学術調査隊, ed. 1999. *Chunichi-Nicchu kyoudou Niya iseki gakujutsuchousa houkokusho*『中日・日中共同ニヤ遺跡学術調査報告書』(The report of Japan-China joint scholarly research of the

Niya ruins). Vol. 2 with an English summary. Kyoto: Nakamura Printing House 中村印刷.

M. Aurel Stein. 1999. *Suna ni umoreta hotan no haikyo* 『砂に埋もれたホータンの廃墟』 [Sand-Buried Ruins of Khotan Personal Narrative of a Journey of Archaeological and Geographical Exploration in Chinese Turkestan] (Seiichi Yamaguchi 山口静一 and Touru Godai 五代徹, Trans.). Tokyo: Hakusuisha 白水社. (Original work published 1904 by Hurst and Blackett)

Zhao Feng 趙豊 and Yu Zhiyong 于志勇, eds. 2000. 『沙漠王子蹟寶』 (The buried treasure of the desert prince). Hong Kong: ISAT/Costume Squad Ltd. 芸紗堂・服飾工作隊.

The Xinjiang Uyghur Autonomous Region Archives 新疆ウイグル自治区档案館 and The Academic Research Organization for the Niya ruins, Bukkyo University 佛教大学内ニヤ遺跡学術研究機構, eds. 2001. *Kindai gaikoku tankenka Shinkyou kouko touan shiryou* 『近代外国探検家新疆考古档案史料』 (The archaeological evidence of modern, foreign explorers in Xinjiang, partially in Japanese or English). Urumqi: Xinjiang Fine Arts Photography Publishing House 新疆美術撮影出版社.

The Academic Research Organization for the Niya ruins, Bukkyo University 佛教大学内ニヤ遺跡学術研究機構, ed. 2002. *Shirukurodo Niya iseki no nazo* 『シルクロード・ニヤ遺跡の謎』 (The mysteries of the Niya ruins on the Silk Road). Osaka: Tohosshuppan 東方出版.

Joshin Shirasu 白須淨眞. 2002. *Otani tankentai to sono jidai* 『大谷探検隊とその時代』 (The Otani expedition team and its age). Tokyo: Bensei Publishing Inc. 勉誠出版.

Lin Meicun 林梅村. 2004. 『絲綢之路散記』 (Essays on the Silk Road). Urumqi: People's Fine Arts Publishing House 人民美術出版社.

Akio Katayama 片山章雄, ed. 2004. *Yo tamatama eikoku rondon ni ari* 『予會々英国倫敦に在り』 (I happened to be in London, the UK). Beppu: Otani Kinenkan 大谷記念館.

The Xinjiang Uyghur Autonomous Region Archives 新疆ウイグル自治区档案館 and The Academic Research Organization for the Niya ruins, Bukkyo University 佛教大学内ニヤ遺跡学術研究機構, eds. 2007. *Sutain daiyonji Shinkyou tanken touanshiryo* 『スタイン第四次新疆探検档案史料』 (The archives of the Stein's fourth expedition to Xinjiang, partially in Japanese and English). Urumqi: Xinjiang Fine Arts Photography Publishing House 新疆美術撮影出版社.

The Japan-China academic research team of the Niya ruins 日中共同ニヤ遺跡学術調査隊, ed. 2007. *Chunichi-Nicchu kyoudou Niya iseki gakujutsuchousa houkokusho* 『中日・日中共同ニヤ遺跡学術調査報告書』 (The report of Japan-China joint scholarly research of the Niya ruins). Vol. 3 with an English summary. Kyoto: Shinyosha 真陽社.

The Xinjiang relics and Chinese characters compiling division 新疆文物漢文編集部, ed. 2009. 『新疆文物・漢唐西域考古－尼雅・丹丹烏里克国際学術討論会専刊』 (Cultural Relics of Xinjiang and the archaeology of the Western Regions in the ages of the Han and the Tang Dynasties–Special edition for the international scholarly conference on the Niya and the Dandanoilik ruins–2009 3Q–4Q, partially in Japanese). Urumqi: the Xinjiang Archaeological Institute 新疆文物考古研究所.

The Bukkyo University Museum of Religious Culture 佛教大学宗教文化ミュージアム and the Academic Research Organization for the Niya ruins, Bukkyo University 佛教大学ニヤ遺跡学術研究機構, eds. 2010. *Kan Tou Seiiki koko–Dandanuiriku kokusai gakujutsu shinpojium happyo youshi youyaku shiryoushu* 『漢唐西域考古－ニヤ・ダンダンウイリク国際学術シンポジウム発表要旨要約資料集』 (The information packet of summaries for the international scholarly symposium on Niya and Dandanoilik–the Western Regions in the ages of the Han and the Tang Dynasties from the archaeological perspective). Kyoto: The Bukkyo University Museum of Religious Culture 佛教大学宗教文化ミュージアムand the Academic Research Organization for the Niya ruins, Bukkyo University 佛教大学内ニヤ遺跡学術研究機構.

Those related with the Dandanoilik ruins

Sven Hedin. 1964. *Ajia no sabaku wo koete*『アジアの砂漠を越えて』[Durch Asiens Wusten] (Fumio Yokokawa 横川文雄, Trans. Vol. 2). Tokyo: Hakusuisha 白水社. (Original work published 1910 by Leipzig/F.A.Brockhaus)

Ancient Khotan 1981, op. cit.

The Xinjiang Archaeological Institute 新疆文物考古研究所, ed. 1998.『新疆文物』(Cultural Relics of Xinjiang, the 4th edition, 1997). Urumqi: the Xinjiang Archaeological Institute 新疆文物考古研究所.

Suna ni umoreta hotan no haikyo『砂に埋もれたホータンの廃墟』(The Khotan's ruins buried in the sand) 1999, op. cit.

The Xinjiang Cultural Heritage Administration Bureau 新疆文物局, the Xinjiang Archaeological Institute 新疆文物考古研究所, The Xinjiang Museum 新疆博物館 et al., eds. 1999.『新疆文物古迹大観』(The overview of relics and ruins in Xinjiang). Urumqi: Xinjiang Fine Arts Photography Publishing House新疆美術撮影出版社.

Kazutoshi Nagasawa 長澤和俊. 2002. *Shirukurodo wo shiru jiten*『シルクロードを知る事典』(The dictionary for the Silk Road). Tokyo: Tokyodoshuppan 東京堂出版.

The Academic Research Organization for the Niya ruins, Bukkyo University 佛教大学内ニヤ遺跡学術研究機構, ed. 2005. *Nicchu kyoudo Dandanuiriku iseki gakujutsu kenkyu purojekuto kokusai shinpojium happyo youshi*『日中共同ダンダンウイリク遺跡学術研究プロジェクト国際シンポジウム発表要旨』(The purport of the international scholarly symposium by the Japan-China joint scholarly research project for the Dandanoilik ruins). Kyoto: The Academic Research Organization for the Niya ruins, Bukkyo University 佛教大学内ニヤ遺跡学術研究機構.

The Japan-China joint scholarly research team of the Dandanoilik ruins 日中共同ダンダンウイリク遺跡学術調査隊, ed. 2007. *Nicchu-Chunichi kyoudou Dandanuiriku iseki gakujutsuchousa houkokusho*『日中・中日共同ダンダンウイリク遺跡調査学術報告書』(The report of Japan-China joint scholarly research of the Dandanoilik ruins). Kyoto: Shinyosha真陽社.

Kan Tou Seiiki koko–Niya/Dandanuiriku kokusai gakujutsu shinpojium happyo youshi youyaku shiryoushu『漢唐西域考古－ニヤ・ダンダンウイリク国際学術シンポジウム発表要旨要約資料集』(The information packet of summarized purports of the international scholarly symposium on Niya and Dandanoilik in the Western Regions in the ages of the Han and the Tang Dynasties from the archaeological perspective) 2010, op. cit.

Those related with international cooperation

Amartya Sen. 2002. *Hinkon no kokufuku–Ajia hattenn no kagi wa nanika*『貧困の克服－アジア発展の鍵は何か』[Beyond the Crisis: Development Strategies in Asia]. (Rira Oishi 大石りら, Trans.). Tokyo: Shueisha 集英社. (Original work published 1999)

Yasuoki Takagi 高木保興, ed. 2004. *Kokusai Kyoryokugaku*『国際協力学』(The studies of international cooperation). Tokyo: University of Tokyo Press 東京大学出版会.

Seiji Utsumi 内海成治, ed. 2005. *Kokusaikyoryokuron wo manabuhito no tameni*『国際協力論を学ぶ人のために』(For those who study the theory of international cooperation). Tokyo: Sekaishisosha 世界思想社.

The Japan International Cooperation Agency 国際協力機構, ed. 2005. *Kokusai Kyoryoku Kikou Nenpou 2005*『国際協力機構年報』(2005) (The annual report of the Japan international Cooperation Agency 2005). Tokyo: Kokusaikyoryokushuppankai 国際協力出版会.

contribution 1

A Summarized Report on Dandan Oilik Ruins

Toshio Asaoka

Representative of Archaeological Sites Researching Group at Rokko

(1) Discovery and rediscovery of Dandan Oilik Site

Dandan Oilik Site, located in Cele County, Khotan Prefecture of Xinjiang Uigur Autonomous Region, China, is an archaeological site from the Tang period (the 7th to 8th century A.D.).

Across the central part of Xinjiang Uigur Autonomous Region stretch the Tian Shan Mountains east and west just like a backbone, on the south of which lies the Taklamakan Desert. In ancient times the area surrounding the desert played a vital role in the East-West trade, and two main highways, Xi-yu Nan-dao (the route along the southern edge of the Taklamakan) and Xi-yu Bei-dao (along the northern edge), enjoyed lively traffic. Dandan Oilik Site is situated in the desert off Xi-yu Nan-dao, approximately 90 km north of Cele urban area.

Dandan Oilik, literally meaning 'the houses with ivory' or 'the land of ivory house', had been only known among 'treasure-seekers' until 1896, when Swedish explorer Sven Hedin made an expedition there and introduced the site to the public. In 1900 M. Aurel Stein, a Hungarian British archaeologist, carried out an excavation at Dandan Oilik, which was the first archaeological excavation in the Taklamakan Desert. He published the results in his report, "The Ruins of Dandān-Uiliq" in *Ancient Khotan*. In the report 17 structures are recorded, labelled by him D1 to D17. The results of the excavation led him to conclude that Dandan Oilik had been an ancient Buddhist sacred place occupied by temples. The absence of evidence for ordinary people's domestic activity discouraged him so deeply that he never returned there.

Since then, with a few exceptional visits by researchers, the site had been paid little attention for a long time, left sleeping under the sand, until even its location became unknown. In 1997, about 100 years after Stein's investigation, an oil exploration in the Taklamakan Desert provided a chance for the researchers of Xinjiang Institute of Cultural Relics and Archaeology to reconfirm the location of the site. Following this, in 2002, a preliminary investigation was carried out by a Japan-China joint team, during which Buddhist wall paintings were discovered. In response Xinjiang Institute of Cultural Relics and Archaeology carried out an urgent excavation and research. Researchers from Japan and China collaborated in restoration and preservation works on the recovered paintings, and in 2005 NHK's TV documentary "Treasures of the Silk Road" introduced some of the vivid paintings from Dandan Oilik to the public.

(2) Extent of the remains

Stimulated by the discovery of the mural paintings, in 2004 a 3-year Japan-China joint project for a distribution survey was launched, aiming to grasp the actual condition of Dandan Oilik Site in defail. It included a partial excavation by a team of Chinese archaeologists and was concluded in 2006.

The investigation revealed that the remains were distributed within an area of about 3 km square as shown in Fig. 1, within which a total of 70 features were discovered and recorded: a circular rampart, 30 buildings, 15 structures related to Buddhist temples or Buddha halls, 2 fireplaces or cooking stoves, 11 kilns, 10 orchards in various sizes, and a fence. While the distribution range of remains was found to be far more extensive than Stein had described, as to the central part the survey results were virtually identical with Stein's record, with an area of approximately 1.2 km square. Each feature was given an ID number beginning with 'CD', 'C' representing 'Cele County', to prevent confusion with Stein's number.

The Chinese archaeologists carried out excavations of the ruins of a Buddhist temple (CD4) in 2002 and three buildings (CD3a, CD1, and CD17) in 2006. The following part briefly describes the excavations of CD4, CD1, and CD17, and the remains of the rampart (CD30).

CD4 is a structure of a 回-shaped rectangular Buddha hall measuring 8.2 m from north to south and 6.02 m from east to west with an entrance on the north. At the center is situated a room measuring 5 m by 6 m, surrounded by a corridor decorated with paintings on the inside face of the outer wall. The wall paintings show the figures of Buddhas, Bodhisattvas, thousand Buddhas, a worshipper on horseback, and a Deva king supporting a Buddha image.

CD1 is a large building measuring about 35 m from north to south and about 20 m from east to west, within which two rooms adjacent to each other were excavated. One of them, Room f2, has wall paintings. The size of the room is 3.7 m from north to south and 3.1 m from east to west, and the surviving standing wall is 1-1.8 m high. On each of its east and west walls is painted a two-eared jug containing flowers, from which leaves and flowers spread out on all four walls.

CD17 is a building with underground beams, measuring 5.6 m from north to south and 13.7 m from east to west. It consists of 4 rooms and 3 of them, Rooms f1, f2 and f3, are each provided with a fireplace. A wooden plate inscribed with a Chinese character '官' was unearthed beside the wall of Room f3. A small piece of paper bearing what seems Khotanese script was found on the ground.

CD30, the remains of a circular rampart, is recorded by Stein as "remains of ancient circumvallation". The rampart, built of rammed clay in the form of a virtually perfect circle, is about 11 m thick and the inside diameter is about 80 m and the outside diameter about 100 m. On the top are found the remains of fences in two rows, built by joining branches of tamarisk and reeds, one row is on the raised inner edge, the other along the outer edge. The fences have posts at intervals of 10-20 m. The wall has a projecting part 15 m long by 10 m wide on the east side. On the projecting part there seems to have been a structure with underground beams and thick pillars, which was most likely burnt down as the red charred floor suggests. It remains unknown what existed within the enclosure due to the thick sand covering there. A similar structure exists in Endere Site, which Stein investigated and concluded to have been a walled fort consisting of brick buildings, a building with basement rooms, a livestock shed, and so on, with a Buddhist shrine at the center.

(3) Recovered artifacts

The artifacts recovered at Dandan Oilik Site include pottery, wooden products, metal products, spindle wheels, beads, stone products, terra-cotta figurines, coins, and foot gear.

Pottery

Most of the pottery unearthed within the site is red pottery, classified as pots, jars, and bowls. The typical type of pot reflecting the characteristic of the time has a straight, slightly longer neck, a rim opening outward, a long body and round bottom, and a handle connecting the shoulder and the rim on either side (Fig. 2, 1). Although there are not many decorated examples, some have wavy line patterns, pricked mark patterns, or small dots arranged in herringbone. Others are a long necked pot of dark brown biscuit-ware marked with white stripes under the rim (Fig. 2, 3), a dark brown glazed pot (Fig. 2, 2), and a small green glazed pot (Fig. 2, 4).

Wooden products

The recovered wooden products are tableware, combs, keys (Fig. 2, 8 & 9), and weaving tools. The tableware includes bowls (Fig. 2, 5 & 6) and plates, all lathed and lacquered in black. The weaving tools include a comb-shaped tool used to pack together the weft in carpet weaving (Fig. 2, 7) and a shuttle Uighurs call 'muka' (Fig. 2, 10).

Copper products

Copper vessels, ornamental fittings, and rings were excavated. A bowl, restored to 16.6 cm in diameter and 8.9 cm high, has a thick out-turned rim and a low, stable base, and four grooves are cut along the rim on the outside, below which is another set of three (Fig. 2, 11). A small portable bottle, of a flat spherical shape with a ring-shaped ear on either shoulder, is 4.4 cm high and has an opening 0.9 cm in inside diameter (Fig. 2, 12). A small spoon has a stem 4 by 4 mm square in section and 8.8 cm long and a flat boat-shaped head 1.7 cm long by 0.7 cm wide (Fig. 2, 13). These utensils were probably Buddhist altar fittings.

The recovered copper ornamental fittings consist of a rectangular plate, a square plate, a tube (Fig. 2, 14), and rings in two types: one with a hole which seems to have been set with a jewel (Fig. 2, 15), and the other without a hole (Fig. 2, 16).

Spindle wheels

Red pottery, black pottery, stone, and jade spindle wheels were recovered. The shape ranges from disk, corn to hemisphere, measuring 2.5 cm to 3 cm in diameter.

Beads

Glass, bone, crystal, wood, and earthenware beads were discovered. The glass beads have three varieties: small balls 2.4-4.5 mm in diameter, a 9-mm cube, and

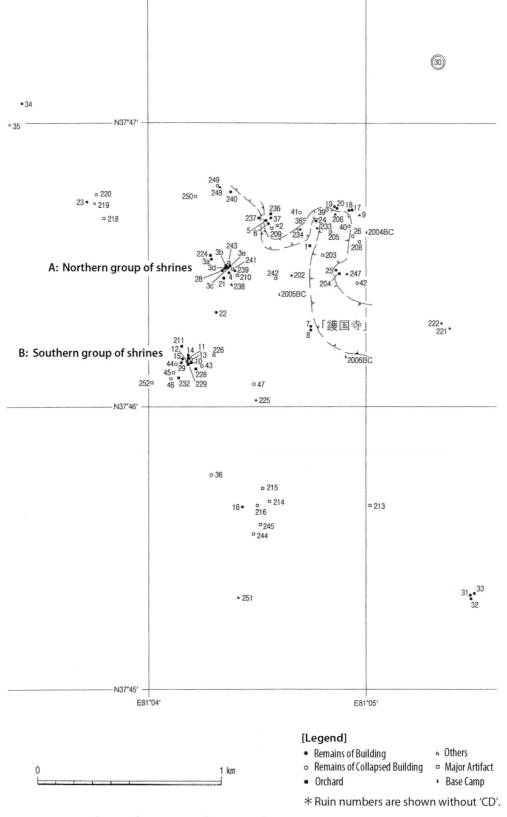

Fig. 1. Distribution of Structures and Major Artifacts

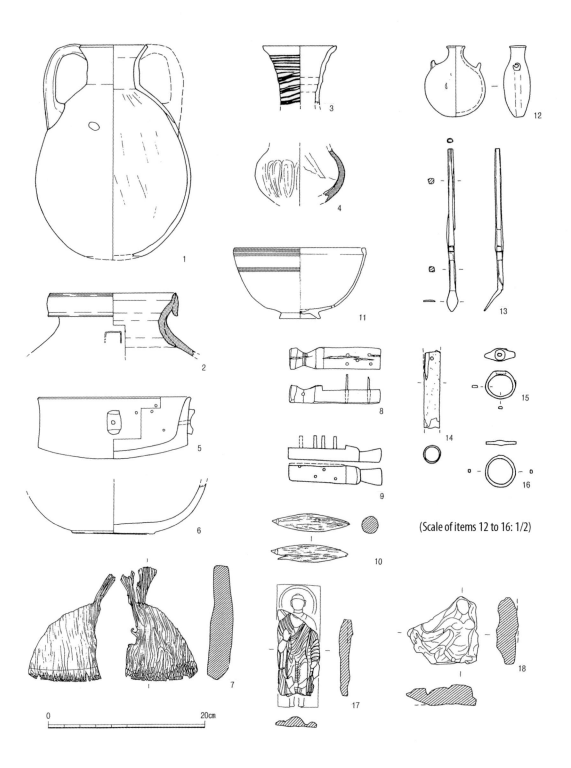

Fig. 2. Major Artifacts from Dandan Oilik Site

a truncated cone 7.5 mm high with a diameter of 7 mm at the bottom. The bone beads are small balls. The crystal bead is a cut work in the shape of a hexagonal column approximately 1.8 cm long. The wooden bead in the shape of a six-petaled flower is 10 mm in diameter and 8 mm high. The earthen beads are spherical and 6.5-10 mm in diameter.

Stone products

Whetstones, stone balls, hammer stones, a stone plate, and stone hand mills were discovered. The stone balls and the hammer stones are spherical and approximately 10 cm in diameter. Among the stone balls, those bearing any use-wear traces of being ground etc. are classified as hammer stones. The stone plate is a disk 22 cm in diameter and 4.4 cm thick, on which no trace of using is observed due to weathering. The stone mills vary in size, two largest ones measuring respectively 55 cm and 80 cm in diameter.

Buddha tiles (Terra-cotta figurines)

Shards of molded terra-cotta include two small relief plates representing a standing Buddha and an Apsaras in flight respectively (Fig. 2, 17 & 18) as well as some ornamental parts probably once fixed on aureoles. The terra-cotta pieces are white, baked fine and hard. They seem to have been colored red and/or black, judging from the pigment still surviving in the pleats and folding on the robes in the relief.

Coins

The 18 coins found there are all copper coins from China: four '開元通宝' ('Kai-yüan tung pao', first minted in 621), one '乹元重宝' ('Ch'ien-yüan', first minted in 758), and the rest are plain coins, most of which seem to be '五銖' ('Wu-chu') coins punched out from official ones.

(4) Characteristics of Dandan Oilik Site

The following are the outlines of the main findings of the archaeological investigation on Dandan Oilik Site and some future research issues.

(i) In the investigation 45 structures were recorded, 15 of which were identified as the remains of Buddhist temples. Temple buildings and temple-related structures account for one third of the whole remains, and further excavation may reveal more. From this, it is possible to consider Dandan Oilik to be a Buddhist site. This supports Stein's conclusion drawn from his 2-week investigation 100 years ago that Dandan Oilik had been a Buddhist sacred place. Some of the temples and shrines were found clustered together in two groups, though the details, including their layout, need to be revealed in further research. One group is what Stain called "southern group of shrines" (CD10-CD15 & CD29). The other (CD3a-CD3e & CD4) is located 500m north of it, here referred to as 'northern group of shrines' correspondingly. In addition, 600-700 m east of 'southern group of shrines' and 'northern group of shrines' is located the temples (CD7 & CD8) where Stein excavated a piece of Chinese document including Chinese characters '護国寺' ('Gokoku-ji', literally meaning 'the guardian temple of the nation'). The two groups of temples and Gokoku-ji are positioned respectively at the vertices of a virtual regular triangle in the middle of the whole site, forming its central core.

The Buddha hall excavated in 2002 has a 回-shaped plan. From this it can be gathered that the building probably had a room enshrining Buddhist images at the center, and that the room was surrounded by a corridor decorated with mural paintings where worshipers performed their clockwise circumambulation.

These findings, including the possible form of worship and the arrangement of the temples, indicate that Dandan Oilik had the character of a Buddhist training seminary.

(ii) Although Dandan Oilik Site clearly shows a character as an ancient Buddhist training seminary, even a trace of stupa has not been found, much less surviving one. The reason that this Buddhist sacred place did not have any stupa should be argued in the context of the changes that took place in the form of Buddhist worship in this area during the Tang period.

(iii) The mural painting of Room f2 found in CD1 represents two vases containing flowers, painted on the eastern and western walls respectively. Although its theme, the reason for painting flower vases there, is unknown, at least it is known that the decorative pattern consisting of lotus flowers sprouting from a vase, called 'purnaghata' (the full vessel), has been revered in Buddhism. In the faith it is believed that the water contained in the vase represents the origin of life and that the lotus flowers in the vase symbolize the origin of the universe as well as fertility and productiveness. The two vases in the wall painting are of the same style, looking just like the pot shown in Fig. 2, 1, having an oblong body with an upright neck and a handle on either side connecting the rim and the shoulder. Thus the pots of this type were probably valued highly at Dandan Oilik.

(iv) A considerable amount of artifacts related to iron and copper goods production, including slag, are widely distributed at a few places in the outskirts of the site, most in the north-western and the southern parts. Around those places were probably situated workshops producing metal articles for use in the Buddhist temples.

References

M. Aurel Stein, *Ancient Khotan: Detailed Report of Archaeological Explo-rations in Chinese Turkestan*, Vol. 1, Oxford University, 1907.

　　日中共同ダンダンウイリク遺跡学術調査隊編　　『日中共同丹丹烏里克遺跡学術調査報告』, 佛教大学アジア宗教文化情報研究所・佛教大学ニヤ遺跡学術研究機構, 2007.

　　浅岡俊夫「ダンダンウイリク ―それは仏教の道場だった―」, 『立命館大学考古学論集』V, 立命館大学, 2010.

contribution 2

Changes in Buddhism and the Styles of Stupa along Xi-yu Nan-dao

Toshio Asaoka
Representative of Archaeological Sites Researching Group at Rokko

(1) The styles of stupa in Central Asia

In early Buddhism, the stupa was one of the most important, indispensable objects. Regarding the ancient stupas in Central Asia, Shoshin Kuwayama, former professor at Kyoto University, points out that the form of stupa changed in three stages as follows: the stupa with a round base (Period I), the stupa with a square base (Period II), and the stupa with a cruciform base (Period III). And Kyuzo Kato, having long been engaged in excavation and research in Uzbekistan, divides the whole change into five stages. The present writer classifies the ancient stupas into five styles, following Kato's theory.

The first style (Style I) appeared in the middle of the third century B.C., when stupas began to be erected in large numbers. Those stupas are supposed to have been hemispherical, just like Sānchī Stupa in India. The stupa in this style is circular in plan, with a circular base on which sits a dome-shaped body. The body is crowned by a 'harmika' (a box-shaped structure or square railing), at the center of which stands a 'chattra' (disk-like stylized parasols attached to a shaft). This style is labeled by Kato as 'the classical hemispherical style'. It corresponds to Period I in Kuwayama's theory.

The establishment of the second style (Style II) is considered to be the epoch-making change in the history of stupa. The form of base underwent a major change from circular into square. In addition, the body has a cylindrical part under the dome, thus tends to take an elongated, bullet-shaped form instead of hemispherical. The square base, which seems to have been only an additional part in the earlier examples, is now terraced with two or three tiers, and the chattra has five to seven disks. Thus stupas have become higher, emphasizing verticality as a whole. This style is called 'the Gāndhāra style', since it was established in Gāndhāra around the first century A.D. during the Kushan period. It corresponds to Period II in Kuwayama's classification.

The third style (Style III) is called 'the Karatepa style' by Kato after Karatepa Buddhist Site in Uzbekistan excavated by him. Although the form of stupa is not very different from that in Style II, the stupa of Style III is characterized by one or two stringcourses (a band-shaped projection with a semicircular section) wound horizontally around the cylindrical part of the body. It is probably in this period that a stairway appeared on one side of the base.

The fourth style (Style IV) is marked by the high, multi-tiered base and a noticeable increase in size. Stairs are provided as access to the terrace on the base. For example, the stupa of Subashi Buddhist Temple in Kucha on Xi-yu Bei-dao has stairs only on the front, while Rawak Stupa in the Khotan area has stairs on each of the four sides. The latter type is referred to as 'the star-shaped type' by Kato and 'the cruciform type' by Kuwayama. Thus Style IV can be divided into two stages: the early stage with stairs only on one side and the later stage with stairs on each of the four sides. It is certain that in the period of the later stage of Style IV worship of Buddhist images was adopted and both stupas and Buddhist statues began to be worshipped.

The fifth style (Style V) is represented by the multi-tiered 'tower-like stupa'. In this style the base has more number of tiers. It probably developed from the stupas with four stairways of the previous style, which had been built widely in Eastern (Chinese) Turkestan, influenced by those in Gāndhāra. In Japan, 土塔 (Doto) of Ono-ji Temple in Sakai and 頭塔 (Zuto) of Todai-ji Temple in Nara were possibly influenced by Style V, though it will need more research in the future to clarify what relation they have.

(2) The styles of stupa along Xi-yu Nan-dao

Stein surveyed a considerable number of ancient Buddhist temples from Kashgar to the area along Xi-yu Nan-dao and put the measured drawings of stupas in his report. In the following part, five stupas comparatively well preserved will be selected from his drawings and each of them will be classified into one of the five styles discussed above.

Style	Subdivision	Stupa
Style I	-	-
Style II	Early Stage	Tōpa-Tim Stupa
	Later Stage	Niya Stupa, Endere Stupa
Style III	-	Maurī-Tim Stupa A
Style IV	Early Stage	-
	Later Stage	Rawak Stupa
Style V	-	Maurī-Tim Stupa B

Table 1. --Development of Stupas in and around the Khotan Area

Any surviving stupa in Style I or 'the classical hemispherical style' with a round base has not discovered so far in the area along Xi-yu Nan-dao, neither along Xi-yu Bei-dao.

Tōpa-Tim Stupa (Fig. 2) in Pishan County, the stupa of Niya Site (Fig. 3 & Fig. 4), and the stupa of Endere Site (Fig. 5) are classified as Style II. Tōpa-Tim Stupa consists of a two-tiered square base, a round base on it, and a hemispherical body on the top. It can be regarded as an early example of Style II. The stupas of Niya Site and Endere Site have a two-tiered square base and a bullet-shaped body standing on it.

Maurī-Tim Stupa in Kashgar (Fig. 1, A & Fig. 7) is an example of Style III. Alongside the stupa A, Maurī-Tim Site has a square terraced structure B (Fig. 1, B & Fig. 7), which Stain considered to have been a Buddhist temple building (the present writer regards it as a ruin of stupa in Style V), as well as the

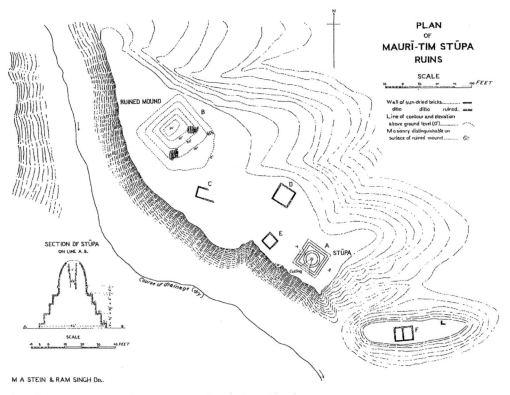

Fig. 1. Plan of Maurī-Tim Site and Cross Section of Stupa (Stain)

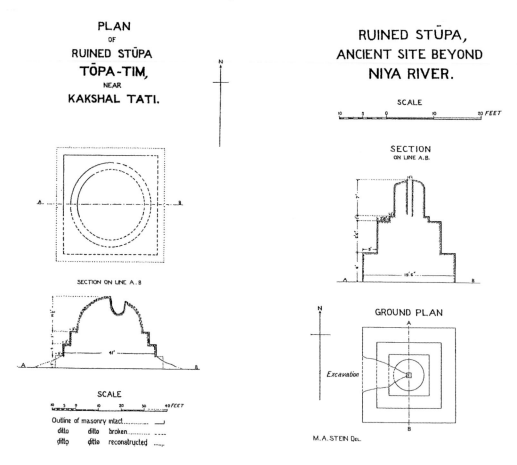

Fig. 2. Plan and Cross Section of Tōpa-Tim Stupa (Stain)   Fig. 3. Plan and Cross Section of Stupa in Niya Site (Stain)

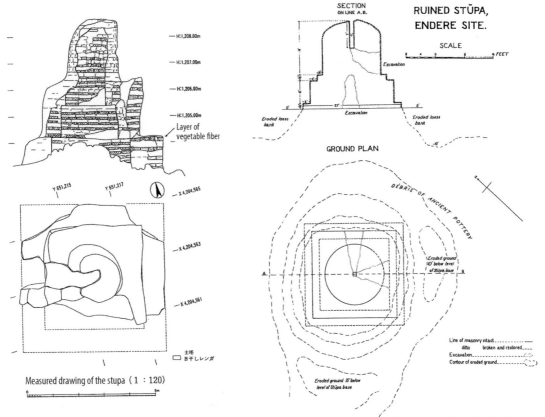

Fig. 4. Plan and Cross Section of Stupa in Niya Site (日中共同ニヤ遺跡学術調査隊)

Fig. 5. Plan and Cross Section of Stupa in Endere Site (Stein)

remains of several buildings (Fig. 1, C-F). The stupa A has a two-tiered square base, a round base on it, and a bullet-shaped body with stringcourses.

Rawak Stupa (Fig. 6) in the Khotan area, a star-shaped (cruciform) stupa with a stairway on each of the four sides, can be classified as Style IV, more precisely, the later stage of Style IV, if the stupa of the early stage has stairs only on the front. This stupa is enclosed by a corridor, whose walls are decorated with rows of Buddhist relief statues in clay. Thus Rawak Stupa indicates the introduction of Buddhist images as objects of worship in addition to stupas and the establishment of 'stupa court', the arrangement of a stupa and an ambulatory around it.

The square terraced structure B in Maurī-Tim Site (Fig. 1, B & Fig. 7) mentioned above is classified as Style V. Although the structure appears to have five tiers in Stein's ground plan, his photographs show it three-tiered. He wrote that it had traces of niches built into the walls, which suggests that it had niches enshrining Buddhist statues.

(3) Conclusion

Considering the change in Buddhism from the styles of stupa in the area along Xi-yu Nan-dao, the introduction of Buddhism into the area can be assigned to the period of Style II, the greatest epoch in the history of stupa. Then, another substantial change is recognized in Style IV. Here the stupa is a remarkably large structure provided with stairs on all four sides of the base. In addition, the

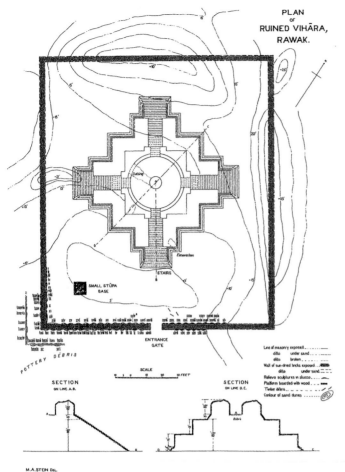

RUINED STŪPA AND MOUND OF MAURĪ TIM, SEEN FROM SOUTH-EAST.

[Picture left]
Fig. 6. Plan and Cross Section of Rawak Stupa (Stein)

[Picture above]
Fig. 7. Photograph of Maurī-Tim Stupa

worship of Buddhist images began in this period. And in Style V, the niches for Buddhist images built into the walls of the tower-like, multi-tiered stupa show the integration of stupa worship and image worship.

Concerning that there is no stupa in Dandan Oilik Site, a Buddhist site, significant clues are found in Domoko Buddhist Site in Cele County contemporary with Dandan Oilik and the results of the excavation in Nāgārjunakoṇḍa Temple Site in central India. The former does not have any stupa either, and in the latter it is revealed that the component of the temple developed in four steps: (1) stupas and viharas (priests' quarters), (2) stupas, viharas, and shrines enshrining stupas, (3) stupas, viharas, and shrines enshrining Buddhist statues, (4) viharas and shrines enshrining Buddhist statues. These things suggest that stupas, which had been the main objects of worship in early Buddhism, were gradually replaced by Buddhist images since the latter's appearance. The change and development in the form of temple in India could have had a great influence on Buddhist worship practiced in Xi-yu (the Western Regions of China.) When Faxian visited Xi-yu in A.D. 399, stupas were still commonly worshipped there. Two hundred years later, stupa worship had become extinct and Buddhist images were the sole object of worship. It is possible to consider that Dandan Oilik Site reflects this epoch-making change in Buddhist faith.

References

桑山正進「Shan-ji-ki Dheri主塔の遷變」,『東方学報』京都第67冊, 1995.

加藤九祚「カラ・テパのストゥーパの起源と特徴　―北伝仏教におけるストゥーパの展開―」,『ウズベキスタン考古学新発見』東方出版, 2002.

M. Aurel Stein, *Ancient Khotan: Detailed Report of Archaeological Explorations in Chinese Turkestan*, vol. 1 text, Oxford University, 1907.

日中共同ニヤ遺跡学術調査隊『日中共同尼雅遺跡学術調査報告書』第2巻, 1999.

張馭寰『中国仏塔史』科学出版社, 2006.

日中共同ダンダンウイリク遺跡学術調査隊編『日中共同丹丹烏里克遺跡学術調査報告』佛教大学アジア宗教文化情報研究所・佛教大学ニヤ遺跡学術研究機構, 2007.

浅岡俊夫「ダンダンウイリク　―それは仏教の道場だった―」,『立命館大学考古学論集』V, 2010.

浅岡俊夫「西域南道における仏教信仰の変遷　―ホータン地区周辺の仏塔を中心にして―」,『立命館大学考古学論集』VI, 2013.

中国社会科学院考古研究所新疆考古隊「策勒県タマゴゥ仏寺遺跡発掘調査報告」註14の付録.

長澤和俊『法顕伝　訳注解説　北宋本・南宋本・高麗大蔵経本・石山寺本四種影印とその比較研究』雄山閣, 1996.

西川幸治『仏教文化の原郷をさぐる―インドからガンダーラまで―』NHKブックス473, 1985, p. 185.

H. Sarkar, "Some aspects of the Buddhist monuments at Nagarjunakonda," *ANCIENT INDIA: Bulletin of the Archaeological Survey of India*, No. 16, 1960.

contribution 3

Lining in the painting of Xinjiang : from Silk Route down to Japan

Yoshika Ando

Professor, Department of Historical Culture Bukkyo University, Kyoto, Japan

Murals found by the Chinese-Japanese joint excavated team in the Dandan-oilik Site in 2010 have shocked the academia field of the Buddhist art with outstanding quality and supreme vast quantity, which in the meanwhile open a new chapter of the study of Buddhist art in Silk Route sub-area. In order to protect and move to further level of study those murals, after being transferred to the Xinjiang Archaeological Research Institute, the Dandan-oilik project had been summoned. Writer of the article had been gladly participated in the project, and able to join the fieldwork of the Dandan-oilik Site in Takla Makan in 2004. Conservation of mural have been jointly completed in 2007 by Chinese and Japanese scholars [1]. Those lately discovered murals bears distinguished features that different them from other Asian Buddhist art, and can be dated between 6th and 7th centuries. From an art historical perspective, the use of lining represents the most profound feature of those murals. The aim of this article is try to link the connection of the use of lining between murals of the Dandan-oilik Site and of Main Hall (Kon-do) of the Horyu-ji Temple in Japan through analysis murals from above sites and murals of Dharmago No.1 niche where near the Dandan-oilik Site.

1. Iron-wire Line Drawing (Tessenbyou; CHN: Tiexianmiao)

Weichi Yiseng was a famous painter from the royal court of the Khotan kingdom. According to Zhang Yanyuan in the famous Lidai- minghua-ji, Weichi Yiseng was regarded as one of the three most renowned painters of the time, and painted murals in various temples in Luoyang from the late 7th century to early 8th century. His brother, Weichi Jiaseng, a talent painter stayed in the hometown of Khotan kingdom while their father, Weichi Bazhi was also renowned painter in Sui dynasty (581-618 AD) [2]. Tremendously contract to his father's bold brushstrokes, Weichi Yiseng delicates to an highly modulate style which Zhang Yanyuan describes as 'bending iron-wire'.

In Japan, iron-wire line drawing is normally employed to describe lining of Main Hall of Horyu-ji Temple, and a number of temples dating to Nara and Heian period are also employed iron-wire lining. Taki Seiichi (1873 – 1945) pointed out that skills as iron-wire lining and chiaroscuro of murals of Main Hall are spread from Xinjiang region, in particular belongs to the style of Weichi Yiseng [3].

Taki mentioned murals of Main Hall resemble a lining style that slim but highly elastic, which he regarded as what Zhang Yanyuan means 'bending iron-wire', however, Taki's statement is only commons without specific examples.

2. Dandan-oilik Site and Dharmago No.1 Niche

Lining of the lately discovered murals of Dandan-oilik Site reminded the bending iron-wire style. Among those murals, the most profound one is the standing Tathagata (fig. 1). Outline drew in depicting the standing buddha is fluent and elastic, which expresses the artist was working in an relax and confident mood. Such style resembles bending iron-wire line drawing, and represents a sense of intense, which is the elixir of the style. It led the viewer walks into a world full of subtle emotions that expressed from lines. Depiction of the hands also represents the elegantly use of lining. Fingertips of the left hand of the buddha full of elasticity (fig. 2), and the rounded depiction of the left hand holding cloth edge (fig. 3).

Outline used in depicting the seating buddha image in the scene of Tathagata with deities (fig. 4) is a fixed highly modulated slim line which resembles the iron-wire line. In other scenes of Tathagata (fig. 5), outlines are also painted in such iron-wire line, but slightly wider than in the figure 4. Those delicate touches are so refine it seems artist was holding breath when depicted them.

In contract with the refine outline, lines used in depicting drapery are bold and full of movements. In the standing Tathagata scene, lines depicting drapery in the torso are expressive and bold. The vast use of draperies also implies the divine body of the buddha. The seating buddha image in figure 4 depicting fluent lines of drapery in collar and elbows, full of energy and movements. There is an obvious distinction between lines used in outline and drapery depiction.

Murals of the Dharmago No.1 Niche near the Dandan-oilik Site are also expresses distinctive use of lines in different sections. The standing figure in the south wall on east side bears outline depicted in strong iron-wire style, which contract to the lines used in the waist to depict the fluent movements of draperies (fig. 6). The Standing image of Vaisravana in the west side of south wall shows dominantly use of iron-wire lines in depiction of outline with minimal amount of soft and delicate brushstrokes in the drapery of left shoulder. Outline of the Tathagata in the north side of west wall is painted in iron-wire style however drapery is fulfill with delicate touches, and same as the Tathagata images in the

Fig. 1. Standing Tathagata (detail), Dandan-oilik Site

Fig. 2. Standing Tathagata (detail), Dandan-oilik Site

Fig. 3. Standing Tathagata (detail), Dandan-oilik Site

Fig. 4. Tathagata and deties (detail), Dandan-oilik Site

Fig. 5. Tathagata, Dandan-oilik Site

Fig. 6. standing celestial being, Dharmago No.1 Niche

east and north wall. In summary, murals of the Dharmago No.1 Niche represents iron-wire outline combines with soft touches in drapery depiction, which is identical to the murals of Dandan-oilik Site.

3. Further research in 'Bending Iron-wire' style

Here the writer wish to analysis the 'bending iron-wire' style (qutie pansi) of Weichi Yiseng as recorded in Lidai-minghua-ji. 'Qutie' refers to bending iron, which as Taki interrupts as 'bending something with great elasticity', however, 'pansi' means wreathe silk thrums refers to soft and delicate lines, which is on the exactly opposite of meaning of 'qutie'. It can be regarded that 'qutiepansi' style is consisted by two parts. The outline lines and refine light lines with movements in drapery section are both employed in murals of the Dandan-oilik Site and Dharmago No.1 Niche.

I'n summary, pansi' or wreathe silk thrum style can be used as a line drawing style that use to depict drapery, and also a comment for group of lines with movements. Thus, Zhang Yanyuan in his work was comment style of Weichi Yiseng in outline of figures and drapery depiction, respectively.

4. Murals of Main Hall (Kon-do) of the Horyu-ji Temple

Out of total twelve large murals in Main Hall, No.6 is the fineness (fig. 7). The mural expresses Gupta style through the depiction of three figures and halo and the Gupta style arabesque pattern in the lotus base of the middle figure [4]. The iron-wire here are wider than usually seen (fig. 8), and lines used to depict fingers are fluent which close to the Tathagate image in Dandan-oilik Site (fig. 9). Lines in the No.1 are wider than No.6 and full of elasticity. No.2 is more delicate

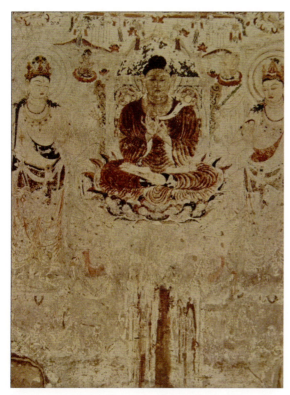

Fig. 7. murals (detail), Main Hall: Wall No.6, Horyuji Temple (The Horyuji temple2, Otsukakogei,1934)

Fig. 8. murals (detail), Main Hall: Wall No.6, Horyuji Temple (The Horyuji temple 2, Otsukakogei,1934)

Fig. 9. murals (detail), Main Hall:Wall No.6, Horyuji Temple (The Horyuji temple 2, Otukakogei, 1934)

Fig. 10. murals (detail), Main Hall:Wall No.1, Horyuji Temple (The Horyuji temple 2, Otukakogei, 1934)

Fig. 11. Sakyamuni descending the mountain after asceticism, (Chinese paintings of buddhism in foreign collections, Hunan Fine Arts Publishing House, 2001)

and expresses soft emotions not seen in the No.6. Thus, from the murals in Main Hall, it is clearly that difference still exists in the general style of iron-wire outline lining.

In depiction of the drapery, the seating buddha image of the No.6 displays a extensive use of fine lines in kumadori style, which empahsis the roundness of the body beneath. Lines in shoulder, sleeves, and belly are almost parallel, while lines of right knee reveal the shape of the body. In close comparison with the middle figure of the No.1, it is obvious that the No.1 tries to conceals the body shape and turn drapery into a stylistic representation (fig. 10). No.6 in the other hand, employs a transformed style of iron-wire lining, which is also a distinctive feature of the Gupta style No.6. It is also seen in Sakyamuni descending the mountain after asceticism (North Song, Washington Museum, fig. 11) in Weichi Yiseng style that details of the drapery are in form of wreathe thrums, and close the middle figure of the No.6.

In conclusion, the article points out that the two lining styles are correspondence to records of the Lidai-minghua-ji through analysis murals of Dandan-oilik Site, and those lining methods are also seen in Main Hall. There should be no doubt that the discovery of the actual examples identifying various contacts between Japan and the faraway Western Regions will lead to further research activities in the future.

Footnote

(1) <Dandan Oilik site, archaeological studies, research report into an ancient town in Xinjiang, China> 2007 ,Center for Asian Religious Culture of Bukkyo University The Academic Research Organization for the Niya Ruin
(2) Zhu jing-xuan <Lidai-minghua-ji>
(3) Taki Seiichi <the Painting of Horyuji Temple> (Vol.1) (Vol.2) < A monthly journal of Oriental art>, No.315, No.316, 1916 (<Taki Setuan bijyutu ronsyu>, 1943, Zauho Kankoukai)
(4) Yoshika Ando < Studies on Solema in Buddhist Art : the eastward spread of the Gupta-style Scroll> Chūōkōronbijutsushuppan, 2003

contribution 4

Topography and Geology of the Niya Site

Shiro Ishida
Former Professor of Yamaguchi University

1. Introductory remarks

During fieldwork conducted in 1997 at the Niya Site as part of a Japanese-Chinese joint research project, the author took part from October 20 to 27 and surveyed the area north of the stupa. The resulting report (Ishida, 2007) showed that the strata at the site are composed of river/lake sediments forming hills, and that these sediments are older than the terrace sediments. Paleomagnetism, diatom, and pollen/spore analysis of mudstone samples from the site was carried out by respective specialists. For the present report, two new samples of pollen and spores have been added, and a new opinion about an equine fossil uncovered at the site has been offered by Prof. H. Nakaya. A vast number of papers concerning the petroleum geology of the Tarim Basin, where the Niya Site is located, have been published in Chinese and English, but for the Basin's general topography and geology, the author here cites various recent Japanese sources.

2. Niya Formation and samples

The hill area of the the Niya Site consists of an alternation of mudstone and sandy layers. The mudstone is fairly well consolidated, but not rock-hard. These sediments were deposited in the delta of a large lake. The beds are flat and show only a low dip.

The sampling sites and kinds of sample taken at each site are shown in Figure 1 and Table 1. The samples for paleomagnetism are designated as A–D, those for diatoms as a–d, and those for

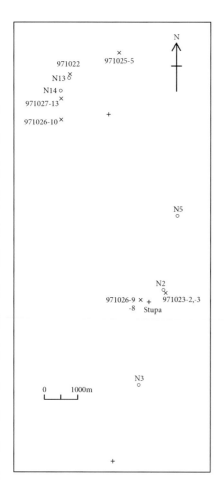

Figure 1 Sampling sites at the Niya Site.

Table 1 Samples of Niya Area.

Sample No.	Pollen	Diatom	Paleomagnetism	Sampling site	Latitude	Longitude	Altitude
971023-2	c		A	Southeast of N2	37°58′ 42″	82°43′ 33″	1,200m
-3		Molluscan fossils		---	---	---	---
25-5	a		B	About 1600m ENE of N13	38°02′ 27″	82°42′ 45″	about 1,190m
26-9	d	a	D	Upper layer of sample-8	37°58′ 35″	82°43′ 09″	1,200m
-8	b		C	WNW of Stupa	---	---	---
26-10		b		About 800m south of N14	38°01′ 29″	82°41′ 35″	1,193m
27-13A		c		Upper layer of sample-13B	38°01′ 49″	82°41′ 35″	1,193m
-13B		d		About 200m south of N14	---	---	---
971022	Equus bone fossil, distal end of right humerus			About 50m NEN of N13	38°02′ 09″	82°41′ 46″	1,192m

pollen and spores as a-d. Molluscan fossils and an equine fossil are also shown.

3. Paleomagnetism (Tadashi Nakajima)

The magnetic susceptibility of the four mudstone samples was almost the same (Table 2). The intensity of natural remanent magnetization was strongest in sample A, but of similar magnitude in all four samples. All samples showed stable magnetic behaviors during alternating-field demagnetization experiments and had magnetic components of normal polarity.

Table 2 Magnetic character of the samples from the Niya Site. (Tadashi Nakajima)

Sample	Magnetic susceptibility ($\mu m^3 kg^{-1}$)	Magnetic intensity ($\times 10^{-5}$ emu/g)
A	0.1245	8.1
B	0.1609	3.2
C	0.1245	1.7
D	0.1635	3.3

4. Diatoms (Yasuyo Noguchi)

Individual diatoms were not very numerous in the four mudstone samples. Eleven genera and 15 species were found, with abundances and ecological characteristics as shown in Table 3. The four samples were similar in numbers of individuals found for each species, with centric and planktonic diatoms comprising

Table 3 Diatom counts of the samples from the Niya Site. (Yasuyo Noguchi)

Species /Samples	a	b	c	d	Ecology
Cyclotella striata	–	–	–	0.9	Brackish-marine littoral plankton
Melosira varians	27.0	48.5	42.1	46.2	Fresh-brackish water, littoral
Cymbella affinis	1.4	3.0	–	2.6	Freshwater periphyton
Cymbella tumida	–	–	2.6	0.8	Freshwater periphyton
Diatoma vulgaris	4.9	1.5	4.0	2.6	Freshwater, psychrophilic flowing water
Eunotia septentrionealis	3.7	–	–	–	Freshwater, mainly inhabiting in peaty moors
Fragilaria construens	37.0	45.5	21.1	42.7	Freshwater littoral
Fragilaria intermedia	2.4	–	15.	–	Freshwater littoral
Fragilaria ulna	7.3	1.5	4.0	2.6	Freshwater littoral
Furustlia amphipleuroides	2.4	–	–	–	Freshwater
Gomphonema olivaceum	2.4	–	4.0	0.8	Freshwater, seems to prefer flowing water
Gomphonema truncatum	–	–	2.6	0.8	Freshwater
Pinnularia submicrostauron	1.5	–	–	–	Freshwater, epipelon
Rhopalodia gibba	–	–	2.6	–	Freshwater, epiphyton
Surirella linearis	–	–	1.2	–	Freshwater, periphyton
Centrale %	37.0	48.5	42.1	47.1	
Plankton %	38.7	45.5	23.7	43.6	
River, torrent species %	18.4	6.0	17.2	10.2	
Psychrophilic species %	4.9	1.5	4.0	2.6	
Peat, swamp species %	3.7	–	–	–	
Adapted salt water species %	39.4	48.5	46.1	47.0	

about 40%, and river species about 10% of the total; 54% of the 15 species were river species. This indicates that the sediment was deposited in a big river or in the delta of a big river in a lake.

5. Pollen and spores (Nobuo Ooi)

The pollen and spores isolated from the four mudstone samples comprised 22 kinds in total, including 11 arboreal pollen types, 10 non-arboreal pollen types, and one type of fern spore (Table 4). Most of the pollen grains were degraded and crumpled, and often difficult to identify, in which case they were recorded as "unknown".

The occurrence of pollen of xerophytic plants such as Chenopodiaceae/Amaranthaceae, *Artemisia*, and *Ephedra* indicates an arid environment. These pollen types were dominant in all samples, and the other, more rarely-occurring types also included several plants that prefer dry environments, such as *Tamarix*, *Allium*, *Salix*, and *Elaeagnus*. The pollen assemblages obtained in this study correspond to a dry environment, such as a desert or steppe.

Table 4 Pollen and spore counts of the samples from the Niya Site. (Nobuo Ooi)

Types	sample no.	a	c	d	b
[arboreal pollen]					
Ephedra		18	20	2	16
Cedrus			3		2
Pinus		1	2		3
Cupressaceae			1		
Salix					1
Quercus					1
Ulmus			2		
Rhamnaceae		1	1		
Vitis			1		1
Elaegnus				1	1
Tamarix					2
[nonarboreal pollen]					
Typha		1			
Gramineae		14	9	2	5
Cyperaceae		4	1		1
Allium		1			
Chenopodiaceae / Amaranthaceae		44	25	8	27
Rosaceae		1	2	2	
Leguminosae					2
Compositae subfam. Carduoideae		2		1	2
Artemisia		30	26	3	23
Compositae subfam. Cichorioideae					2
[fern spores]					
monolete spores		3	5	6	
Unknown		71	26	13	70
total arboreal pollen		20	30	3	27
total nonarboreal pollen		97	63	16	62
total fern spores		3	5	6	0
total pollen and spores		120	98	25	89

6. Molluscan fossils

The southeast cliff at the site of the N2 ruin crops out as thick claystone with intercalated thin beds of sand. The claystone contains the casts of shells of freshwater Bivalvia belonging to the Legion Paleoheterodonta: Order Unioida: Superfamily Unionacea.

 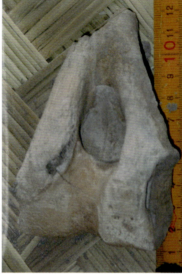 

Fossil distal end of the equine right humerus

Dorsal view   Caudal view   Distal view

Caudal view of distal end of right humerus embedded in laminated clay stone and fine sandstone.

Caudal view from slightly medial side   Caudal view from slightly distal side   Caudal view from slightly lateral and distal side

Figure 2 An equine fossil from the Niya Site.

7. An equine fossil

The distal end of an equine right humerus was found in laminated claystone and fine sandstone about 50 m northeast of the N13 ruin (Figs. 1, 2, 12). Prof. H. Nakaya (Kagoshima University) believes, based on his examination of photographs, that this fossil is not of the extinct genus *Hipparion*, but represents the extant genus *Equus*. The maximal distal width of humeri of Pliocene to Lower Pleistocene *Hipparion* of China is 73–75 mm whereas that of the extinct *Equus sanmeniensis* is 85 mm (Qiu *et al*., 1987). The comparable measure of the specimen from the Niya Site is 80–85 mm, judging from photographs. Direct observation and measurement of the specimen is desirable.

8. Geological setting of the Niya Site

The Niya Site is situated in the lower reaches of the Niya River, which flows to the north from the Kunlun Mountains in the southern part of the Tarim Basin. The Basin is a tectonic platform, part of the continental shield, covered by flat-lying Paleozoic to Mesozoic strata that are underlain by Precambrian basement rocks.

Continental China is situated in the East Asian part of the Eurasian Plate and consists of the Sino-Korean platform, the Yangtze Platform, the Tarim Platform, and others. The platforms are surrounded by folded and faulted sediment zones of Paleozoic to Mesozoic accretion. Large earthquakes occur in these zones, well within the continent. Taira and Tashiro (1987) presented a simplified accretionary tectonic map of East Asia (Fig. 3). In the continental domain, the geotectonic units consist of blocks, accretionary fold belts, suture zones and thrust fold belt etc. The Siberian block is composed of shields, a platform, and the Sajany early Paleozoic accretionary fold belt. The Junggar Block is probably an early Paleozoic accretionary fold belt. The Tsaidam and North Tibet blocks may be platforms.

The Indian Plate moving to the north has collided with the North Tibet platform of the Eurasian Plate, and the oceanic sediments between the two blocks have been compressed, folded, faulted, and accreted to the Eurasian Plate to form the Himalaya Mountains. The Kunlun Mountains, with an ice cap at elevations higher than 6000 m, represent a late Paleozoic Kunlun accretionary fold belt situated between the North Tibet and Tarim blocks. The Tarim Basin sits north of the Kunlun Mountains. It is spindle-shaped, extending about 1400 km east and west and about 550 km north and south.

The Tarim Basin is a platform on which strata since the Paleozoic have been piled up on Precambrian basement rocks. The North Minfeng Upheaval (Yang *et al*., 1995) is located on the left bank of the lower reaches of the Niya River, which flows into the Basin, and Mazar Tagh Mountain is located on the left bank of the lower reaches of the Hotan River, which also flows into the Basin from the Kunlun Mountains. The upheaval consists of Precambrian rocks and Neogene strata, while the mountain is composed of strata deposited since the Paleozoic. This pattern shows that an east-west belt of older rocks rose to the earth's surface from deep underground along faults running WNW to ESE, and that the northward movement of the Indian Plate resulted in a rupture of the basement rocks of this Eurasian Plate platform.

The following geological profile of the Tarim Basin is from Matsumoto (2006). The Cenozoic Erathem is not shown in Cai (1997), but has been added to Kang's (1996) isopach map of the Neogene and Quaternary system by the author (Fig. 4). The Neogene and Quaternary sediments are over 8000 m thick in the western part of the Basin, less than 500 m thick in the western central part, and 1000–2000 m thick over a wide area of the Basin.

In the northern foot of the Kunlun Mountains, Pleistocene gravel beds are mainly found underground, dipping northwards from about 3000 m elevation. Fifty km farther north, the slope surface is lower, at 1500 m, and 30 km still farther north, it is at 1350 m. The Niya Site is situated at about 1200 m elevation. The lowest point of Lop Nur at the east end of the Tarim Basin, the lowest point in the Basin, is 780 m.

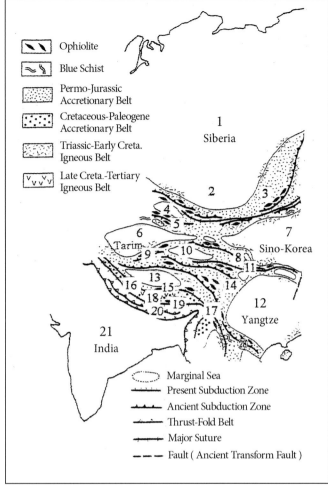

Figure 3 Simplified accretionary tectonic map of east Asia
(adapted from Taira and Tashiro, 1987)

Continental domain geotectonic units: 1: Siberian block, 2: Sajany early Paleozoic accretionary fold belt, 3: Altay-Hinggan late Paleozoic accretionary fold belt, 4: Junggar block, 5: Tien Shan accretionary fold belt, 6: Tarim block, 7: Sino-Korean block, 8: Qilian-Northern Qinling accretionary fold belt, 9: Late Paleozoic Kunlun accretionary fold belt. 10: Tsaidam block, 11: Southern Qinling-Dablei Shan suture zone, 12: Yangtze block, 13: Northern Tibet block, 14: Baryanhar Shan accretionary fold belt, 15: Southern Tanggula-Gerze accretionary fold belt, 16: Rutog-Dengqen suture zone, 17: Lancang River suture zone , 18: South Tibet accretionary fold belt, 19: Yarlung-Zanbo River suture zone, 20: Himalayan thrust fold belt, 21: Indian block.

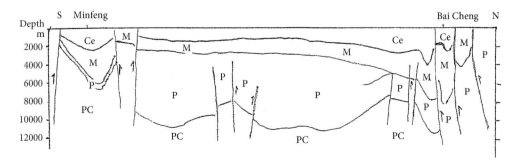

Ce : Cenozoic Erathem   M : Mesozoic Erathem   P : Paleozoic Erathem   PC : Precambrian Rocks

Figure 4 North-south geological profile of Tarim Basin
(simplified from Cai, C. , 1997 in Matsumoto, 2006)

9. Geologic age of Niya Formation

The basic evidence for ascertaining the geologic age of the Niya Formation is as follows:

1. The mudstone and claystone are consolidated as soft, not hard rock.
2. Casts of fossil shells are present.
3. A fossil of the equine genus *Equus* was found.
4. The paleomagnetism is normal.
5. The landform is hilly.

10. Niya Formation and the K1 core at Lop Nur

The pollen profiles of the Niya samples and the K1 core at Lop Nur are compared in Fig. 5. They more or less resemble each other. In the Niya sample, Tamarix and Typha were rare, and Picea and Abies were absent, but Cedrus was found.

Yan *et al.* (1997: table 1) described the lithology and layer thickness of the Lop Nur core. Above layer 17, there are 17.05 m of clay, and below layer 18 there is only mudstone. The clay is of Upper Pleistocene and Holocene age, while the mudstone is Middle and Lower Pleistocene (Fig. 6). The mudstone, lithology, and normal paleomagnetism of the Niya Formation indicate a Middle Pleistocene age.

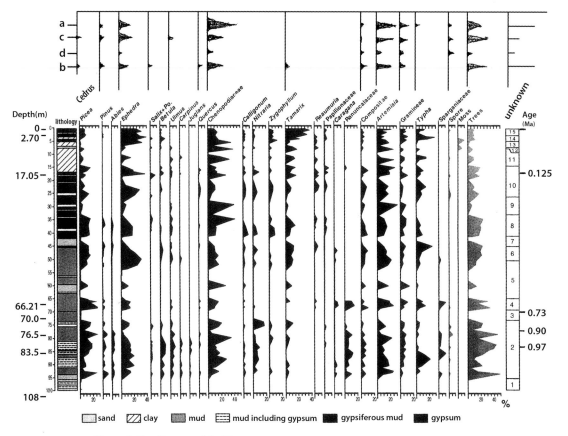

Upper: Pollen diagram of the Niya site

Lower: Pollen diagram of the K1 core at Lop Nur (from S. Yan, G. Mu *et al.*, 1997)

Figure 5 Pollen diagram of the Niya samples and the K1 core at the Lop Nur

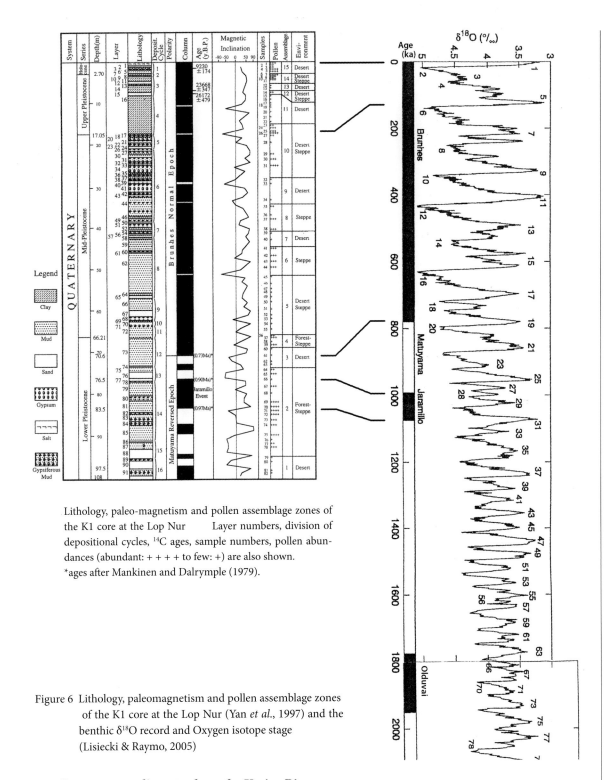

Lithology, paleo-magnetism and pollen assemblage zones of the K1 core at the Lop Nur   Layer numbers, division of depositional cycles, ¹⁴C ages, sample numbers, pollen abundances (abundant: + + + + to few: +) are also shown.
*ages after Mankinen and Dalrymple (1979).

Figure 6 Lithology, paleomagnetism and pollen assemblage zones of the K1 core at the Lop Nur (Yan et al., 1997) and the benthic $\delta^{18}O$ record and Oxygen isotope stage (Lisiecki & Raymo, 2005)

11. Quaternary sediments along the Keriya River

Compared to the Niya River, the Keriya River has a larger catchment area in the Kunlun Mountains and longer lower reaches (Fig. 7). The river terraces in its upper to middle reaches were described by Sohma et al. (1993) (cf. Fig. 8A and Fig. 9A). Five terraces (I–V) were discriminated between elevations of about 2200 m and 3000 m. The terrace-III plain at about 2600 m is correlated with the wide fan plain in the river's middle reaches. The age of relics recovered from loess on the terrace-II plain is 14.86 ka, and this plain is correlated with the terrace-E plain in the river's lower reaches (Fig. 8B). The river terraces of the lower reaches were designated as F to A from higher to lower, and they are younger than Oxygen Isotope Stage 6 (Fig. 6). Terrace IV is correlated with Oxygen Isotope Stage 5, the Last Interglacial Stage.

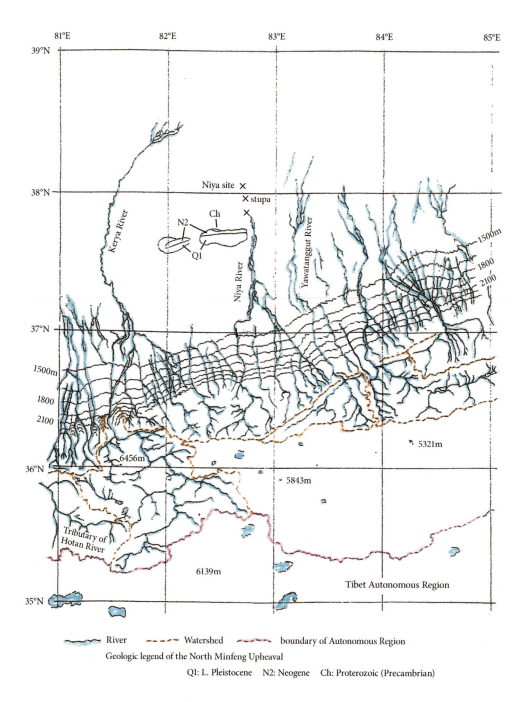

Figure 7 Map of Keriya, Niya, and Yawatanggut river systems

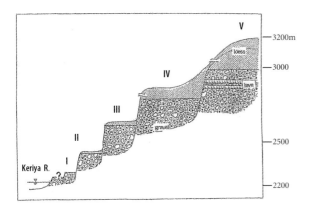
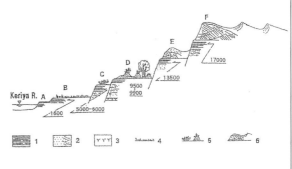

A Schematic profile of river terraces from Pulu to Kangsulak in the upper to middle reaches of the Keriya River (from Endo *et al.*, in print)

B Schematic profile of river terraces with ^{14}C age from Yutien to north of Bulak in the lower reaches of Keriya River (modified from Endo *et al.*, in print).
1. silt, clay, 2. fluvial sand, 3. organic material, 4. reeds, 5. vegetation (*Tamarix*) cones,
6. large linear sand dune, barchan dune.

Figure 8 River terraces in the upper to middle reaches of the Keriya River (Sohma *et al.*, 1993)

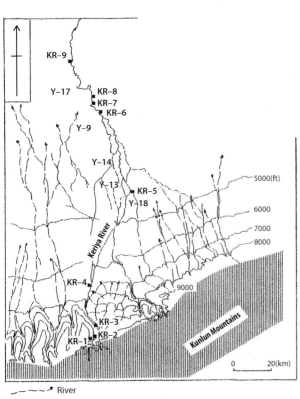
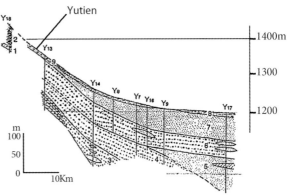

[Fig. left] A Survey area and locality of geological sites (modified from Sohma *et al.*, 1993)
KR–1 Pulu, KR–3 Kangsulak, KR–4 Nuerlankan,
KR–5 Yutien, KR–6 Yougantaklak,
KR–8 north of Bulak, KR–9 Chunmazer

[Fig. above] B Geologic profile of the southern part of Tarim Basin, based on borehole data along middle to lower reaches of Keriya River
(added to Cao and Xia, 1993 in Endo *et al.*, 1997)
Y7–Y18, borehole numbers
1–9, stratigraphic divisions

Figure 9 Borehole data along middle to lower reaches of Keriya River

The following geologic profile of the middle and lower reaches of the Keriya River was reproduced by Endo *et al.* (1997) from Cao and Xia (1993) (Fig. 9 B). Stratigraphic division 4 is 1.2–1.4 Ma (Lower Pleistocene, Matuyama Reversed Epoch), and division 6 is Middle Pleistocene. The relevant borehole sites were not shown in Cao & Xia's (1993) figure, but the present author has added the elevations and the site of Yutien to it based on the slope profile.

12. Niya Formation and the Niya riverbed

The Niya lake sediment consists of mudstone and sand and forms a hilly landscape. The sediment at the Niya Site was deposited more than 100 km north of the foot of the Kunlun Mountains in a delta of the big lake that then filled the Tarim Basin. It may include sediment transported by two rivers from the east and the west, the Keriya and Yawatanggut Rivers, respectively.

The Niya riverbed at the foot of the mountains consists of gravel, changing into finer particles farther north. The photograph in Fig. 10 shows the Niya Formation eroded by the Niya River, not Niya riverbed sediments per se.

In conclusion, a photograph of the locality at which the equine fossil was found (Fig. 11) and the geological profile along the Niya River (Fig. 12) are presented. The photograph, taken from the N30°E direction, shows laminated sediments tilted to the southeast with a low dip as well as the N13 ruin on top of the hill.

Acknowledgements

The author thanks T. Nakajima, Y. Noguchi, and N. Ooi for their laboratory work and also H. Nakaya for his opinion concerning the equine fossil. The English of an earlier draft was checked by Mark J. Grygier, Lake Biwa Museum.

Figure 10 Niya, through the dried up Niya River to the Ruins of the Southern Castle Walls (Matsumoto, 2006)

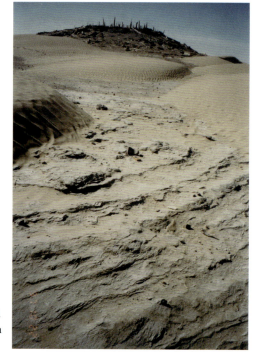

Figure 11 Locality of the equine fossil and N13 ruin viewed from N30°E

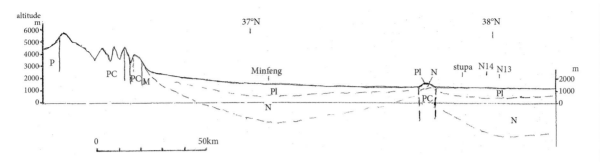

Pl: Pleistocene Series   N: Neogene System   M: Miocene Erathem   P: Paleozoic Erathem   PC: Precambrian Rocks

Figure 12 Geological profile along Niya River

References

Endo, K., Yan, S., Kanemaki, M., Sohma, H. and Mu, G. 1997 Evolution of Paleoenvironments in Tarim Basin—Focussed on the development of Taklimakan Desert—   Jour. Geography Vol.106, No.2, pp.145–155

Ishida, S. 2007 Topography and Geology of Niya Site   Research Report of the Sino-Japanese Joint Research of the Niya Site Vol.3, pp.203–212 (in Japanese)

Matsumoto, Yukio 2006 Phantom Lou Lan Mystery of Lop Nur   Touka Book 459p. Fukuoka (in Japanese)

Qiu, Z., Huang, W. and Guo, Z. 1987 The Chinese Hipparionine Fossils   Palaeontologia Sinica   Whole No. 175   New Series C, No. 25   Science press 249p. 47 plates (in Chinese and English)

Sohma, H., Endo, K., Watanabe, M., Kanemaki, M., Fujikawa, K., Hamada, S., Xia, X.-C., Cao, Q.-Y., Mu, G.-J. and Zhao, Y.-J. 1993 Environmental Change in the Taklimakan Desert since the Latest Pleistocene Based on Terraces and Sand Dunes, in the Case of Kerya River Region   Transactions, Japanese Geomorphological Union Vol.14, No.3, pp.245–263 (in Japanese with English abstract)

Taira, A. and Tashiro, M. 1987 Late Paleozoic and Mesozoic Accretion Tectonics in Japan and Eastern Asia   in Taira and Tashiro ed. Historical Biogeography and Plate Tectonic Evolution of Japan and Eastern Asia   Terra Sci. Pub., Tokyo 221p., pp.1–43

Yan, S., Mu, G., Xiu, Y., Zhao, Z. and Endo, K. 1997 Environmental Evolution of the Lop Nur Region in Tarim Basin since Early Pleistocene   Quaternary Res. (Daiyonki Kenkyu) Vol.36, No.4, pp.235–248 (in English with Japanese abstract)

Yang, Y., Zhou, X., Zhao, J. and Li, S. 1995 Comparing Research of Geology and Geomorphology of Two Highlands (Mazar Tagh and North Minfeng Upheaval) in the Interior of Taklimakan Desert   Environment and People of the Southern Taklimakan Desert (Hosei University) 225p., pp.169–175 (in Chinese with English abstract)

contribution5

Remains related to Buddhism at the point 93A35 (N5), Niya, Xinjiang

Kiyomi Tanaka

Tezukayama Gakuin University

Sir Marc Aurel Stein overtook three excavations at the city site of Niya and gathered a lot of relics, including literal materials such as wooden records with a Chinese chronical remark of AD. 269, and with Kharosthi letters.

In 1995 and 1996, a century after Stein's excavations, Japan-China joint scholarly research team carried out an excavation at the point of 93A35 (N5) and made some new discoveries: Buddhism painting such as of Amitabha were gathered; from the building called N. Xv, which Stein previously excavated, four statues with bodhisattvas on both sides were discovered; from a newly excavated building and while cleaning the building of N. Xv, the relics Stein left on the floor were collected. On this paper, the author will analyze the date and characteristics of the buildings of 93A35 (N5) according to the report of Stein's excavations and the results of Japan-China joint scholarly research.

1. New result of the expedition's and its differences from that of Stein's expedition

The point 93A35, which Stein called N.V, is located on a slightly elevated hill whose south-west and south east part had been rounded by long-termed weathering when Stein carried out his excavation[1]. There were three buildings, two cattle sheds and orchards (Fig. 1). The building N, Xv was at the northern part, while the building N. Xvi and sheds were at the southern part. A fence made of tamarisk twigs was stretched from the south-western toward the south-eastern corner. It was probably surrounding the buildings and sheds on the hill, but most part of

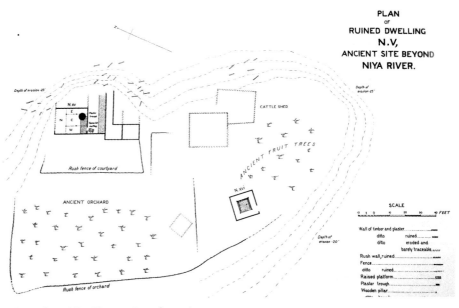

Fig. 1. Stein Niya N5 remains schematic

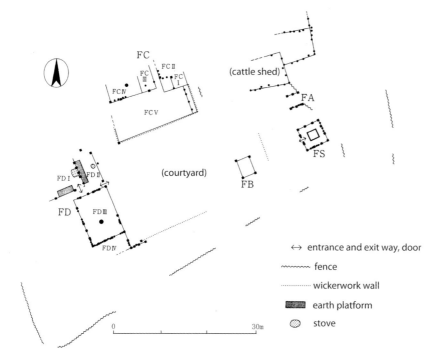

Fig. 2. China Japan joint expedition tram 92A35 (N5) remains schematic

it was broken by quicksand, and the part near the eastern three-lined street running north and south was covered with a large amount of sand. Japan-China joint scholarly research revealed that the building drawn on Stein's report is wrongly directed almost by 90 desrees, and that there was another building on the place between the building N.Xvi and the building N.Xv, which Stein reported as an orchard [2]. Furthermore, the locative relationship among two cattle sheds near the N.Xv, a building of four pillars and walls of wickerwork was different from that drawn on Stein's report (Fig. 1). These facts imply that the drawings facts imply that the drawings on his report provide us with less reliable information than previously expected. However, as for the point N5, the pictures and some reference on his report still have academic importance. The author will make a brief review on the buildings Stein reported from the point 93A35 (N5) [3].

The building N. Xvi, called FS by China Japan expedition, is a small rectangular building like a gallery with its entrance on the western side. N. Japan-China joint scholarly research newly found a rectangular platform and recognized it as a dais for Buddhism images, and revealed that the corner pillars were standing on underground beams [4]. The beams were constructed by jointing components vertically at their ends. Small pillars with two mortises on each stand, on each of the beams and in each space between the small pillars three mortises to stand props for building a wall (Fig. 3). In fact on the outer side of the northern wall the expedition found a broken wall containing props in each 35 cm in space (Fig. 3). On the floor of the gallery pieces of wall with drawings of Amitabha and flowering plants were collected, indicating that on the inner side of the walls colorful paintings were drawn.

Stein reported the entrance of the building was located on the south-western

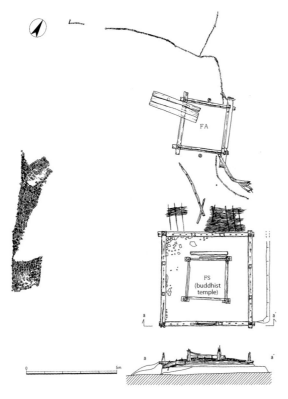

Fig. 3. Fs measure drawing

corner. It it seems that he did not cleaned the floor of the gallery while he deeply dug at the corner of the dais, this is why he did not mention the wall paintings on his report. In addition, Japan-China joint scholarly research discovered a gate facing east, which has three pillar's length and two pillar's width. The gate, called FA by the expedition, was not mentioned on Stein's report. The expedition replaced the 60cm depth of sand to reach those days' surface and then found a part of a door at the point westward of FA. On his report, Stein said that at some points he replaced 1.8 to 2.4m depth to reach the ancient surface while the other points the depth of sand was about 0.3 to 0.6m. This situation is similar situation to that the expedition saw at the point 93A35. A long amount of sand may have prevented him from finding any structure there. He probably could not find structures because of a large amount of sand. He said that there was a large orchard with a fence covered with sand at the west of N. Xvi and south of N. Xv, where the expedition found constructions such as FA and a large buildingFD .

As for the building N.Xv, according to his pictures and drawings, Stein found several pillars including ones taller than a man while its eastern part was destroyed together with its underground beams. Japan-China joint scholarly research also found some of the pillars. In addition, the expedition found components of construction at the northern and the north-eastern side of the building, and found its underground beams and walls preserved at the western part of the building. Furthermore, they found a fence like wickerwork of tamarisk, which Stein recognized as a horse enclosure. The expedition excavated inner partitions, walls and pillars, and proved that the situation of the building was not so different from that mentioned on Stein's report, excluding destruction of the southern underground beams and some of the pillars. It is in the building that Stein found 52 pieces of wooden Chinese record including a chronical remark of AD.269, and 200 pieces of wooden record in Kharosthi letters, which still preserve extraordinary academic importance for understanding the date of activities of Niya and its relationship with interacting countries [5].

Japan-China joint scholarly called the building N. Xv as FC, and clarified its rectangular plan and its composure which consists of two wooden buildings and a garden partitioned by a southern fence. In addition, in cleaning the floor inside a building (Fig. 2), they found a milky white piece of roman glass, pieces of wooden Chinese record, pieces of felt and silk, potteries, ceramics, wooden spindle bases, and living remains including props of grape, turnips and seeds of apricot. Furthermore, from a pit on the floor they found Stein's lost articles such as wooden relics with writings in Roman numbers by pencil, a piece of an iron scoop and pieces of a printing in Roman letters. At the eastern part of the inner garden, they found a lot of livestock's feces, and leaves and stems for laying. The two sheds in the south of the building N.Xv was recognized as those found by the expedition though the western part was destroyed. In addition to this, a construction of four pillars [6] and fences running north and south were drawn in the northern side of the building N.Xvi on Stein's report, while its direction was different from that proved by the expedition. These facts suggest that Stein investigated only some large buildings probably preserving literal materials at the point 93A35 (N5), as these days they say that his investigations were aiming at collecting valuable literal materials and ordinarily so rough as to be recognized almost as robbing.

2. Results of the joint expedition at the point 93A35 (N5)

The expedition newly found two sheds at the northern side of FS, a Buddhist building (called FS) running east and west near southern walls of buildings, a building (called FB) in the western side of FS beyond a fence, and a large building (called FD) with thick columns in the southern part of its center. In addition, they also excavated the floor and the fences of the building FC, and found that clatified directional line was a little different from the buildings above (fig. 2). As a result, they found that the buildings FS, FB, and FD were systematically located. For example, the south-eastern corner of FS and the south-western corner of FD (FD III) are distant by 55m on the drawing of the plan, which is close to 226 units of length used by Western Jin dynasty, China (about 24.3cm par a unit). In addition, the pillars of the northern wall of FS, those of FB and the columns inside FD (FD III) stand in a line. Furthermore, the direction of the line of FA's pillars is almost same with that of the pillars of FD (FD III)'s northern wall. The deliberate plan found in the buildings above implies that these buildings were systematically build at the same era. The measurement of the buildings closely related to the unit of Western Jin suggest that the buildings of the point 93A35 (N5) date back to the Western Jin era, although there still remain some problems in the accuracy of measuring. It does not conflict with the fact that a piece of wooden record with a chronical remark of AD.269 was found from the building N. Xv.

As for the building FC, the fact that it had several partitions and spaces for enclosing camels, which are necessary to travel through the desert, and that Chinese wooden records including administrative records and Kharosthi wooden records were found suggests that it is probable that the building was an official facility of the point 93A35 (N5). When thinking again of the locative relationship between FC and the other buildings above and of the relics and remains from these buildings, the building FS can be recognized as a Buddhist building characterized by its dais and wall paintings of bodhisattvas, the building FB as a tall building like a tower. As for the building FC, it is quite a large building and has two rooms with a line of thick columns standing in a line inside d room. the relics indicate that, the northern room can be recognized as a room for everyday life, and the central room, from which four statues of standing bodhisattvas were found

Fig. 4. Statues of standing bodhisattvas measure drawing

(Fig.4), as a room for Buddhism rituals.

The result of the analysis on the buildings above reveal their functions. On entering the gate FS from a eastern street of the point 93A35 (N5), one can find a Buddhist building FS in the left side, a tall tower FB in the right side beyond a fence, and another building for Buddhist rituals and everyday life for monks in the western side of the central garden. The point 93A35 (N5) can be recognized as a temple or as a set of buildings playing a role of a temple.

3. Significance of the excavation of the temple

As indicated by the report of the expedition, the Buddhism building FS is an important material for understanding of the penetration of Buddhism into the noble rank and the common people in Niya.

The point 93A35 (N5) is the first example around Niya which is conficmed to have played a role of a single complex of Buddhism as a whole, although a stupa was already found around Niya as well as some relics and remains related to Buddhism at the point of 97A5. Interestingly none has been around the point 93A35 (N5), while several cemeteries around the stupa and one at the point near the point 97A5 has been found. This fact implies that the temple at 93A35 (N5) played a different role from that played by ordinary temples, since it has a building recognized as an official facility.

Thinking of its scale, deliberate planning and possession of FC, a non-ritual facility. We can assume that the temple at 93A35 (N5) was probably a private religious facility owned by such noble ranks as a king or a ruler with his rank next to a king.

4. Conclusion

From the point 93A35 (N5), where Stein carried out the first investigation at the beginning of 19th century, a lot of literal materials including Chinese and Kharosthi records were brought abroad. However, accurate date and characteristics of its buildings were not clarified. As explained above, Japan-China joint scholarly research revealed the systematic construction of buildings such as a Buddhism building FS, a building for both everyday life and Buddhism rituals FD and an official building for governance FD. This discovery indicates extraordinary academic importance such as for understanding the penetration of Buddhism into the city of Niya, and so on. And it also clarified the necessity of further investigation on remains of the point and around.

Picturer1. Steine excavation N.xv The whole view

Picturer2. China Japan joint expedition 93A35 (N5) The whole view

Notes:

(1) Sutain, A, 1907 *Ancient Khotan: Detailed report of archaeological explorations in Chinese Turkestan*, 2 vols. Clarendon Press. Oxford

(2) The Sino-Japanese Joint Research of the Niya Site1999, NIYA SITE: Archaeogical Studies Number 2.

(3) Stein, op.cit.

(4) The Sino-Japanese Joint Research of the Niya Site, op. cit

(5) NAGASAWA, Kazutoshi1979, An introductory essay on the history of Loulan Kingdom, *Studies on the history of the Greater Silk Road*, pp.190–198, Kokushokankokai, Tokyo

(6) The expedition recognized the building as a room for preserving ices.

contribution 6

The remains of manufactories in the north of The Ruins of Niya

Shin Yoshizaki

Investigation Section Manager of Kyoto City Archaeological Research Institute

1. Introduction

The distribution survey of the ruins of Niya has revealed the remains of 17 manufactories, including the remains of furnaces and kiln [1] (Illustration 1,2). Within these 17, including the remains of furnaces 93, 95A9, The Remains of NN Manufactory 1 through 8, 96A11 and others, 11 of them are located in the north area of the ruins. Among these 11, The Remains of Manufactory 93 and 95A9 are considered to be in the same structure group by the excavation survey in 1995, and were named 93A9 (N14 [2]). They were located in the south area of the buildings, and reported as 93A9 (N14) The Remains of Manufactories [3].

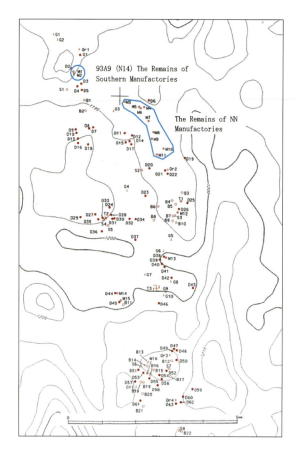

Fig.1. Distribution map of the remains in The Ruins of Niya (the north half)

Fig.2. The list of the remains of manufactories in The Ruins of Niya

Number in the map	Name of the ruins	Remains / Relics	Notes
M 1	Remains of Furnace 93	Remains of furnace	93A9 (N14) The Remains of Southern Manufactories
M 2	95A 9	Remains of kiln / shape of pond	93A9 (N14) The Remains of Southern Manufactories
M 3	Remains of NN Manufactory 2	Scattered sheep bones / iron scraps / metate / potsherd	The Remains of NN Manufactories
M 4	Remains of NN Manufactory 2	Scattered iron scraps / metate / iron dregs	The Remains of NN Manufactories
M 5	Remains of NN Manufactory 3	Scattered sheep bones / iron scraps / metate / potsherd	The Remains of NN Manufactories
M 6	Remains of NN Manufactory 1	Remains of kiln, scattered coins / potsherd / beads	The Remains of NN Manufactories
M 7	Remains of NN Manufactory 5	Scattered potsherd / metate / iron dregs	The Remains of NN Manufactories
M 8	Remains of NN Manufactory 6	Wooden poles, scattered potsherd / iron dregs	The Remains of NN Manufactories
M 9	Remains of NN Manufactory 7	Wooden poles, Scattered potsherd / iron dregs	The Remains of NN Manufactories
M10	96A11 Manufactory	Remains of kiln or 2 furnace/ buildings, scattered iron dregs / potsherd	The Remains of NN Manufactories
M11	Remains of NN Manufactory 8	Wooden poles, scattered potsherd / iron dregs / metate	The Remains of NN Manufactories

On the other hand, The Remains of NN Manufactory 1 through 8, 95A9 and 96A11, which are located in the south of the above mentioned, have been discovered with the remains of their production sites, furnaces and kiln, intensively located in the traces of the riverbed of Niya. I would like to refer to them as The Remains of NN Manufactories, since they are considered as a series of ruins. In this paper, I would like to study the characteristics of the ruins of Niya's handicraft industry through the investigation of their remains of manufactories in the north area.

2. 93A9 (N14) The Remains of Southern Manufactories

93A9 (N14) The Remains of Southern Manufactories are located in a small basin which was created by the bed of Niya River. Remains of 4 furnaces, 2 kiln, the buildings constructed with adobe bricks and a pond shaped remains have been discovered (Illustration 3). Among these, the remains of fireplace (fireplace 2) and the furnace (furnace 1) have been investigated.

Especially this furnace 2 is an important part of the study of this manufactory. However, its condition is not well enough to disclose what it was used to produce. Only the foundation is left of this furnace, which was built in a square shape with clay bricks on a hillock surface of a mound of dirt (Illustration 4/5). The remnants of the superstructure of the furnace were scattered in the surroundings. With its configuration, it is presumed to be a vertical type furnace which is known as a cupola furnace. It is certain that it was used for some kind of casting due to the scattered slags in the wide surrounding area and the found earthenware which could possibly have been a crucible. There are many remnants found from the remains of manufactories which include glassware, bronze ware and ironware. These remnants require melting furnaces for their production. Furnace 2 may be considered as the remains of one of these productions[*4].

Incidentally, many remnants in varieties of material have been found from 93A9 (N14) The Remains of Southern Manufactories, including glass, bronze, iron, earthenware, coral, shell, bone, stone and wooden products. When you compare them by the different type of works, you can see that there are relatively few ironworks, and there are some tools such as arrowheads and small knifes.

On the other hand, a majority of the finished goods are in bronze: small metal ornaments, glass: bead products such as small cylindrical beads, polyhedron beads and tonbo dama (glass beads), stone: beads products using gem stones such as agate and turquoise, coral and shell: beads and coral branches with some holes in a sections (Illustration 6,7). These items may be considered as articles of adornment. There were many unfinished items in those found articles. This allows us to consider that 93A9 (N14) The Remains of Southern Manufactory was mainly processing those materials to produce articles of adornment.

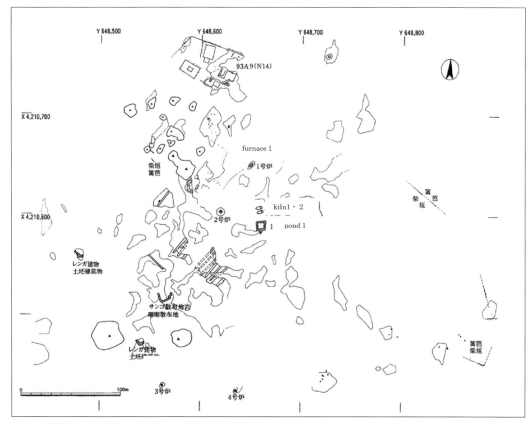

Fig.3. Distribution map of 93A9 (N14) The Remains of Southern Manufactories

3. The Remains of NN Manufactories

The Remains of NN Manufactories are located at the altitude 1990 to 1995 meter, along the valleys stretched in southeast of 93A9 (N14) The Remains of Southern Manufactories, in total of 10 remains of manufactories are almost in a line which runs from north to south in the length of 2km. There were many remains of kiln and furnaces found by the distribution survey (Illustration 8, 9). However, like above said, its true purpose has not been revealed. Its products are still unidentified, but it is presumed that it mostly had something to do with producing iron products from the scattered iron scraps and dregs around the manufactory.

Fig.4. The condition of the furnace 2 before the investigation

Fig.5. Discovery condition of the furnace 2

Fig.6. Relics collected from 93A9 (N14) The Remains of Southern Manufactory (1)

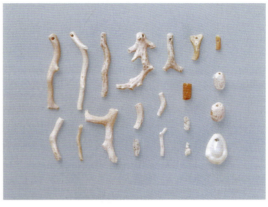

Fig.7. Relics collected from 93A9 (N14) The Remains of Southern Manufactory (1)

Fig.8. The Remains of NN Manufactories

Fig.9. The remains of furnace at The Remains of NN Manufactory

4. Characteristics of The Remains of Northern Manufactories of The Ruins of Niya

In the north area of the ruins of Niya, there are two different groups of the remains of manufactories, 93A9 (N14) The Remains of Southern Manufactories, and The Remains of NN Manufactories. They are both located along the same valleys of the Niya river. Considering this fact, it shows a strong connection in between these two groups of the remains. Although it has not been identified as to what they were producing, they may have been sharing roles. Considering the fact that 93A9 (N14) The Remains of Manufactory could possibly have been producing decorative items with glass, bronze, gem stone and coral, and The Remains of NN Manufactory working mostly with iron. Also the number of furnace and kiln as well as the amount of scattered relics and slags around the remains suggests that they could possibly have been producing the large amounts of products surpassed by Niya's demand.

Agate, turquoise, coral and sea shells were used at 93A9 (N14) The Remains of The Southern Manufactory. These materials were not being produced in Niya. It must be examined furthermore, but I predict that bronze and iron were the same case. Considering these points, I presume that they were importing those materials and exporting the finished products after adding extra value by processing them in their manufactories. I believe that Silk Road had much to do with making this kind of trade possible.

Moreover, some charcoals, which seemed to be used as fuel, were found inside of the furnace 2. The examination had revealed that it was Euphrates Poplar, a species of Populus. Euphrates Poplar is distributed in the Niya River valley, and is the main wood which supports life there. It was used for building houses, furniture, coffin and other things. It shows how important this industry was to Niya, considering that they kept the manufactories which consumed a large amount of precious fuel, Euphrates Poplar, when desertification was progressing in that area.

Note

*1 The Ruins of Niya Japan-China Joint Scientific Research Group: The Ruins of Niya Japan-China Joint Research Report Volume 2 (1999)
*2 The name and number used in parenthesis were named by British explorer Sir Aurel Stein in the early 20th century.
*3 Same as *1
*4 I analyzed the remains of furnace 2 which had something to do with producing glass products, however, there are some opposed opinions. "The Ruins of Niya, 93A9 (N14) The Remains of Southern Manufactories" in The Ruins of Niya Japan-China Joint Research Report Volume 3 (2007)

contribution 7

The Whole Story of Sir Marc Aurel Stein's 4th Expedition To Xinjiang in Central Asia

Yasutaka Kojima

Representative of Academic Research Organization for Niya, Bukkyo University, Japan

The purpose of this thesis is to clarify some questionable points in regard to the 4th expedition to Central Asia, specifically China Xinjiang, by Sir Marc Aurel Stein (1862-1943), the archaeological explorer born in Hungary and naturalized later in England. He spent 326 days for the expedition, leaving Srinagar in Kashmir on Aug. 11, 1930, and arriving back there July 2, 1931. During this period, even though Sir Aurel Stein encountered such troubles as "the cancellation of the visa and an immediate deportation" directed by the Government of the Republic of China, he struggled to reach the Niya ruins where he had established "glorious achievements" through three previous expeditions. He managed to excavate there and collect 150 or so antiquities, all the while avoiding the Government's observers.

I have visited Xinjiang more than 140 times since 1982 and worked on numerous Japan-China joint activities, including the restoration and preservation of the Kizil grottoes, archaeological research of the Niya ruins, archaeological research of the DandanOilik ruins along with the conservation of its wall paintings, a network to raise awareness of cultural property protection (www.wenbao.net.), and a provision of a grant for researchers engaged in conserving cultural relics. The results of this research and these studies were disclosed via reports and symposiums, and the efforts of Chinese as well as Japanese researchers are still being made. I also had an opportunity to present much of the research about the Niya and DandanOilik ruins at the "International Conference-Archaeology of the Southern Taklamakan: Hedin and Stein's Legacy and New Explorations," which was held in November 2012 at the British Library.

Stein's reports helped me greatly as useful references in the course of researching in the Taklamakan Desert, which led me to become interested in his way of life and to write this thesis. As I have been fortunate to know Xinjiang very well along with the desert research noted above, I am in a somewhat better position to come to grips with Stein's undertakings than the academic scholars of Central Asia and the so-called "Silk Road enthusiasts."

While Stein's first (1900-1901), second (1906-1908), and third (1913-1916) expeditions were well known because a massive volume of his reports on those expeditions was published due to the great success of them, the report of his fourth expedition (1930-1931) was not issued due to a humiliating failure. Thus his expeditions to Central Asia were thought to be only three until recently and the fourth expedition was not well-known. As information of this expedition has gradually spread in recent years, the archival records of the fourth expedition were beginning to be disclosed. Yet there remain a number of unclear points.

As references for my research, I have mainly used the following materials. *The Xinjiang Archaeological Archives of Modern Foreign Explorers, Archives of Stein's Fourth Expedition to Xinjiang, and Historical Archival Documents of Sino-Sweden Scientific Expedition to North-West China*, all of which were published jointly with Xinjiang Uygur Autonomous Region Archives. "Stein's Diary" was acquired from the Bodleian Libraries of Oxford University, and the "Stein-related Archives" was acquired from the British Museum – both of which deserve deep thanks and support. I also refer to Jeannette Mirsky, SIR AUREL STEIN: ARCHAEOLOGICAL EXPLORER published by University of Chicago Press in 1977; Susan Chan Egan, A LATTERDAY CONEFUCIAN: Reminiscences of William Hung published by Harvard University in 1987; Shareen Blair Brysac, *Last of the Foreign Devils Archaeology* published by the Archaeological Institute of America in 1997; Annabel Walker, AUREL STEIN-PIONEER OF THE SILK ROAD published by University of Washington Press in 1998; Helen Wang, *Sir Aurel Stein in The Times* published by Saffron Books in 2002; and Wang Ji Qing, *Deliberations on Stein's Diary of the Fourth Archaeological Expedition to China* published by Gansu Educational Publisher in 2004. I would like to express my sincere appreciation to all parties mentioned above, as they provided me with important information and inspiration.

Why did people like Professor Paul J. Sachs at the Fogg Art Museum of Harvard University, who understood how the views on cultural heritage were drastically changing among the Chinese (specifically scholars in Peking), propose the Xinjiang expedition to Stein with a $100,000 grant? Especially considering that the funds were proposed following the Great Crash at the New York Stock Exchange (Oct. 24, 1929), which triggered the Great Depression? Harvard University envisioned filling the Fogg Art Museum with relics excavated in Central Asia. Langdon Warner at the Fogg Art Museum was not allowed to remove some parts of a wall surface on his second visit to Dunhuang. To make their wish come true they hired Stein as a "professional" explorer. America, a country with a short history, was longing for ancient cultural heritage. During the "Museum Era," when museums were being built one after another, people satisfied their desires with a variety of art pieces and antiques.

Why did England, including its Indian Empire, continue to support Stein's Xinjiang expedition? Stein had brought a large volume of Central Asia's relics, including those from Niya, DandanOilik, Loulan, and Dunhuang, to the British Empire while championing the norms of the Imperialism Age. He was considered a great hero in terms of culture, similar to a general winning a war. To seize those relics by endorsing him was one of the best ways to show how great this imperial power was.

I am wondering why a person such as Stein, who was superb in collecting information and familiar with Chinese affairs, misread the situation in those days. Harvard University invited Stein to deliver a series of lectures at the Lowell Institute at the age of 67 just one year after he retired from the Archaeological Bureau of the Indian Empire. We can sense the desire of both Stein and Sachs for relics through their correspondences. Mirsky referred to Stein's attempt to climb Mount Mustagh Ata on his first Central Asia expedition in a rivalry with Hedin. While Hedin was proceeding with comprehensive research of the Chinese northwestern area jointly with China, Stein thought he could single-handedly manage this expedition with British diplomatic power as well as his own exploring capabilities overriding objections from John Leighton Stuart and William Hung from the Harvard side.

Breakdown of Harvard University's contribution of USD 100,000, Appendix to Sachs' letter on Jan. 4, 1930 (At the British Museum)

Notification from Stein to Sachs to request for revision and addition (a part), Stein's letter on Jan. 9, 1930 (At the British Museum)

In the end of April the next year, he arrived in Nanking to discuss acquisition of a visa with British Minister Miles Lampson on the 28th. The following day, the minister visited the director of the Nanking Government's Foreign Affairs, Wang Zhengting, to submit memorandums regarding both Stein's expedition and arms exports requested by the Xinjiang Province. He pressed for the issuance of Stein's visa. On May 1, Stein, along with Minister Lampson, visited the Director of Foreign Affairs, Wang, to explain the expedition plan and request the visa. The visa was issued on May 6th and received 7th. The reason Stein asked the British Museum to subsidize the Harvard proposal was that he focused more on Great Britain's diplomatic power rather than on financial assistance. The visa could not have been issued without British involvement.

The interpretation of this visa was widely different between the Chinese side and Stein, which led to the subsequent turmoil. The visa was described as "遊歷

護照", meaning "a travel passport." Minister Lampson also cited in his telegram of June 12, 1930, to the Secretary of Foreign Affairs of the Indian Empire, "Stein has merely been furnished with a passport for ordinary travel in Hsinchiang and Inner Mongolia … and if he intends to collect antiquities and remove them from the country, he should submit to the Institute a statement of the object, scope and plans of his proposed research and obtain their approval."

However, according to Stein's counterstatement (dated May 10, 1931) sent from Kashgar during his exploration to address reproaches from both the Chinese Foreign Affairs and the National Commission for the Preservation of Antiquities, "I received a passport authorizing me to travel in Hsin-chiang and Inner Mongolia for archaeological purposes, this permission being understood to include needful surveys…. It was on a definite understanding that I was to be allowed to examine and, where necessary, to clear any ancient ruins traced." He stated in "The Times" on July 16, 1931 on his way back to Srinagar: "Passport authorizing me to trace and closely investigate." And in the preface of the research report conducted in India and Iran, Archaeological Reconnaissance's in North-Western India and South Iran (1937), he stated, "…to obtain the issue by the Chinese Ministry of Foreign Affairs of a passport authorizing me to trace and investigate ancient remains in Hsing-chiang and Inner Mongol."

Thus, both parties argued on different planes, and Stein was thwarted from entering China. Minister Lampson worked hard to successfully let him enter the country, but he was stuck in Kashgar. Finally, thanks to the tremendous efforts made by Consul General George Sherriff and others, Stein could proceed eastward on the South Road of the Taklamakan Desert on November 11, 1930. Observers dispatched by the Government accompanied him. Every trick came into play on the Stein side, wishing to reach neighboring Keriya without letting them know their true destination -- the Niya ruins. The Xinjiang side wanted to summon Stein to Urumqi to check on his intention. The scene was described in lurid detail in the Xinjiang archives, Stein's diary, and in the British Government's archives. Developing bronchitis, Stein had to stay in Keriya for treatment for 20 days or so. Soon afterward he advanced to the Niya ruins to research there for about a week and collected a number of relics.

In spite of being summoned to come to Urumqi by Jin Shuren, the Chairman of Xinjiang Province, Stein ignored it because he may have anticipated that it was risky to return to Kashgar via Keriya carrying the relics. Thus he took a detour by circling the Taklamakan Desert and stopping at Cherchen, Charkliq, Korla, Kucha and Aksu. He finally returned to Kashgar on April 25, 1931. Stein negotiated through the Consul General to bring back the relics he had collected from the Niya ruins for research and then return them to China. But as his request ended in rejection, Stein had no choice but to leave Kashgar for home on May 18.

Why did Stein "dig up" the Niya ruins despite the fact that research and excavations were forbidden? The collections of the ruins in Niya and other places rewarded him with the title of "Sir" as well as being naturalized in Britain. He needed to secure that honor first of all. He also had to perform "the relics

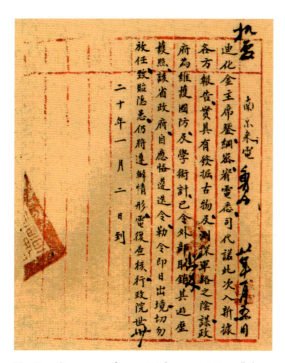

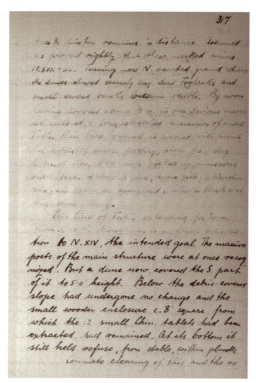

Nanjing Government's secret telegram stating, "There is a plot to excavate antiquities and make a survey of military roads. Revoke his visa and issue an immediate departure order." Issued on Dec. 31, 1930 (Excerpt from Archives of Stein's Fourth Expedition to North-West China)

Noted "Compete cleaning" at the Niya ruins on Jan. 20, 1931, Stein's Diary (At the Bodleian Library)

providing agreements" with Harvard University and the British Museum. Stein also put the words "complete cleaning" in his diary in place of "excavation" and let his Indian and Uygurian subordinates work ahead of him. Meanwhile, he kept records in a tent to keep the observers off guard. He also made investigations while the observers were sleeping.

And what kinds of actions were taken domestically in China, including by the Central Government, Xinjiang and local regions? Social turmoil was prevailing there soon after the establishment of the Republic of China, intensive intrusion by foreign powers, and rivalry between the local warlords. In fact, the Xinjiang Province took a different tack from the Central Government. Concerning local treatment for Stein, a welcoming response was recorded thanks to the issue of an arms import in some quarters. Within Xinjiang, conflicting ideas were observed among local governments of Urumqi and other regions. Even among ethnic groups, different views were expressed. Stein received a big welcome from old friends, but some local supporters from the first expedition were arrested and cast into prison.

Where are the relics collected by Stein now, as they were forbidden from being removed by the Chinese Government? Is the rumor true that some parts of the banned relics are stored at the British Museum? Though we can verify by Chinese archives that the relics Stein left at the British counsel in Kashgar were actually

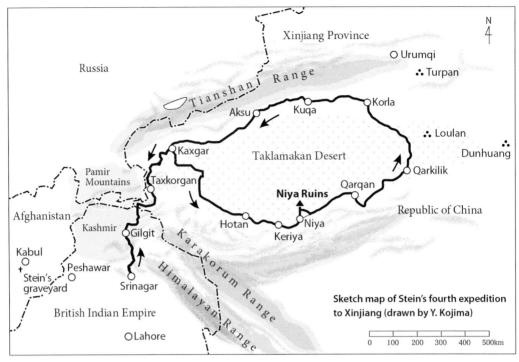

Sketch map of Stein's fourth expedition to Xinjiang (drawn by Y. Kojima)

transported to Urumqi, no one knows their current whereabouts. That is because rumors have been spread that they are at the British Museum, in Beijing or were sold within China. The pictures that were banned from leaving along with relics are now stored at the British Museum and at the Library of the Hungarian Academy of Sciences.

In addition, how should we come to grips with the activities of bringing out cultural materials by explorers from abroad, including Stein's Britain, Germany, Japan, the U.S., and France? From the end of the 19th century through the beginning of the 20th century, when the "exploration boom" was being exploited by the major powers, excavations and removal of artifacts were partly allowed for research purposes. That is why every explorer from any country could hire people at the site and work together with them. However, that way of thinking had changed by the time of Stein's fourth expedition. We have to recognize that the activities conducted up until the third expedition should be clearly distinguished from those of the fourth expedition. It is no wonder that the fourth expedition to Xinjiang is denounced. While ideally cultural materials should be stored where they actually were, we often see examples where removed relics have been preserved, yet those left at sites were destroyed or scattered.

England and Russia (the Soviet Union) raged an intelligence-gathering battle to expand territory across the entire Central Asia including Xinjiang after the middle of the 19th century. The explorers of each nation could be called vanguards in the intelligence-gathering battle to acquire territory. Because so many people from England and Russia lived in Xinjiang, some records show that it is similar to a settlement, which is the so-called "Great Game." Though we can see an old example of "The Great Game" in the area of the Wakhan Corridor in Afghanistan, it continues now not only in Central Asia but across the world.

While the protagonist of Stein's fourth expedition was nobody but Stein himself, the "scriptwriter" and director were Harvard University and the British Empire, respectively. Stein's expeditions and research, which extended over a wide variety of fields, have been highly valued. Their spectrum, depth and volume are almost superhuman. We cannot discuss the history of Central Asia without referring to him just as we cannot easily pass over a huge mountain. It is also noteworthy that he offered what he had done to the public through a massive volume of books. Whereas Stein has been highly regarded in Europe as well as in Japan, the Chinese people consider him to be the epitome of a looter.

"The lifetime explorer wandering around strange lands" who turned "his inferiority complex and defiant spirit against an irrelevant discrimination" into his own energy source is sleeping in Kabul.

This paper is the summary of a thesis titled as The Whole Story of Sir Marc Aurel Stein's 4th Expedition to Xinjiang in Central Asia which I released in The Research Bulletin of Bukkyo University in March 2014. It comprises some 110,000 Japanese characters, 169 notes, and 65 illustrations.

Kizil, Niya, and Dandanoilik
Commemorating World Heritage Designation of
Silk Roads: the Routes Network of Chang'an-Tianshan

Copyright © 2016 by Academic Research Organization for Niya, Bukkyo University, Japan

Edited by: Yasutaka Kojima
Published by: Toho Shuppan
　　　　　　2-3-2, Osaka, Tennoji-ku, Osaka 543-0062 Japan
　　　　　　URL: http://www.tohoshuppan.co.jp
　　　　　　Tel +81-(0)6-6779-9571 Fax +81-(0)6-6779-9573
Issued by: Bukkyo University Museum of Religious Culture／
　　　　　　Academic Research Organization for Niya, Bukkyo University, Japan
Designed by: Hideko Nakagawa (Yorozu Design)
Printed by: Graphic Corporation
ISBN978-4-86249-274-6